THE BANK WAR AND

THE PARTISAN PRESS

The BANK WAR *and the* PARTISAN PRESS

NEWSPAPERS, FINANCIAL INSTITUTIONS, AND THE POST OFFICE IN JACKSONIAN AMERICA

Stephen W. Campbell

Hey Daniel,
Very honored to be on your
podcast and part of your
world. All the best
— Steve

University Press of Kansas

Published by the University Press of Kansas (Lawrence, Kansas
66045), which was organized by the Kansas Board of Regents and
is operated and funded by Emporia State University, Fort Hays State
University, Kansas State University, Pittsburg State University, the
University of Kansas, and Wichita State University

Library of Congress Cataloging-in-Publication Data is available.

ISBN 978-0-7006-2744-8 (cloth)
ISBN 978-0-7006-2745-5 (ebook)

British Library Cataloguing-in-Publication Data is available.

Printed in the United States of America

10 9 8 7 6 5 4 3 2 1

The paper used in this publication is recycled and contains 30
percent postconsumer waste. It is acid free and meets the minimum
requirements of the American National Standard for Permanence of
Paper for Printed Library Materials Z39.48-1992.

Contents

CONTENTS

Acknowledgments

Throughout the long, strange trip that has been the life of this book, I have incurred numerous debts to individuals and institutions. It would be nearly impossible to do justice to all of them, but what follows is the next best thing. Growing up in northern California I was lucky to have "Philosopher Dave" Danielson and Richard Braun as intellectual role models. Steven Deyle, Brian Schoen, and Charles Postel challenged and nurtured my instincts during my formative years as a historian. A. Glenn Crothers, Jeffrey L. Pasley, Jerry Koufeldt, the Franciscan friars of Louisville, and Richard Kilbourne Jr. deserve praise for their companionship and hospitality. My research trips would have been much more difficult and isolating without them.

I wish to recognize Liz Covart, who introduced me to my editor, Kim Hogeland, at the University Press of Kansas. Kim's flexibility and professionalism were a godsend as I confronted life's curveballs and a demanding teaching load. The staff, copy editor, and anonymous reviewers at Kansas were helpful in shepherding this book toward completion. And thanks go out to the editors of *American Nineteenth Century History* and *Ohio Valley History* for permission to reprint parts of articles that have been published in their journals.

This is a book about how historical actors appropriated public and private subsidies while navigating through the boundaries of political and economic institutions erected by their predecessors, and I would be remiss if I did not consider the individuals and institutions that helped me. The University of California, Santa Barbara (UCSB) History Department, Filson Historical Society, All-UC Group in Economic History, and Phi Alpha Theta extended generous financial support in the form of travel grants and fellowships. Innumerable historians, archivists, and other specialists working at the Western Historical Manuscript Collection at the University of Missouri, the Historical Society of Pennsylvania in Philadelphia, the Library of Congress, and several other archives were always ebullient and receptive. Staff members at the Interlibrary Loan offices at California State University, Sacramento, UCSB, and Cal Poly answered my requests dutifully and enthusiastically. I appreciate the time that Becky Imamoto took out of her busy schedule at the UC Irvine Langson Library to help me find records of obscure congressional debates.

Among the search engines and electronic databases that have proved immensely valuable in not only sharpening the factual basis of this book but also enabling the keyword searches that saved much-needed time, energy, and money compared to the tools that were available to my intellectual forebears were ProQuest, Measuring Worth, electronic census records through ancestry.com, Google Books, and the American Periodical Series Online. The publication of three volumes of the *Andrew Jackson Papers* by Dan Feller and his colleagues at the University of Tennessee Press occurred while this book was coming together. These volumes enhanced the evidentiary basis of this book, from bringing some issues into clearer focus, to providing additional texts and passages to bolster certain claims, to leading me toward entirely new directions. From the *Jackson Papers* I have come to appreciate—rather than dismiss—the multitudinous critiques of the Second Bank of the United States, even if I did not always agree with them.

A number of esteemed scholars, friends, and colleagues have offered valuable suggestions and critiques. Fellow political historian Donald J. Ratcliffe read this entire manuscript from start to finish. In addition to his encouraging presence, he alerted me to new sources and phrased concepts in ways I had not imagined. Petra Shenk and Karen Kelsky helped me clarify the importance of this project in ways that were direct and unpretentious. Robert E. Wright patiently answered all of my questions about the esoteric financial instruments that comprised the antebellum-era economy. I thank Nicole Pacino, Jill Jensen, Matthew Schoenbachler, Mark Cheathem, Jessica Lepler, Richard John, Mary Furner, and Gavin Wright for reading earlier versions of these chapters. Any mistakes or weaknesses that have eluded their perceptive eyes are entirely my own responsibility.

At UCSB, Patricia Cline Cohen was an inspiration not only for her tremendous ability to juggle a hundred different responsibilities but also for always giving me her complete and undivided attention. John Majewski was an early supporter of this project, consistently respecting my own inclinations and projecting an amiable disposition. I am fortunate to have supportive and pleasant colleagues at Cal Poly Pomona. For their generosity, care, and friendship, I give a warm embrace and special thanks to Alicia Rodriquez, Oliver Rosales, Katie Datko, Henry Maar, and Brian Ernst.

The most important honor is saved for last: this project would have never come to fruition without the unconditional love and support of my parents, Barbara and Tom Campbell, for whom I am eternally grateful. I dedicate this book to them.

Stephen Campbell
La Verne, California

Introduction

Amos Kendall, a New Englander-turned-Kentuckian, was being torn in two directions. It was the mid-1820s, and the country was increasingly fracturing along partisan and regional lines. Kendall had to decide whether he would continue to support fellow Kentuckian Henry Clay, whom he had backed in the 1824 presidential election, or Clay's nemesis, Andrew Jackson. Although Kendall did not see eye to eye with Clay on many of the leading issues of the day, including support for the Second Bank of the United States (BUS), Clay, the old war hawk and Speaker of the House, had helped Kendall during a particularly vulnerable period of his life. After moving to Kentucky in 1814, Kendall had struggled to find consistent work and was beset by recurring health problems. Clay and several of his contemporaries provided crucial help. It was through Clay that Kendall acquired both valuable political connections and financial assistance in the form of public printing contracts. These contracts—in effect state subsidies for printing legislative debates in the state capital of Frankfort—helped sustain Kendall's newspaper enterprise, the *Argus of Western America*. They demonstrated the ways in which white men of modest means in Jacksonian America blended public and private sources of money to manage thriving newspaper enterprises and launch successful careers in party politics.[1]

The transition was gradual, but by the next presidential election in 1828,

Kendall had come over to the Jackson camp and would eventually become a major party stalwart. A legal dispute over money that Clay had lent to Kendall, combined with aggressive lobbying from Martin Van Buren and Kentucky Jacksonian Richard M. Johnson, facilitated Kendall's conversion to Jacksonianism. Through cutting editorials and vigorous campaigning, Kendall worked on Jackson's behalf, helping to spread allegations that the 1824 presidential election was scandalized by a "corrupt bargain," the unverified accusation that Clay had arranged the House votes necessary to secure John Quincy Adams's rise to the presidency in exchange for Clay's appointment as secretary of state.[2] Kendall's friends credited him with helping Jackson carry the Bluegrass State in the election. To reward him, they asked the incoming president to find Kendall a job in Washington as an auditor. "Mr. Kendall, we all *believe*," they wrote, "is a man of exemplary purity in his private life" who operated an "efficient" public journal and who maintained a character "highly distinguished for probity, consistency and uniform devotion to the best interests of his country."[3] On March 19, 1829, Jackson appointed Kendall fourth auditor of the Treasury Department, a position in which Kendall would manage the account books for the navy.[4] Kendall was erudite, talented, organized, detailed, and deeply committed to enacting the president's vision for fiscal reform, including the reduction and eventual elimination of the country's public debt. But in his personal life, financial difficulties remained. He had acquired property and slaves through marriage but also had a large family to support and significant debts owed to numerous creditors. At one point Kendall's total debt exceeded $10,000.[5]

Neither his health problems nor his financial struggles would go away entirely, but within just a few months of arriving in Washington, Kendall began to make a name for himself. He loathed public speaking but operated effectively behind the scenes, quickly becoming a leading voice in administration policy. One notable achievement was the establishment of the *Globe*, a state-subsidized party organ in Washington edited by his friend, Francis Preston Blair. The two men benefited not only from executive department printing contracts, which helped sustain the *Globe*'s business during its infancy, but also from an army of party loyalists and influential political allies in the federal bureaucracy who recruited new subscribers. As an administration press, the *Globe* mobilized support for the emerging Democratic Party, underscored Jackson's leadership qualities, and mounted a successful assault on the "Monster Bank." By the end of Jackson's second term, Kendall could count an impressive list of accomplishments that included a successful presidential reelection in 1832, a newspaper enterprise with national appeal, the formation of a state banking system designed to replace the national bank, pro-Jackson grassroots political organizations scattered throughout the nation, and his own appointment as postmaster general in 1835. Jackson's famous veto of the bill to recharter the BUS in July 1832 carried Kendall's polemical editorial style. A great deal of Jackson's success in the Bank War can be attributed to Kendall's skills and, just as significantly, to institutional support from the federal bureaucracy.

The "monster" that Jackson and Kendall worked so hard to destroy was a uniquely powerful financial entity chartered by Congress in 1816. Its president was a brilliant if overly confident Philadelphia patrician named Nicholas Biddle. The bank was endowed with a capital stock of $35 million. Private investors subscribed to 80 percent of these shares while the U.S. Treasury owned the remaining 20 percent. This made it a hybrid public-private corporation. At once a for-profit commercial bank, a repository for the nation's public money, and the country's main fiscal agent, the BUS helped to collect and distribute federal money and serviced the national debt. It accounted for about 20 percent of the nation's banking capital, bank lending in the form of discounts, and bank notes in circulation. Of the nation's entire stock of specie—gold and silver bars, ingots, and coins—the bank owned between 30 and 40 percent. As part of a complex, decentralized, and highly seasonal economy comprised of hundreds of financial institutions, the BUS stood alone in its national reach. There was no standardized national currency at the time like today's Federal Reserve notes, but BUS notes had some of the same characteristics.[6] They circulated widely from hand to hand and were payable for all public debts, including customs duties and land sales. At a time when most businesses were small partnerships operating with only a local or regional presence at best, the BUS employed a nationwide army of over 500 agents and over 200 directors through its network of 30 branch offices and commercial agencies. Serving below the numerous presidents, directors, and cashiers of each branch office were various tellers, porters, bookkeepers, discount clerks, note clerks, and other employees.[7]

Flexibility and regulation were key to Biddle's leadership. From the bank's headquarters in Philadelphia, Biddle communicated his preferred monetary policies to the branch offices. The intent was to curb excessive lending among the country's numerous state banks and stabilize variations in prices and trade. Because of the national bank's large specie reserves, Biddle could relieve the inconveniences of temporary shortages of liquidity. On a handful of occasions he even rescued state banks from collapse. These actions made the BUS a "central bank," though only in the early nineteenth-century understanding of the term, as today's central banks possess regulatory and monetary powers that are far more expansive. Those who subscribed to the orthodoxy of minimal governmental intervention in an economy, which included many leading financiers and merchants in Great Britain and the United States, criticized Biddle's unconventional means. But to the bank's backers, the Philadelphia prodigy was bold and innovative.[8]

Economic nationalists linked the bank's regulatory functions with prosperity and stable commerce, but for strict constructionists and states' rights advocates, the bank raised a multitude of serious moral, legal, and philosophical issues. Anti-BUS Jacksonians cried foul over the bank's foreign stockholders, most of whom were British, for their potential to meddle in the financial affairs of a relatively young nation that had twice fought wars against Great Britain. Then there were looming questions over the bank's constitutionality, the financial instruments it circulated that seemed to prioritize the interests of merchants and speculators above those of farmers and artisans, and, especially, the bank's ability to wield its enormous financial resources to bribe newspaper editors and buy off members of Congress. Corrupting the press and stealing elections, opponents held, made the bank a dangerous threat to liberty. Added to this was the bank's monopolistic financial relationship with the federal government. There could be only one national bank according to its charter, and individual states could not tax its branches. For the advantages of storing the nation's public deposits, the bank paid interest and a $1.5 million bonus to the Treasury—a financial marriage, according to critics, that enabled the bank to oppress state banks and leverage public money for private gain. In addition, the BUS concentrated large sums of money in a few hands, which smacked of European aristocracy and violated the spirit of a nation founded on equal rights.[9]

Only a few months into his first term, Andrew Jackson began to voice these objections, reigniting controversies that had been lying dormant for most of the 1820s. He began working with his inner circle of advisers for a substitute national bank and criticized the current one in an address to Congress. The general storyline of what historians call "the Bank War" typically begins around this time. Against the wishes of much of his initial cabinet, the commander-in-chief began criticizing the BUS at least in part because he harbored a deep-seated opposition to all banks and paper money, stemming from earlier investments in a stock bubble gone awry.[10] Biddle responded to Jackson's critiques by launching a nationwide public relations campaign designed to secure a new BUS charter. There were still four years left on the bank's charter in 1832, but Biddle and his congressional allies confronted the president by sending a recharter bill to his desk. This strategy backfired. Citing a long list of grievances, Jackson handed down one of the most consequential presidential vetoes in American history.[11] The bank question took center stage in the upcoming presidential election whereby Jackson overwhelmingly defeated Clay. With renewed energy in his second term, Jackson again attacked the bank, this time by removing the institution's federal deposits. The president, encouraged by Kendall and other close advisers, placed the deposits in a series of state banks that were politically and financially connected to prominent Democratic Party newspapers and postmasters. Biddle wanted to force the president to come to terms with a more limited recharter, so in the fall of 1833 he deliberately induced a mild economic contraction. But once again, Biddle's political instincts proved misguided. Public support for the BUS fell precipitously. Biddle and his political allies continued to push for a new bank charter, but their plans never came to fruition. The bank's federal charter expired without renewal in 1836. As a state-chartered institution, the bank stayed open for a few more years, but it collapsed for good in 1841 amid a prolonged financial panic.

The Bank War was a major political issue with lasting consequences for the relationship between Congress and the presidency, the development of what historians and political scientists have dubbed the "Second Party System" of Democrats and Whigs, and the trajectory of the nation's banking system and larger political economy. Thus, it should come as no surprise that the controversy has generated a vast scholarly literature among historians, economists, political scientists, and those who straddle these disciplines.[12] Starting in the post–World War II era, an outpouring of monographs, articles, and synthetic works gave rise to vibrant discussions regarding the wisdom of Jackson's destruction of the BUS, the amount of criticism that Biddle deserved for his dealings with the press and Congress, and the degree to which the Bank War was responsible for the Panic of 1837. Class conflict, liberal entrepreneurialism, and classical republicanism were among the analytical tools employed by experts to frame these issues.[13] At the same time, the very nature of the topic meant that specialists often discussed the personality traits of the Bank War's two chief antagonists, Jackson and Biddle. Robert V. Remini, Jackson's most prolific biographer, portrayed the Bank War as a personal struggle "between two willful, proud, and stubborn men" that helped inaugurate the modern presidency.[14] In recent decades, the national bank has been described as a test case of Americans' conflicting attitudes toward the "market revolution," or as a vital player in the global history of capitalism with particular attention to the mutually reinforcing booms in land, cotton, and slavery.[15] Measured by the publication of monographs, scholarly interest in the Bank War peaked from about 1950 to 1970. Historians today continue to cite books and articles from this era (and even before) as definitive accounts. Economists, meanwhile, have refined their statistical analyses of the handful of economic crises that transpired between 1819 and 1843 in which the BUS played direct and indirect roles, but among political historians the Bank War is usually relegated to an article in an edited volume or a chapter or two in the latest Jackson biography. Scarcely any politically focused monographs have appeared since the publication of Remini's work over fifty years ago. This may have been linked to the expanded opportunities for research in new subfields that have replaced—or at the very least complemented—publishing within the realm of what might be considered traditional political history. There is plenty of room for a fresh approach.[16]

The Bank War and the Partisan Press, the latest contribution to a long-studied but recently neglected topic, advances a new political interpretation of the Bank War through its focus on the funding and dissemination of the party press. It brings together insights from the subfields of political history, the history of journalism, financial history, and administrative history to demonstrate how newspaper editors mixed public and private sources of capital to fund their businesses. Through its study of newspapers, this book brings to light a revolving door of editors, financiers, and postal workers who appropriated the financial resources of preexisting political institutions, and even created new ones, to enrich themselves and advance their careers. Both sides in the Bank War sought political advantage by using interregional communications networks funded by public and private money. The BUS financed the dissemination of newspapers and kept track of public opinion through its system of branch offices, while the Jacksonians did the same by harnessing the patronage networks of the Post Office.

Parts of this book draw upon a group of historians, political scientists, economists, and historical sociologists sometimes categorized under the school of thought known as American political development (APD), who share in common a fundamental belief that the state exists as an autonomous actor with the ability to shape social, political, and economic developments in significant ways.[17] From setting up courts to collecting revenues from tariffs; from issuing patents and thereby protecting inventors' intellectual property rights to distributing veterans' pensions; from establishing the General Land Office to managing the Bureau of Indian Affairs; from subsidizing transportation companies, banks, and newspaper enterprises to funding public schools; and from authorizing federal marshals to return fugitive slaves to carrying out Indian Removal, there is no doubt that the state established powerful boundaries between which society and markets developed. It was not so much a question of *whether* the American state was weak or strong, but of what segments of the population benefited from government largesse.[18]

Within this tradition, a more select group of scholars, many of them with backgrounds in media history and communications, argued for the establishment of the early federal bureaucracy as an important historical agent. Once the founders created the federal bureaucracy, according to these authors, the bureaucracy could create new institutions and narrow the range of possibilities available to future individual actors. Richard John, in *Spreading the News* (1995), posited that the Post Office Act of 1792 helped initiate westward expansion, a burgeoning market economy, the creation of a public sphere, and later advances in transportation and communication. The essential public subsidies established by the founders—including the franking privilege, printing contracts, free exchange of newspapers among editors, and cheap postage—enabled widespread newspaper circulation and readership. By the Jacksonian era, the nation's leading partisan newspapers came to rely heavily on federal subsidies from Congress and executive department agencies, especially the Treasury, State, War, and Post Office Departments.[19] These policies reflected the founders' conviction that the news was a public good that required public money, as well as a belief that a healthy republic depended on an informed citizenry. Although the past thirty years have shown signs of a growing consensus among academics regarding the importance of the state, this is arguably less true among the general public. It remains as important as ever to overcome what one historian called the "collective amnesia" among the American public regarding the role of government in their nation's past, and to remind them that government has almost always picked winners and losers.[20]

In this book, I am concerned less with characterizing the early American state along the traditional binaries of weak versus strong or liberal versus republican, and more with showing how state institutions interacted with individual actors in complex ways to shape the Bank War. Placing a definitive label on the early American state runs the risk of oversimplifying a fluid, multidimensional phenomenon.[21] In the same vein, it can be fruitless to apply the classically liberal assumption of arbitrarily separating the state and market. As one recent study of the complex political and economic relationships of chartered corporations in New York's early statehood revealed, the boundaries between public and private were often so thin as to be indistinguishable.[22]

Suffice to say that for the purposes of this book, the early American state was *influential*, but not so prohibitive as to overpower the role of individual agency, and not so one-dimensional as to mask the ways in which public and private, liberal and republican, and polity and economy were intertwined. Printing contracts and other public subsidies were institutional factors that framed the boundaries through which the Bank War unfolded, but business practices, party attitudes, and personality traits were also important. The role of political institutions was not deterministic. Contingency and choice still mattered. A major contention of this book, therefore, is that there was a dual relationship between editors as individual actors and the institutions within which they operated. Editors in the Bank War could simultaneously influence—and be influenced by—the public-private institutions established by their predecessors.

This book approaches the Bank War by considering questions that have been underreported in the literature: How did this controversy morph from a seemingly simple question of renewing the bank's charter to a highly charged, nationwide sensation that divided the American public into ideologically polarized political parties? How did the institutional structure of the bank (e.g., its interregional network of branches), the federal and state bureaucracies, and the national and international economies shape the Bank War? What factors allowed some partisan editors to succeed financially while others floundered? Answering these questions holistically requires us to spend some time looking into the broader political economy that prevailed between roughly 1820 and 1840.

Most of the political and economic institutions discussed here mixed public and private sources of money to some degree on a nationwide scale. Defined broadly, these institutions ranged from formal branches of government like the presidency and Congress, to financial institutions like the BUS and state banks, to executive department agencies like the Post Office. Considering how transportation improvements at the time were only beginning to erode long-established patterns of regionalism, the national character of these institutions was significant indeed. Among nonreligious organizations, the BUS, Post Office, and party newspapers like the *Globe* and *National Intelligencer* were unique in commanding a nationwide presence. The degree of governmental involvement in these institutions was often indirect and at times imperceptible to the undiscerning eye. Newspaper editors relied on printing contracts drawn from the public purse and appropriated public subsidies in transmitting their products through the mail, but the advertisers, bank loans, and subscriptions that paid for printers' wages and sustained their businesses were of a private nature. Editors sought government patronage, but much of what financed the delivery of newspapers came from those who paid higher rates of postage to send letters through the mail. Similarly, the Post Office was an executive department agency, but the government itself did not directly transport the mail. Rather, it hired private contractors to manage postal routes and paid private conveyance companies, postmasters, and editors to deliver the mail. State governments, moreover, might raise capital for bank and transportation companies by purchasing shares of stock or by backing the full faith and credit of their bonds, but strictly speaking, government employees did not manage the day-to-day operations of the companies that helped fuel westward expansion and the spread of newspaper readership. We might say, then, that local, state, and federal governments provided a helping hand in encouraging a certain type of environment in which economic growth and civil society could flourish.

Beyond providing a lens through which one can see the broader, pre-1840 political economy, the study of newspaper editors in the Bank War purveys a number of other analytical advantages. Too many accounts of the Bank War focus almost exclusively on Jackson, Biddle, and their closest allies. Editors appear from time to time, but they are implicitly reduced to the role of being passive actors. While any telling of the Bank War must necessarily deal with the letters of Jackson and Biddle, and this book is no exception, *The Bank War and the Partisan Press* brings some of the lesser-known and midlevel editors, postmasters, financiers, public officials, and party surrogates to the fore. Many of the central figures, advisers, and civil servants caught up in the Bank War were editors, and it was through newspapers primarily that Jackson and Biddle promulgated their messages. Without these crucial actors, Jackson's and Biddle's ideas would not have reached a mass audience. Without probing Kendall's quick rise through the ranks of the Jacksonian Party, for example, we might miss the opportunities that existed for social advancement among ordinary white men through patronage networks, exploding the myth that one's success or failure in life is derived exclusively from one's choices and work ethic.

In addition, studying the business model of partisan newspapers helps us understand the hypercharged rhetoric that made the politics of the Jacksonian era famous. Anyone who has read an editorial from this period can recognize immediately that editors did not adhere to the professional standards of objectivity and neutrality that are more commonly associated with twentieth-century journalism, but it is only through studying the economic incentives of the newspaper business in this period that we gain an adequate understanding of *why* the editorials were so vicious. Even the most successful editors contended with the financial instability and uncertainty of low profit margins and long hours of arduous labor. Much of this resulted from delinquent subscribers and others who consumed newspaper content without paying. Failure was common. In this environment, state support in the form of public printing contracts and other types of political patronage could spell the difference between profit and loss. And the best way for editors to win these contracts was to demonstrate loyalty to the party through vituperative commentary.

By focusing on the partisan press, finally, we can uncover a broader, multisided view of the Bank War; one that complements—and in some ways moves beyond—the traditional narrative of the boxing match between Jackson and Biddle. As it played out on the ground level throughout the country, the Bank War was marked by violent duels, inflammatory letters to the editor, politically orchestrated bank runs, assassination attempts, raucous public meetings, and destructive riots. These developments constituted a "Second Bank War" of sorts; one that was related to—but distinct from—the one unfolding in the elite corridors in Washington, Philadelphia, and New York. If we did not pay attention to newspapers and communications networks more broadly, we would not see the interplay between these two phases of the Bank War.

The Bank War and the Partisan Press follows a general storyline over a roughly seven-year period from Jackson's election in 1828 to 1834, at times eschewing a strict, linear chronology to take thematic considerations into account. Chapter 1 explores the newspaper business with particular attention to how struggling editors competed for printing contracts and other forms of patronage to achieve sustenance in a financially uncertain environment.

Amos Kendall's experience in founding and contributing to the *Globe*, the subject of Chapter 2, tells us about the statist undercurrents of Jacksonian ideology. While the Jacksonians viewed themselves as exponents of states' rights and limited government, they harbored no reservations over using the tools and resources of the federal bureaucracy to carry out the destruction of the BUS. In eviscerating a public-private, federally chartered corporate monopoly like the BUS, the Jacksonians elevated their own institutional base of support—the Democratic Party, Democratic Party newspapers, the executive branch, and state banks—at the expense of the institutions that opposed them, especially Congress and the Supreme Court.

Biddle did not go quietly into the night in the face of a sustained Jacksonian onslaught. Chapters 3 and 4 revisit traditional sources and emphasize newer ones to challenge or complicate many of the long-standing interpretations in the Bank War literature that have been passed down, uncritically, over the generations. These chapters interrogate congressional reports, newspapers, and epistolary evidence to show how the BUS used interregional communications networks to enact monetary policy and assess public opinion. Biddle, demonstrating his forward-thinking impulses, engaged the latest advances in transportation and communication to transmit articles, essays, treatises, and petitions that conveyed a pro-BUS message to voters living in all sections of the union. The nationwide character of Biddle's public relations campaign stemmed from the bank's vast financial holdings and institutional structure in the form of branch offices, and the mobilization of newspaper editors, economic theorists, branch officers, state bankers, vote counters, and confidential agents. At times Biddle covertly marshaled BUS funds as bribe money in this endeavor.

Included in this part of the book are a reassessment of the politicians and financial actors who pushed Biddle into recharter and a detailed estimate of how much the BUS spent in this endeavor. I estimate that the bank spent somewhere between $50,000 to $100,000 in printing orders for circulating pro-BUS media and lent about $100,000 to editors and perhaps $100,000 to $150,000 to congressmen from the start of Biddle's campaign in early 1830 to Jackson's veto in July 1832. These figures exceed historians' previous estimates. Large newspaper enterprises with nationwide subscription lists—including the *New York Courier and Enquirer*, *United States Telegraph*, and *Intelligencer*—were some of the most noteworthy recipients of these loans. Furthermore, *The Bank War and the Partisan Press* contests the received wisdom that Clay and Daniel Webster were central to pushing Biddle into an early application for recharter. In my view, Thomas Cadwalader, a senior BUS officer and director, along with the rest of the bank's board, were just as important in influencing Biddle's thinking, if not more so.

Chapter 5 examines the interactions between members of the bank's board in Philadelphia and the cashiers and presidents of the branch officers in the South and West during the enactment of loan reductions that contributed to a mild economic contraction from the fall of 1833 to the summer of 1834. It concludes that this interaction, facilitated by an interregional communications network, resembled Biddle's back and forth with newspaper editors prior to Jackson's veto. There were many reasons why Biddle's efforts did not secure a new BUS charter, and one of the key findings in this book, shown in Chapter 6, is that the Jacksonian-administered Post Office was one of them. An 1834 Senate report linking the Post Office with the establishment of the deposit banks and Democratic Party newspapers illuminated the degree to which Jacksonian loyalists appropriated mechanisms of the state to promote their party and defeat the BUS. Like the Jacksonians, Whigs criticized the manipulation of public money for partisan purposes. Instead of attacking the BUS, though, they directed their ire toward the Post Office, which could mold public opinion by controlling a vast patronage system, by rewarding editors and contractors with public money, and by determining the accuracy and speed with which it delivered newspapers through the mail. By linking the Post Office with the deposit removal controversy, Chapter 6 offers a new interpretation on an often-told story.

As the year in which the interrelated deposit removal scheme and Post Office scandal came to light, 1834 proved to be a pivotal moment for the Bank War. Around this time, Biddle lost significant public support because the economic contraction he engineered caused genuine economic hardship and did not force Jackson to acquiesce. Biddle would try to procure a new charter several more times, but he could never count on the enthusiastic support among merchants, politicians, planters, and financiers that he had once enjoyed. In addition, 1834 marks a suitable end point for this book because the following year, Kendall enacted a series of administrative reforms in the Post Office that supplanted much of the spoils system that had prevailed during much of the Bank War. These reforms, which sought to depersonalize and more formally organize much of the spending and management practices in the federal bureaucracy, were intended to prevent the sorts of inefficiencies and abuses of public money that characterized the management of the Post Office under Postmaster General William Barry. And while it is common to link the policies of Jackson and Biddle to the Panic of 1837, a trend that has increased in the past two decades as economists have returned to the American origins of the panic, this book is primarily concerned with the successes and failures of partisan editors, in which the larger developments of economic history play important but secondary roles.[23]

ONE

༄

Public Printers, Private Struggles: The Party Press and the Early American State

During his first year as president, Andrew Jackson dismissed dozens of civil servants in the federal bureaucracy, replacing many of them with partisan newspaper editors who had written on his behalf during the recent election. As Jackson saw it, there was an opportunity to root out corruption and at the same time promote social advancement for the underprivileged. John Randolph of Virginia, one of the president's longtime friends and political allies, asked Jackson to defend these actions, which were causing serious political blowback. In response, Jackson criticized those who would "make the calling of an editor a disqualification for the possession of those rewards which are calculated to enlarge the sphere of talent and merit, and which are accessible to other callings." The president asserted that "the respectability of the humblest vocations in life cannot be maintained" under the presumption that editors were unfit to serve in federal office.[1] There were elements of truth in Jackson's explanation, but a different rationale for what was known as "rotation of office" to its practitioners and "the spoils system" to its detractors came from Kentuckian William Barry, Jackson's pick for postmaster general, who, in the safety of being able to communicate candidly with his wife, wrote, "It is right and politic to encourage and reward friends."[2] With the possible exception of Thomas Jefferson, no president had before used the appointment process for party-building purposes to the extent that Jackson did.

In order to promote greater turnover and accountability in the federal bureaucracy, Congress had passed the Tenure of Office Act in 1820. This statute required Senate approval for commissioned officers like customs collectors who wished to serve longer than four-year terms. Rather than fire certain collectors outright, Jackson achieved his desired end by declining to renew their commissions, which ended at the beginning of each president's term.[3] If Jacksonians saw the opportunity for social advancement in this process, Jackson's opponents, the National Republicans, saw tyranny and despotism. Many of the civil servants that Jackson dismissed had spent their entire careers in Washington with creditable records of service. Previous administrations had established an unspoken precedent that working for the state should be independent and nonpartisan; something greater than the selfish reaches of any individual or political party. Absent grave misconduct, civil servants were supposed to retain their positions.[4]

National Republicans chided Jackson for corrupting the public trust of government by hiring based on loyalty and friendship, not competency and merit. A classically educated Henry Clay spoke for the opposition in declaring that the ultimate consequence of Jackson's arbitrary removals was "to convert the nation into one perpetual theatre for political gladiators" where "some Pretorian band would arise" from the destruction of free government. Jackson's appointments, according to National Republicans, threatened not just the independence of the civil service but also the authority and autonomy of Congress and the press. For all of these reasons, the U.S. Senate voted down many of the editors that Jackson nominated to fill the vacancies left by his removals. That Jackson continued to receive negative feedback for his actions from friends and foes alike shows the degree to which he had struck a deep nerve in the country.[5]

This chapter examines the ways in which appointment to federal office, and political patronage more generally, provided a means of economic security and social advancement for partisan newspaper editors. It analyzes the factors that facilitated the funding and dissemination of party newspapers and links these factors to some of the key issues involved in the Bank War. It starts with the premise that financial insecurity was endemic in the newspaper business. Editors endured long hours of arduous labor and low profit margins. Many antebellum Americans read newspapers without paying for subscriptions, and even some of those who did subscribe were delinquent in their payments.[6] And while many editors willingly accepted the self-sacrifice and meager standard of living out of the profession's higher calling, failure was common. Most newspapers, like most businesses back then and today, went bust after only a few years in operation.[7] Because private methods of funding newspapers—loans, advertising, and subscription revenue—were tenuous and unpredictable, political patronage drawn from public dollars provided essential financial stability, enabling newspaper businesses to grow. State legislatures, for example, paid editors to print legislative debates for public record, and at the federal level, the State, Treasury, and Post Office Departments paid editors to print official documents. These contracts were often profitable enough to allow editors to start side projects or expand their current operations. When their printing contracts ended, editors' private businesses often suffered too.[8]

To be clear, patronage was not the only factor that determined the success of newspaper businesses. Most editors survived without patronage, which was never so overwhelming as to prevent meaningful competition.[9] Business practices, personality traits, and ideological commitment were always at play, and it is difficult to isolate any single variable as universally determinative. In addition, the practice of awarding printing contracts to the lowest bidder, reinforced by the Jacksonians' aim of reducing what they viewed as wasteful and corrupt spending practices in government, ensured that editors could never maintain a life of luxury off of the public dime. Nonetheless, the importance that editors attached to public printing contracts—competing vigorously to win them and characterizing them as an important selling point to those who wished to move up the ladder in the business—is revealing. Contracts may not have always provided the path to material success and political power that editors desired, but a good deal of evidence suggests that editors believed they would.

Over fifty years ago, Jackson biographer Robert V. Remini identified "the creation of a vast, nation-wide newspaper system" during the administration of John Quincy Adams as "perhaps the single most important accomplishment" of the Jacksonians in Congress and in the states.[10] Indeed, party newspapers were the glue that held the political system together. They galvanized voters, informed readers of upcoming political meetings, broadcast candidates' stances on leading controversies, and showcased editorials that helped shape public opinion. Before the telegraph, they were practically the sole medium for communicating political ideas on a mass, nationwide scale.

Americans' prodigious consumption of newspapers in post offices, coffee houses, libraries, and hotel rooms contributed to a vibrant public sphere in which politically active citizens read up on the latest news and exchanged ideas in spirited debates. In fact, newspapers were a key part of a more general increase in the consumption of political media at this time that included broadsides, handbills, and political cartoons.[11]

The men who edited newspapers were indispensable political actors who organized rallies, set up county meetings, and served on a party's central committees and conventions, which were suitable venues to recruit subscribers. Effectively, they were middlemen between party elites and ordinary voters. By recommending party loyalists for positions of public office and by endorsing candidates, editors exercised sway over the political process. If a candidate wished to run a successful campaign, having his name appear at the top of a friendly newspaper was essential.[12] The bipartisan opposition to Jackson's appointments reflected the real or perceived personality traits exhibited by many partisan editors. Younger editors, especially, seemed to lack the decorum and comity of their predecessors from the early republic. A more vocal, vituperative, and aggressive editorial style was both an influence and symptom of the partisanship and polarization that helped to define Jacksonian-era politics. Party leaders needed newspapers to mobilize voter turnout, enforce party discipline, and draw recalcitrant voters back into line, so it made sense to recruit strong-willed, combative personalities to run papers.[13] On the other hand, the ascent of newspaper editors in American politics evinced a measure of social advancement and democratic inclusion. Many of them hailed from artisanal social backgrounds, or in the words of one historian, they were "recent graduates from manual to intellectual labor." Their election to Congress and appointment to federal office helped to erode the deference and elitism that characterized the politics of the founding generation.[14]

Struggle, self-sacrifice, long hours of laborious work, and financial insecurity were defining features of the business. Samuel Harrison Smith, the renowned Jeffersonian editor and founder of the Washington-based *National Intelligencer,* gave up the trade when he sold his business to Joseph Gales Jr. in 1810. The demanding line of work was taking a toll on Smith's health, and his wife, distinguished socialite and author Margaret Bayard Smith, implored him to devote more time to his family.[15] Success could be elusive for even the most talented. Clay expressed sympathy to an editor who had resigned from the *Daily National Journal* when he wrote, "The situation of Editor . . . appears to me far from desirable," and that of all partisan editors in the country, few "have made a comfortable provision for themselves!"[16] These struggles were not confined to National Republicans. Pennsylvania Jacksonian Simon Cameron, joint owner of the Harrisburg *Pennsylvania Reporter and Democratic Herald* and one of Old Hickory's earliest support- ers as a presidential candidate, described the struggles of operating a news- paper without patronage in a letter to the president. Cameron wanted his friend and business partner, Samuel C. Stambaugh, to receive the appoint- ment of district marshal for "the health of Mr Stambaugh by a devotion to his editorial duties, was much injured."[17]

Unfortunately for the hundreds of enterprising editors who tried to stake out a decent livelihood, hard work often yielded little material reward. It was common for partisan newspaper editors in Jacksonian America to take second jobs as postmasters, customs officials, clerks, and cashiers. One might assume from this moonlighting that the profits from the newspaper business were insufficient to make ends meet. This was partially attributable to the countless numbers of Americans who read papers without paying for subscriptions, as well as the untold numbers who either could not or chose not to pay on time. Hotels, taverns, libraries, and banks often made free copies of newspapers available for customers. If one subscriber paid for delivery, the paper might pass through five or six hands before the next edition. Historian Charles G. Steffen posited that Americans in the early re- public demanded access to free newspapers as a right, a trend that grew out of a republican priority of an informed citizenry as well as a liberal tendency toward greater consumer choices.[18]

Complaints about unpaying customers among editors were pervasive. In September 1833 the *Saturday Evening Post* printed a story about a delin- quent customer who demanded an end to his subscription. The editor of the *Post* explained: "We wanted money to pay for paper—to journeymen—for printing—for the thousand articles necessary for our publication—and we sent him a bill." The customer forwarded $13, equivalent to overdue sub- scription money that had accumulated for five years, but "flew in a pas- sion." Exasperated, the *Post* editor asked, "What are subscribers worth who will not pay?" The column ended with a firm admonition: "We ask no man's patronage who, by his acts, declares that the 'labourer is not worthy of his hire.'" In the minds of editors, free access to newspapers degraded the dignity of hard work.[19]

A constant tug-of-war developed between editors, who struggled for sus- tenance, and readers, who eagerly sought the latest and most exciting politi- cal news at the cheapest rate possible. Leniency on the part of editors was key to this negotiated relationship. Subscribers often paid editors in foreign coins, which were legal tender at the time, but when coins were in short supply, they sometimes bartered for newspapers or paid in agricultural goods.[20] Some editors floated the idea of a national convention to craft uniform rules for delinquent customers, including the proposal that all new subscribers pay in advance, as well as the termination of delivery to customers whose delinquency exceeded one full year. But as the *Fayetteville Observer* put it, any editor who enacted uniform policies that penalized delinquent subscribers "would soon find himself without subscribers." Withholding delivery could backfire. The editor had to strike a delicate balance so that customers would not take advantage of him.[21]

Other techniques ranged from more psychological maneuvers, as in threatening delinquent customers with public exposure, to more forceful methods, as in dispatching bill collectors to peoples' houses or issuing lawsuits. The publication of delinquent lists in newspapers was an effort to publicly shame customers into paying. The hope was to appeal to readers' sense of honesty, integrity, fairness, and compassion for the plight of struggling editors. The *National Intelligencer* reprinted an urgent message from the *Portsmouth Journal*: "*Newspaper Borrowers.*—Reader, if you borrowed this paper, send it right back—as you may feel *cheap* after you have finished this paragraph." The *Journal* then offered several analogies to reinforce its headline, including the sarcastic rhetorical question, "If the baker leaves you a *hot loaf*, should you like to lend it to your neighbor, and have it returned cold with corners gnawed off?"[22] Local authorities and postmasters sometimes helped editors recover payments, but there was frequent pushback. According to John Cook Rives, the business partner of *Globe* editor Francis P. Blair, some recalcitrant subscribers in New York "den[ied] the authority of the Agent to collect." The agent asked Blair to remind readers in print that agents were authorized "to receive all dues to the Globe in Brooklyn, Tomklesville, and the city of New York."[23]

One wonders why so many editors joined the business if it entailed such hardship and hassle.[24] Some evidence indicates that purely profit-driven motives and sustainability in a business sense may have been secondary to artistic passion and the conviction that writing for a party newspaper was not only an honorable profession but a way to remake the world in a better light. When describing the extensive financial sacrifices he experienced in establishing the *Globe* in Washington, Amos Kendall told Jackson, "It is not for my own sake that I have taken any part in political affairs." Rather, it was "obligations to my God and country" and a conviction that if he had not started the *Globe*, "So far as newspapers are concerned, [Jackson] would have been at the mercy of enemies and traitors."[25] After becoming proprietor of the Anti-Jacksonian *Daily National Journal* in Washington, William Prentiss "deemed it a duty under all hazzards to sustain that press so far as pecuniary means would enable [me]." Prentiss even advertised his "stock of Jewelry watches silver ware for sale at auction" for the purpose of standing up for "vital principles" and for helping Clay become president. There was a common assumption among editors that merely by establishing a newspaper business in a certain locale, one had the opportunity to mold public opinion for the better. F. H. Pettis sought a newspaper editorship that would allow him to support Clay for president, especially in "some state where there is a chance for a victory and not where the majority is already Anti-Jackson." Some of those in the U.S. Senate who voted down Jackson's appointments may have felt that because of their heated and propagandistic rhetoric, partisan editors were unfit for the job of public service. But plenty of editors saw the profession as a noble calling and an opportunity to contribute to something larger than the self.[26]

Because the career of a partisan newspaper editor entailed low profit margins at best, public printing contracts and other forms of political patronage assumed critical importance. In early 1833 Kentucky printer Albert Gallatin Hodges became co-proprietor of the *Frankfort Commonwealth*. Hodges's new ownership responsibilities brought "very heavy expenses" and "anxiety." He pledged the utmost fidelity and "workman-like manner," thanked members of the Kentucky General Assembly for providing him with public printing contracts, and appealed to his friends "for a liberal patronage."[27] Patronage greased the wheels of the political system and allowed editors to survive financially. Its critics pointed to corruption, inefficiency, and fraud, and with good reason, but it did prove mutually beneficial for those involved. In its simplest form, patronage was the exchange of hired work for political loyalty. For newspaper editors, this could mean that a patron (literally, a fatherly figure) was sponsoring the arts (or in this case newspapers). Alternatively and more commonly, it implied the procurement of patrons, or customers, for the newspaper in the form of paying subscribers. Editors had done much to get Jackson elected, and to return the favor, he appointed them to public office or rewarded them with printing contracts.[28]

Among the commissioned officers appointed by the president and requiring Senate approval were Treasury bureau chiefs, land office registers and receivers, judges, customs officers, territorial officials, postmasters, Indian agents, and district attorneys and marshals. If an office-hunter (sometimes known as an "office seeker" or "place hunter") wanted Jackson to consider him for a particular position, there were semiformal expectations that another person(s) would write a letter of recommendation on his behalf, testifying to his loyalty, character, hard work, experience, qualifications, temperament, moral compass, and contributions to the party. A petition with numerous signatures might accompany the application.[29] Assuming the president was convinced, either by the application, word-of-mouth, or some other means, that a particular candidate would make a good fit for an opening, the president would instruct or encourage one of his department heads (e.g., secretary of the Treasury) to carry out the selection. As practiced during Jackson's presidency, the goal in many cases was to reward a struggling editor who had sacrificed his time and energy in helping the party.[30]

A letter to Jackson from *United States Telegraph* editor Duff Green, written on behalf of John Silva Meehan, demonstrated a consistent theme of advancement through patronage for the lower to middling rungs of the white male social ladder. Green depicted Meehan, former *Telegraph* founder now in Green's employ, as "a faithful friend," a "pious Christian," ardently devoted to Jackson's principles, and perhaps most crucially, "the father of an amiable family, who are entirely dependant upon his earnings for support." After detailing the lengths to which he had gone to help Jackson get elected, his own debts, and the $1,200 per year salary he paid to Meehan, Green compared Meehan's financial position to another man who was lobbying Jackson for the same position. Because the competitor was the nephew of a man "of boundless wealth" who could "obtain for him other and better employment," Green stated unequivocally that Meehan should get the appointment. There were a limited number of openings in federal office, and it would be wasteful, according to Green's thinking, to appoint someone who was already comfortable. It was much better to hire the man who needed it. When it came to formulating policy on federal support for internal improvements and reducing the public debt, the Jacksonians often preferred to appropriate classical liberalism in characterizing government spending as wasteful and inefficient. Yet when it came to staffing state and federal bureaucracies, they saw no contradiction between hard work, social advancement, and a career in government.[31]

If the president could not appoint editors to federal office, he could persuade executive department heads to provide editors with printing contracts, guaranteed subscribers, or some other type of income. The State

Department, for example, hired editors to print treaties and diplomatic correspondence. Each executive department appropriated public money to fund editors with advertising insertions in their papers as well as printing contracts for the production of large quantities of official documents. At the beginning of Jackson's first term, Ohio Jacksonian Caleb Atwater requested patronage for one editor by writing, "If a few advertisements could be sent to him for insertion, in his paper by members of your cabinet, he would be satisfied."[32] In printing official documents, advertisements, and over-the-top editorials under the same newspaper establishment, antebellum-era party presses blended public policy, profit concerns, and partisanship in interesting ways. Editors were expected to demonstrate their value to the party by endorsing candidates, organizing political meetings, donating to a campaign, or writing editorials on behalf of their patrons. If their preferred candidates won, editors could claim some right to consideration for printing contracts. Decades before professional journalists adopted standards of balance and objectivity, editors did everything within their power to get their party leaders elected. The built-in business model of party presses, thus, lent a powerful incentive to heated rhetoric.[33]

The specific terms of a printing contract, including whether the position was appointive or elective, varied based on the context. Typically the dollar amount of a printing job reflected costs for labor, time, and material. Some editors received money for publishing a monthly list of unclaimed letters at the local post office while others earned cash by printing public notices from the courts. At the beginning of each session of Congress, the president, working with the State Department, selected about eighty editors in various cities across the country to print the laws.[34] At least two phenomena ensured that the monetary value of these contracts did not become excessively profitable for the beneficiaries. One was the Jacksonian push to limit public spending, which was founded on the belief, articulated by Jefferson, Franklin, and many others, that debt equaled dependency, waste, profligacy, and corruption. This was embodied in Jackson's decision to retire all of the public debt during his second term. The other was a practice commonly employed in the Post Office Department in the disbursement of contracts for delivering the mail to private conveyance companies: public contracts were supposed to go to the lowest bidder.[35]

These two factors—the competitive bidding process and the Jacksonian goal of limiting public spending—were ideals that often failed to materialize in practice. As much as the Jacksonians may have railed against the corruption in Washington when John Quincy Adams was president, abuses of public spending also occurred under their watch. This was especially true if there was a question of party loyalty or the possibility of rewarding political allies (see Chapter 6). It might be said, then, that the Jacksonians were most concerned over the accountability of public spending when public dollars were awarded to their opponents. In March 1833 the House of Representatives appropriated a contract for two printers, Peter Force and Matthew St. Clair Clarke, who were to work under the direction of the secretary of state in compiling 1,500 copies of diplomatic correspondence for a seven-volume project called the "Documentary History of the [American] Revolution." Force had briefly edited the pro-Clay *Daily National Journal* while Clarke had been clerk to the House. The House contract stipulated that the two printers would complete the project at a rate of $2.20 per volume, which had been the standard rate for some years.

But after discovering that other printers were willing to complete the same job at a much cheaper rate, the Jacksonian House rescinded the contract. The partnership, Carey, Lea, & Co., of Philadelphia, quoted a rate of $1.67 per volume while printer Charles Hendee of Boston offered to do the work for as low as $1.00 per volume. The Senate ultimately paid $15,000 to Force and Clarke for their troubles and partial completion of the project, but the House insisted that the contract came with the assumption of a "*fair and reasonable publication price*" based on the cost of paper, printing, binding, composition, presswork, copying, editing, and collecting material. Blair and Rives eventually won the contract for $1.71 per volume, printing 1,000 copies for a total of $11,968.88. This was not the cheapest rate and may have reflected the desire of the Jacksonian-controlled House to reward Jacksonian editors. Partisanship cut both ways, potentially inflating or limiting the dollar amount of the contracts. Politicians of both parties took seriously their classically republican duty to guard the public trust, though the degree to which they honored this duty, unsurprisingly, depended on whether they or their opponents were the ones benefiting from public dollars.[36]

The most lucrative printing contracts were for recording and distributing the legislative debates in Congress. For most of the 1820s and 1830s, these were doled out to Green, Blair, or Gales, all of whom managed major party presses. Gales, an English-born North Carolinian who hailed from a family of authors and printers, had published and owned the *National Intelligencer* along with his partner and brother-in-law, William Winston Seaton, since 1810. Initially a de facto administration press for President Thomas Jefferson, the *Intelligencer* had by the 1820s come to espouse the nationalist economic policies articulated by Clay and Adams, including support for the

BUS.[37] When they were not managing the *Intelligencer*, Gales and Seaton spent most of their careers covering congressional debates—the *Annals of Congress* was the nation's official record of debates from 1798 to 1824, and the *Register of Debates* picked up where the former left off, lasting until 1837. The two editors earned $84,217.93 for printing for both houses of Congress for the year 1834 and approximately $75,000 the following year. For their work on the *American State Papers*, an ambitious, multi-year project that sought to record the poorly kept congressional debates from the early republic, Gales and Seaton grossed $219,172.26 for a period covering July 1834 to November 1836.[38] The exact profits that Gales and Seaton took home from these projects are unknown. One journalism historian estimated that two-year congressional contracts typically entailed profit margins between 20 and 55 percent, which, given the scale of the projects, would have meant many thousands of dollars of profit. But Baltimorean editor Hezekiah Niles believed that once Gales and Seaton had paid off the principal and interest on the loans needed to initially finance their project, the profit "would hardly buy a year's bread for a single family."[39]

Because printing the laws and debates for Congress was a major undertaking involving numerous hours of preparation, equipment, materials, and the employment of scores of workers, the editors in charge of such projects required significant capital investment, paid up front. This came most often in the form of bank loans. Sometimes Gales and Seaton borrowed from state banks like the Patriotic Bank in Washington, though most state banks refused to lend to the editors because of their pro-BUS stance. The BUS, therefore, functioned as an intermediary of both necessity and political mutualism. As both a for-profit financial institution and fiscal arm of the Treasury, the BUS helped to disburse public funds when Congress awarded printing contracts, and it issued loans to the two editors during intervening months or during lean times.[40] Typically the Second Bank advanced to Gales and Seaton funds secured by liens on their real estate, press, and materials. The assumption was that once the public funding for the project came through, the editors would then have the means to repay their initial private loans. In printing for Congress, Gales and Seaton established a relationship with the Second Bank that blended public and private money.[41]

Interestingly, the public money that Gales and Seaton received from Congress for printing the laws and debates seemed to predict the financial health of the *Intelligencer*, the editors' private business. Like most party presses, the *Intelligencer* obtained the bulk of its revenue from subscription money, advertising, and bank loans, but the importance of public money in the editors' financial affairs is perhaps best shown by its absence. When Gales and Seaton lost their appointment as printers in 1829, their debt to the bank was $37,609.96.[42] Richard Smith, the cashier of the Washington branch BUS, testified before Congress that since Gales and Seaton could not pay the interest on this debt, let alone pay down the principal, the BUS would take possession of the *Intelligencer* establishment, including all of the lots, housing structures, and printing materials. The metaphor of the revolving door might best characterize the close personal and financial relationships involved in these agreements. The president of the Washington branch at the time was *Intelligencer* founder Samuel Harrison Smith (no relation to Richard), who had trained Gales as an apprentice during Jefferson's presidency.[43]

According to several deeds of trust signed with the BUS in the 1820s, Gales and Seaton would pay rent to the bank in a dollar amount roughly equivalent to the interest on the full property value of the *Intelligencer*. While this financial relationship effectively made the *Intelligencer* the de facto media outlet of the bank—a point that Blair constantly flagged as evidence of bribery and corruption—what is noteworthy from the standpoint of running a newspaper business was that the paper's debt to the BUS more than doubled, to $80,000, by March 1833. Their debts ballooned in the very same years that their public printing contracts dried up. To erase these debts and securitize additional loans, the bank assumed ownership of Seaton's house and Gales's farm and residence. No doubt part of the reason that the two editors had accumulated significant debts stemmed from Biddle's desire to finance newspapers that would help him wage the Bank War, but the loss of public printing was also crucial.[44] Gales owned and operated the *Intelligencer* for almost fifty years, and in the words of the author of the sole monograph on this illustrious newspaper, "for most of its life the *Intelligencer* depended on the federal government for its financial support."[45] The man who replaced Gales and Seaton as printer for Congress, Duff Green, encountered similar financial difficulties once the bounty of the public treasure ran out. From 1829 to 1835, Green enjoyed well-paying printing contracts from the House, Senate, and both. Soon after losing the congressional printing, however, Green conspicuously relinquished editorial control over the *Telegraph*.[46]

Printing contracts could, thus, provide a significant boost to the business prospects of party newspapers. But just as easily, good fortunes could run out if the political party with which an editor was aligned lost power. When Kendall experienced financial difficulties during his youth as editor of the *Argus of Western America*, becoming public printer for the state legislature in Frankfort elevated his standing to the point that he "acquired a strong influence in the affairs of the state." But in 1825, as Kendall put it, "the party to which I belonged was defeated in the elections and I lost public printing." Kendall subsequently entered a phase where his personal life became "disordered." He was "entirely broken up" and had to sell his property. In 1828 Jacksonians regained control of the state legislature and restored Kendall's public printing. The ups and downs of Kendall's professional and personal lives seemed to correlate—and even depend upon—the availability of public printing contracts.[47]

None of this is to suggest that patronage alone determined the entrepreneurial success of party presses. By no means could printing contracts guarantee long-term profits or eliminate competition. Green abandoned the *Telegraph* soon after losing congressional printing, but he had numerous other personal failures. His explosive personality alienated allies. He did not manage the *Telegraph* prudently—overextending his operations and hiring too many workers.[48] Alabamian Enoch Parsons described William Travis, a young lawyer then editing the *Claiborne Herald* who would later go on to fight and die at the Alamo, as a "worthy young man . . . who has a family, and is poor." If Travis was to print the laws, Parsons wrote to the president, "it would aid him materially."[49] When explaining that Travis's current paper did not have many subscribers, he referenced the previous editor's personal disposition: "The predecessor being intemperate, lessened the use of the paper." Social capital could matter as much as financial capital. And to win contracts in the first place, editors had to demonstrate at least some business acumen. Parsons was confident that Travis "would faithfully perform the duty, [but] Candor compels me to say his paper does not circulate as much." Before doling out contracts, party leaders usually wanted some assurances that new ventures could survive on their own. This may have been due to the high failure rate for newspapers. Understandably, politicians would not want to grant public funds to an editor who had yet to prove himself capable.[50] If they managed to cross this minimum threshold, however, editors who won the contracts could witness an expansion of their business; in other words, an investment of public funds could lead to private profits. "If the laws are published in the Claiborne paper," Parsons told Jackson, "it will at once circulate more freely."[51]

It might be reasonable to conclude that in patronage, editors had a potentially viable path to financial success if only because contemporary politicians and editors claimed as much for those who thought of joining the trade. When Nicholas Bailhache, editor of the *Guernsey Times* of Cambridge, Ohio, informed readers of the *Scioto Gazette* that he wished to sell his establishment, he wrote confidently that he had "no doubt but it would yield a handsome profit." As the only paper in Guernsey County, the paper had a monopoly, but as a crucial selling point, it also had "the advantage of being located at the county seat, and consequently does all the public printing for the county which in the course of a year amounts to a considerable sum, and is sure to pay."[52] Nicholas's father, John, had edited the pro-Clay *Ohio State Journal* and served as co-chair of the National Republican Central Committee of Ohio for the 1832 elections. As was the case with Gales and Philadelphia printer William Duane, the job of an editor was a family trade of sorts passed down from father to son.[53]

The degree to which editors sometimes battled with one another in acrimonious terms over the distribution of printing contracts provides additional testimony to the importance of public money to the newspaper business. Calvin Gunn, editor of the *Jeffersonian Republican*, was the main recipient of contracts to print debates in the Missouri General Assembly between 1824 and 1845.[54] The editor maintained a long editorial career, in part, because of printing contracts, and also because of his decision to downscale the *Republican* when the assembly was in session. Nathaniel Patten, editor of the *Missouri Intelligencer* and one of Gunn's competitors, wrote, somewhat humorously, "When the teats of the *two* Treasuries [the state and federal] are pulled from him, [Gunn] will be apt to find himself a little wiser—and a little poorer."[55] In a few cases, the granting of contracts generated uproar. Missourian Finis Ewing, a federal land office employee and anti-BUS political ally of Senator Thomas Hart Benton, penned Jackson in September 1833, assessing public opinion in his home state with the following statement: "The people here feel the greatest indignation at the election of public printers, especially the election of Duff Green." Frustrated and angry, Ewing continued, "The idea of the *people's* money going to the support of a paper which is scattering poison & political death, is almost too much to bear." The Missourian was incensed that "the people be *compelled* to pay money for the support of Nullification."[56]

Ewing's letter got to the heart of the complex relationship between the state, newspaper businesses, and public opinion in antebellum America. Green devoted considerable space in his *Telegraph* to publishing the laws and debates, which appeared on the surface to be an innocuous practice. But given the profitability of congressional printing contracts, he also had extra money to write antitariff editorials. Public money and private business intersected in innumerable ways when it came to the newspaper business. Ewing saw a flagrant conflict of interest. He could not stomach the fact that public money—extracted from the pockets of all Americans—was supporting a certain political perspective, and a potentially incendiary one at that when one considers that the nullification crisis of 1832 nearly drove the nation to civil war. Ewing's outrage, however, may have been selective. Many party presses throughout the country drew from public money in some form or another. Whether they knew it or not, antebellum Americans paid revenues, principally through tariffs and land sales, to fund a bureaucracy that in subsidizing newspapers did much to shape the development of mass political parties and public opinion.

The same tariff concerns referenced in Ewing's letter haunted Blair, who was one of Ewing's employers and political allies.[57] In April 1833 the election of public printer to the House of Representatives was extremely close, involving several rounds of votes. After fourteen ballots over a two-day period, Gales and Seaton narrowly eked out a one-vote victory. Blair was apoplectic. He wrote letters to *every* House member, demanding to know who had voted against him. One Jacksonian representative, Mark Alexander of Virginia, responded to Blair's inquiry on April 11: "It was not until you came out in approbation of the principles of the President's proclamation [on nullification] that I determined not to vote for you." But when subsequent ballots revealed a close contest between Blair and the two editors of the *Intelligencer*, Alexander decided that he could not support either side. "I declined voting," he said, "on the several last ballotings and was not present in the House when the election was made, having retired to the Senate."[58]

Blair could have used Alexander's vote. Characteristically, the *Globe* editor blamed the BUS for bribing the congressmen who voted for Gales and Seaton.[59] The leading political issues of the day, especially nullification and the Bank War, were so convulsive that they inflamed and spilled over into the seemingly mundane tasks of electing public printers for Congress.[60] In addition to the potential profits at stake, it may have been the case that printing legislative debates gave editors a certain degree of power, however subtle, of shaping public opinion. Legislative printing contracts like those for Congress came with the influential perk of deciding what issues to cover and how to cover them. Editors did their best to report congressmen accurately, but there were numerous accusations at the time that a public printer allied with the opposing political party could, either deliberately or mistakenly, misquote or misconstrue a congressman's words and thus influence how voters felt about them.[61]

Political conflicts in Missouri under the governorships of John Miller and Daniel Dunklin showed how the business struggles of partisan newspapers were linked with how the Bank War unfolded in various parts of the union. On February 25, 1832, newspaper editor John Steele composed a letter to Dunklin, a prominent anti-BUS Jacksonian and soon-to-be governor. Steele solicited Dunklin's financial assistance in establishing a new Jacksonian newspaper in St. Louis, which would tackle a variety of issues, including the BUS. To distance himself from the more moderate *St. Louis Beacon*, which had endorsed pro-BUS candidates for Congress, Steele considered publishing one of Senator Benton's recent anti-BUS speeches. He wondered if printing and disseminating 10,000 copies of this speech would win Dunklin's support. Steele enclosed a prospectus of his new paper, the *Missouri Free Press*, in his letter to Dunklin. "Anything you do for this paper," Steele wrote, "will be appreciated and in a proper manner reciprocated in the impending contest." If Dunklin gave his financial support to the *Free Press*, then Steele would back him in the upcoming gubernatorial election.[62]

Hard-money Jacksonians like Dunklin, Benton, and Miller had struggled endlessly to find loyal newspaper editors and elect anti-BUS Jacksonians into office. For many years, commercially oriented Jacksonians who were friendlier to Clay's American System had benefited by attaching themselves to Jackson's larger-than-life persona, by mobilizing proto-Whig voters, and by running in elections with multiple candidates, thereby splitting the anti-BUS vote. Miller derided these politicians as "counterfeit Jackson men" because of their support for the BUS.[63] For Miller, having a loyal anti-BUS Jacksonian press was essential for the growth of the party he represented. In a confidential letter written to Dunklin on March 8, 1832, the governor complained of the *St. Louis Beacon*'s "duplicitous" tactics. "It is of the first importance," Miller wrote, "to the best interest of the Democratic party as well as of the country that an ably Edited paper should immediately be established at St. Louis." In the event that this paper required an initial advancement of funds, Miller recommended that Dunklin, "in connection with a few other confidential friends," should "furnish the necessary aid." Miller believed that if only five or six individuals pooled their resources together, "it would not require an advance of more than some two hundred dollars from each," which would eventually be repaid from the paper's profits. But time was of the essence for the governor. "A paper at Postosi

[Missouri]," he said, "would be highly beneficial, and should you delay in establishing one," a National Republican editor would fill the void.[64]

An opportunistic Steele aggressively courted Dunklin's support with numerous letters. In one letter from April 16, Steele warned Dunklin of the *Free Press*'s precarious financial position: "Nothing short of our extensive circulation of this paper can sustain it in its infancy." It needed state support to survive. "If the Party will do what I know my perseverance" deserves, he continued, "I have no fears of success."[65] On April 24 Steele again wrote to Dunklin: "I am your *friend* & will not be unfaithful—your confidence is not misplaced in me." This proclamation of unwavering loyalty seemed fitting for Dunklin, who had recently opined that "to secure anything like patronage in this county the man who undertakes must show himself worthy of it first."[66] Steele's letters documented the self-sacrifice and financial struggle experienced by countless party newspaper editors. He confessed that he did not have enough time "to review or revise anything save only the Editorial." He typically wrote letters "in the night at late hours" and apologized for sentences that might have contained missing words. Steele concluded his missive by stating, "It is now 3 o'clock in the morning. I am much fatigued, must stop should have done so sooner."[67]

Over two years later, Dunklin solicited another editor, Alonzo Manning, to serve alongside Calvin Gunn as public printer for the Missouri General Assembly in Jefferson City. Manning declined because his career was taking off in St. Louis and Dunklin's offer, which was modest, did not justify relocation. But there was also some hesitation before he rejected the offer. Manning believed that the state of Missouri's political affairs were "in the midst of a greater crisis than ever known since the days of the Revolution." Just as Jackson had done in his veto message of 1832, Manning cast the Bank War as an epic metaphorical struggle for liberty against British oppression. "The many-headed monster," Manning wrote, "is secretly and not less vigilantly feeding upon the vital spirit of Democracy and to throw in my small mite towards the accomplishment" of defeating the bank "would, indeed, be a proud consolation."[68]

Dunklin offered financial support to Manning, in part, because he was never enthusiastic about working with Steele, who criticized some of the pro-BUS Jacksonians in Missouri with whom Dunklin had a working relationship. Steele moved ahead anyway, inaugurating the *Free Press* in the spring of 1832, endorsing Dunklin for governor, and echoing his views on states' rights, the BUS, the tariff, and slavery. Dunklin eventually rewarded the editor, albeit modestly. Steele received state contracts for printing legislative debates in Jefferson City and also secured a small amount of federal patronage. Unfortunately for Steele, the *Free Press* never took off in the manner he had hoped. Extant records do not indicate the precise dollar amount that Steele garnered from printing contracts, but it was probably not higher than a few hundred dollars. Most of the contracts were at the state level, which paid much less than those at the federal level. And in Steele's case, editor Calvin Gunn had already claimed much of the state printing. Dunklin opted to spread out state printing contracts among as many editors as possible, but in doing so, he may have shortchanged Steele.[69]

While Steele's particular experiment failed, the larger mission to shape anti-BUS public opinion in Missouri eventually succeeded. After losing several close congressional races in the early-1830s, Missouri's anti-BUS Democrats moved to unify their party by purging pro-BUS members from their ranks in what might be likened to a party purity test. Hard-liners like Dunklin and Benton used the press to attack the "counterfeit Jackson men," including Representative William Henry Ashley. The attacks were vicious and spearheaded by authors who wrote pseudonymously in Democratic newspapers.[70] The pseudonyms were often covers for editors and other prominent politicians seeking to speak for—or influence—public opinion. In the Democratic *Missouri Argus*, "Justiciary" characterized Ashley as "aristocratic and anti-Democratic" and claimed that a large number of voters had switched their allegiance because Ashley had gravitated toward the Whigs, and was now "too plain to deceive them any more." Another correspondent cited Ashley's purported campaign donations from the BUS.[71]

In part because of his support for the BUS in a Missouri electorate that had become increasingly polarized by 1836, Ashley could no longer run on the Jacksonian label that had helped him win three elections to Congress. In the gubernatorial contest, Ashley ran as an independent candidate against Lilburn W. Boggs, a hard-money Democrat.[72] Boggs defeated Ashley by a fairly healthy margin. Four years of Democratic attacks against Ashley, many of them centered on the bank question, finally caught up with him. Ashley's defeat exemplified a nationwide trend of increasing ideological orthodoxy when it came to Democrats and their opposition to the BUS. It seemed that few, if any, politicians by the mid-1830s could run as Jacksonians, support the bank, and win election.[73] Intraparty fights among Missouri's Jacksonians tell us that the Bank War became a nationwide phenomenon whose precise permutations depended on local and regional conditions. The bank issue may have originated in Washington and Philadelphia, but newspaper editors, aided by state subsidies and improved transportation, helped broadcast it to various states so that the Bank War became intertwined with more local conflicts over printing contracts and differences of personality.

Wrapped up with the most convulsive political issues of Jackson's presidency—rotation of office, nullification, and the Bank War to name a few—were questions of how newspaper editors earned a living. These questions, in turn, evoked passionate debates over who was most deserving of guarding the public trust. Opting to become a newspaper editor entailed a career of constant financial uncertainty, but state-supported printing contracts and other forms of patronage prolonged and advanced the careers of editors who might have otherwise failed. Historians have long known that public subsidies, when combined with private means of raising capital, were indispensable to western settlement. Newspaper enterprises were no exception to this hybrid public-private political economy. It would be misleading therefore to argue, as some earlier theorists like Tocqueville did, that the public sphere, civil society, and public opinion were distinctly separate from the state.

If the underlying assumptions of free labor ideology stressed hard work and individualism, ostensibly free from governmental assistance, the Jacksonian work ethic as practiced through the system of patronage, with all of its potential for abuse and corruption, stood for something qualitatively different. For at least some white men of humble origins, state and federal governments could provide opportunities for social advancement and material prosperity. There was no better illustration of this phenomenon than Jackson's hand-picked mouthpiece, the anti-BUS *Globe*.[74]

❧

TWO

"A Very Able State Paper": Amos Kendall and the Rise of the *Globe*

The first issue of the *Globe*, a Jacksonian Party newspaper in Washington headed by two Kentucky editors, Amos Kendall and Francis Preston Blair, appeared in December 1830. From the outset, it communicated the president's hardline anti-BUS views to a nationwide audience, which was noteworthy for an administration that had sometimes been reluctant to tackle the bank question head-on.

This chapter explores the institutional precedents, party attitudes, and business practices that enabled Kendall and Blair to launch and expand the *Globe*. It balances the individual actions of newspaper editors against the larger institutional background that predated Jackson's presidency. Political institutions erected by Americans during the founding generation and early republic framed the range of possibilities available to Americans during Jackson's presidency.[1] At the same time, Jackson, Kendall, and Blair, exerting their own individual agency within this institutional context, established a newspaper whose chief objectives included defending the president's policy priorities and reelection, mobilizing support for the emerging Democratic Party, and helping to defeat the national bank. Jackson took a lead role in finding new subscribers and in prodding his executive department heads to patronize the paper. For their part, Kendall and Blair enlisted crucial financial and political support from members of the federal bureaucracy and Post Office. The result was a state-subsidized party organ and de facto mouthpiece for the administration that proved financially successful.

The story of the *Globe*'s founding and expansion reveals important insights about the workings of the federal bureaucracy, the development of Jacksonian ideology, and the political economy of the antebellum era. Those who seek a basic understanding of where the two major parties of the antebellum era stood on key issues typically learn that the Jacksonians (later, the Democrats) resisted—or were at the very least ambivalent about—accumulated wealth, broad constitutional powers, and an expansive federal government. To preserve their notion of liberty, they favored states' rights and a weak or negative state. Their opponents, the Whigs, safeguarded liberty, in contrast, through state-sponsored economic development at the national level. This paradigm is useful insofar as it captures the essence of the two parties' platforms and what major party figures said about themselves.[2]

Kendall's actions in setting up the *Globe*, however, portray a more complicated story than initially meets the eye. Despite their professed antistatist positions on slavery, tariffs, internal improvements, and banks, the Jacksonians successfully appropriated mechanisms of the state through public subsidies to newspapers, political patronage, and the federal bureaucracy to build what is often considered the world's first mass political party.[3] A Democratic Party committed to localism and limited government in theory often embraced significant aspects of federal power and statist undercurrents in practice. When we evaluate the antebellum era in its entirety, noting the numerous instances in which Democratic presidents like James K. Polk and Franklin Pierce appropriated state powers to support slave interests and westward expansion for whites, Kendall's use of the bureaucracy during the Bank War appears not as an aberration but as part of a larger trend.[4]

Many of the institutional preconditions that helped to enable the *Globe*'s success were established during the mid-1820s, about halfway through the Adams administration. Angered by what they saw as a "corrupt bargain," Jackson's allies in Congress worked assiduously to set up party organizations at the national, state, and local levels. A group of them that included Polk, John Eaton, and Martin Van Buren lent $3,000 to Duff Green to edit the *United States Telegraph* as their official party organ. Pro-Jackson members of Congress, aided by governors, state legislators, and county leaders, also raised money through fund-raising campaigns and public dinners in order to subsidize newspapers in various states and more enthusiastically rally voters on the ground. Their central aims were to thwart any substantive policy victories in the Adams administration and make Old Hickory the overwhelming favorite heading into 1828.[5] As later events would show, Green made for an unreliable editor and one not entirely attuned to Jackson's beliefs on the bank question, but his *Telegraph* started out as an integral part of a quasi-permanent campaign structure that would prove valuable in the hands of a more capable editor like Kendall.[6]

When he arrived in Washington to work as fourth auditor of the Treasury Department, Kendall distinguished himself as a principled Jacksonian. As he described in one newspaper column in March 1829, Kendall, upon entering the fourth auditor's office, discovered a pile of sixteen different newspapers, twenty letters, and three pamphlets sitting on his desk. He learned that many of these letters were intended for other Treasury Department officials but were sent to the fourth auditor's office to avoid paying postage. For Kendall this was an unnecessary drain on the Treasury Department's—and therefore the American people's—funds and an abuse of the franking privilege. He convinced Secretary of the Treasury Samuel D. Ingham to change the department's subscription policies and quickly composed a circular, which he forwarded to all of the newspaper editors, stating, "Not believing that I am authorised to charge the government with subscription . . . which are not useful to me in the discharge of my official duties . . . I have to request that you will discontinue" sending newspapers to this office. Hezekiah Niles, editor of the eponymous *Niles' Weekly Register*, and Isaac Munroe, editor of the *Baltimore Patriot*, complied with the request but criticized the manner in which Kendall comported himself. It was a bit odd, they said, that Kendall, himself a former editor who had relied on government patronage in Kentucky, was now terminating other editors' public subsidies. But in order to reduce spending, corruption, and "[prove] that reform is not an empty sound," Kendall adhered to a strict reading of the law.[7]

Kendall's boldness left a lasting impression on the president, who possessed a compatible personality and shared vision of reform. Jackson appreciated Kendall's intellect and ability to construct arguments.[8] Counting on the president's trust and support was crucial because Kendall could sometimes rub people the wrong the way. Tenacious, detail-oriented, frugal, and even rigid, Kendall would soon emerge as a leading administration voice. He authored a report for the War Department arguing that marine officers were getting paid improperly with allowances and reimbursements for fictitious expenses, beyond what statutory authority warranted.[9] Not one to shy away from disagreeing with his superiors in the federal bureaucracy in the relentless pursuit of fiscal reform, even when it invited discord, Kendall underscored that "when I entered this office I determined to do justice to the country regardless of men. . . . To make the administration pure is my only aim, if I know my own heart."[10] It was perhaps because of his divisive reputation, but more likely because of the piercingly effective editorials he had written on Jackson's behalf during the recent presidential election, that Kendall's nomination as fourth auditor stalled in the Senate. Kendall had come to Washington under Jackson's recess appointment, but it was not until May 1830 that Vice President Calhoun cast a tie-breaking vote in the Senate to more permanently confirm Kendall's nomination.[11]

The official, state-sponsored newspaper for the Jacksonian Party at the time of Kendall's confirmation was Green's *Telegraph*. A former postal agent, medical student, and land surveyor, Green had been instrumental in setting up an enduring Jacksonian coalition. But in Washington, his presence had quickly become a major headache for the new administration. Unreliable, irascible, and caustic, he gravitated toward conflict.[12] He was also intensely loyal to Vice President Calhoun, who controlled a major faction within the Jacksonian coalition and competed with Secretary of State Martin Van Buren to become the president's successor. When Calhoun changed his tune on some of the leading issues of the day, Green usually followed suit. Green's inconsistency and reticence on the bank question, in particular, infuriated Jackson, Kendall, and many of their allies, leading to calls for Green's replacement.[13]

These calls grew louder in the middle months of 1830. James Alexander Hamilton, son of the famous founding father, noted in a letter to Jackson that Green had published both pro- and anti-BUS speeches and reports. "Among other Changes required at Washington," Hamilton argued, "it is indispensably necessary that [t]he administration should change its *official organ*."[14] Kendall knew that many others had criticized Green as "faithless" and "more devoted to Mr. Calhoun than to General Jackson." For him the BUS was "a question upon which there will be no compromises," and he strongly recommended a "*real* administration paper" that could stand by the president.[15] The man who mattered the most in setting up a new party press—Andrew Jackson—was no easier on Green, denigrating the editor as a puppet of "his idol," Calhoun, and writing later, "Duff Green has violated his pledge on [the bank question], & is nutralised."[16]

Postmaster General William Barry suggested that Kendall connect with Blair about editing a newspaper that would replace the *Telegraph*.[17] The three men had been friends and political allies in Kentucky going back to the relief controversy in the aftermath of the Panic of 1819. At the *Argus* in Frankfort, Kendall and Blair had both penned anti-BUS editorials. Kendall's offer would take some massaging as Blair was not very enthusiastic about leaving Frankfort, where he enjoyed a comfortable existence. Blair was nearly forty years old, married, the father of four children, the owner of slaves and valuable property, and president of the Bank of the Commonwealth.[18] Key to convincing Blair to come to Washington was a business arrangement predicated on political patronage and state subsidies. Like so many other editors of the day, Kendall and Blair lacked the investment capital to start a new business. But they did have numerous political allies in Kentucky and Washington who commanded not only extensive social networks but significant financial resources both private and public. "I will undertake to make such arrangements," Kendall wrote to Blair, "that it shall require no advance of funds to start the paper." Former Kentucky governor Joseph Desha and U.S. Senator Richard M. Johnson of Kentucky facilitated loans to help cover some of Blair's debts. Van Buren's political clique promised to give the *Globe* an initial circulation of 2,000 subscribers who could pay in advance. Before expending any significant amount of their own capital, Kendall and Blair already had a guaranteed subscription list and source of profit.[19]

From the Post Office Department, Kendall secured approximately $2,500 per year in patronage, as well as the entire backing of the War Department, State Department, and General Land Office. In addition, Kendall solicited financial aid from several members of the Treasury Department and Congress. It took some negotiating, but Kendall persuaded Blair to come to Washington to start the *Globe*. Its first issue was released on December 7, 1830, and immediately its editors started castigating the BUS. Indeed, killing the "Monster" seemed to be the *Globe*'s raison d'être. The total amount of patronage available to Blair's newspaper started at $4,000 per year and would eventually increase to $10,000. Over half of this initial amount came from the Post Office.[20]

Most editors combined public and private funding—usually, loans and printing contracts—to start their papers. Kendall and Blair may have been unique in relying to such a significant degree on state funds to start a major party newspaper. The practice of appropriating public subsidies in order to shape public opinion in the pursuit of lasting partisan gain was by no means novel in the Age of Jackson, as editors had done much the same in the 1790s and 1800s. Indeed, there is a growing consensus among political historians that many of the features traditionally linked with "Jacksonian democracy" were readily apparent in Jefferson's era.[21] Nonetheless, there was something both quantitatively and qualitatively different by the 1820s and 1830s. Now, dozens of pro-Jackson papers were linked and coordinated through a nationwide network that one historian described as a "journalistic pyramid." From this point forward, future presidential campaigns would follow the model jump-started by Green and perfected by Kendall and Blair.[22]

Kendall had done much of the hard work in securing funding for the *Globe*, but success was by no means a sure thing. He had to work unobtrusively and navigate through difficult waters for explosive events were threatening to derail the administration's agenda. Part of Kendall's elusive and enigmatic workings stemmed from personal limitations: he was terrified of public speaking. Then there was the fear of provoking the intemperate Green. Blair would serve as the paper's editor while Kendall did the heavy lifting in getting the newspaper off the ground. While he wrote anonymously for the *Globe*, Kendall instructed Blair on appropriate political behavior.[23] The fallout from the Margaret Eaton scandal, or petticoat affair, was peaking right around the time that Kendall and Blair were launching the *Globe*. Related to this was Calhoun's shocking rupture with Jackson. The vice president had encouraged Green to publish secret correspondence revealing Jackson's illegal military action against the Seminole Indians in Florida during the administration of James Monroe. Rumors also circulated that Calhoun intended to supplant Jackson as president in 1832. Jackson was now convinced that Calhoun, and cabinet members loyal to Calhoun, were blatantly defying the president.[24] By the spring of 1831 all but one of Jackson's initial cabinet members had resigned. Throughout all of these chaotic developments, Kendall and Blair retained the president's utmost confidence, which redounded to their benefit. The cabinet breakup created a power vacuum where Jackson turned to men like Kendall, Blair, and other upstarts for advice. Anti-Jacksonians sensed that the two editors had become part of the so-called Kitchen Cabinet—a pejorative term describing an informal, rotating body of presidential advisers lying outside the traditional cabinet positions—that exerted a powerful influence over the administration's position toward the Second Bank.[25]

The *Globe*'s launch coincided with the president's second annual message, which he delivered to Congress on December 6, 1830. Jackson again called on Congress to address his concerns over the bank's constitutionality and threat to liberty, much as he had done one year previously.[26] There is no doubt that Jackson took a lead role in finding subscribers for the new paper. He included a copy of the *Globe* prospectus with his annual message and sent them out to numerous political allies, friends, and relatives. The franking privilege enabled him to disseminate these copies for free. Jackson urged all of the recipients to patronize the paper and find new subscribers, which many of them did willingly.[27] To several of his correspondents in Alabama and Tennessee, Jackson expressed his conviction that the *Globe*, unlike the *Telegraph*, would not be advocating nullification or a wishy-washy position on the BUS. This was "the true faith." Using the White House as headquarters, Jackson and his assistants coordinated with other Jacksonian editors in numerous states, encouraging them to start copying extracts from the *Globe* and to locate more readers.[28]

The significance of the paper's public subsidies and attachment to the administration was not lost on Jackson's friends and foes. William Prentiss, a Clay ally and proprietor of the *National Journal*, referred to the *Globe* as "the Government paper" while another anti-Jackson editor labeled the *Globe* "a state paper of the highest merit."[29] Former Tennessee congressman and senator George Washington Campbell, writing to Jackson from Nashville in January 1831, offered similar praise in concluding that the *Globe* was "a very able State paper" that would be "well patronized in this quarter."[30] Not only was Jackson directing financial resources from the federal government to give the *Globe* a wide circulation, but he was also establishing a litmus test for loyalty to the party that bore his name. If one wanted to be a loyal Jacksonian, one had to subscribe to the *Globe*.[31]

From the standpoint of political institutions and the relationship among the three branches of government, Kendall regarded the *Globe* as a platform to push for the concentration of power in the executive branch. This was based on his view that Congress and the BUS were fundamentally hostile to Jackson's vision of reform. A pro-BUS majority prevailed in Congress, many of the executive department agencies were staffed by lifelong civil servants who opposed Jackson, and many Jacksonian politicians had either supported the bank or not yet taken a firm position on the subject. Kendall hoped Blair could secure enough patronage from the executive branch so that the paper would not need printing contracts from Congress, which might compromise their editorial integrity.[32] Under Kendall's vision, the executive would be the dominant branch of government. If the national legislature continued to stymie Jackson's wishes, Kendall held, "It must be known that the views of the Executive have not been met and that our Representatives have not given the President the means of doing the good he would."[33] Referring to his plans for the *Globe* in a letter to Blair, Kendall declared, "We will shortly furnish materials for comment which, if properly used, will bring public opinion to operate on Congress with irresistible force."[34]

In other words, the *Globe* was a state-sponsored institution designed to mold public opinion according to Jackson's views. Hard-line Jacksonians effectively utilized existing institutions in the federal bureaucracy—and even created new ones like the *Globe*—to weaken Congress and the BUS. To this end, Kendall wisely fused much of the *Globe's* anti-BUS rhetoric with Jackson's popularity. He knew that Congress commanded solid majorities in support of the bank and that arguing on the economic merits of the bank alone would not settle the conflict in Jackson's favor. Highlighting Jackson's personality was a necessity in the initial phases of the Bank War because if Jackson was too heavy-handed in his denunciations of the BUS, he would risk losing many of his supporters.[35] William Stickney, Kendall's son-in-law and first biographer, echoed this view: "The more intelligent adversaries of the Bank" recognized that "the only hope of success therein lay in making [the bank] a direct issue between the Bank and President Jackson, backed by his invincible popularity."[36] This task was somewhat easy for Kendall since Old Hickory had a reputation that long predated his rise to the presidency. Jackson was a famous dueler, Indian fighter, and slave trader whose personal popularity rested to a large extent on military prowess.[37]

As a business, the *Globe* amassed a large, nationwide subscription list of readers stretching over a vast geographical area in just a few short years, siphoning away customers from competing newspapers in the process. Jackson had given the paper an important start, but Kendall and Blair, with nearly two decades of experience in the newspaper business, had also honed their business skills. Kendall found a job printer in Washington and negotiated a salary with him based on monthly payments. Alexander Kyle, Kendall's father-in-law, and Kyle's son, Alexander Jr., helped with folding papers, directing them to post offices, and collecting subscription fees.[38] Though Blair had yet to turn the *Globe* into a legal partnership, he did enter into an informal agreement with Kendall that split much of the paper's duties, with Blair adopting the title of chief editor and proprietor. Blair would retain most of the profits while Kendall would take home $800 per year "for furnishing original matter for the Globe." As an incentive, Kendall would earn a bonus of $100 for every thousand subscribers gained above the initial base of 3,000 subscribers.[39]

According to a confidential missive he addressed to the president, Kendall maintained that Blair did not compensate him monetarily for his efforts in establishing—and writing anonymous editorials for—the *Globe*. He sought Jackson's help in settling the matter. Kendall recounted the general storyline of the *Globe*'s founding, including the business arrangements he established with Blair, which would later emerge as a source of dispute between the two men. The lengthy account illuminated the financial travails experienced by partisan editors at the time. "With a wife and five children," Kendall said, "I am very poor. If I were to die this moment, it would take all I have on earth, disposed of as it would be, to pay my debts," which Kendall described as "a weight which often puts me to inconvenience and sometimes make me momentarily unhappy."[40] He deliberately denied to his family the "comforts of life" while his feeble health and child-rearing responsibilities added to an already packed schedule.[41] It is possible that Kendall exaggerated his financial difficulties to win Jackson's sympathy. Kendall had twelve children through two marriages and a $3,000 per year salary as fourth auditor, which he divided equally between paying off his debts and supporting his family.[42] He was not wealthy by any stretch of the imagination, but his family labor arrangement, not unusual for the time, did provide benefits. Having inherited four slaves through marriage with his wife, children, and the elder Kyle managing the day-to-day affairs of the family, Kendall had at least some time to concentrate on his duties with the Treasury Department, *Globe*, and Kitchen Cabinet.[43]

Thus, Kendall may have informed those above him that he was constantly struggling with debt, and while this was true to a certain extent, it is also true that Kendall developed a certain shrewdness in matters of business that proved rewarding when it came to the *Globe*. Kendall was "decidedly in favor of rigidly exacting advance payment" from customers. "Experience has taught me," Kendall posited, "that it is better to have 2000 potential subscribers at advance than 4000 paying on credit." As an editor in Kentucky, he had lost "many thousands" of dollars because of customers paying on credit. In comparison to the business habits of Green, Kendall's were first-rate. The Kentuckian stated, "I am told that Green does not collect enough from his subscribers to pay for his paper," which provides at least one explanation for why Green, in spite of lucrative congressional patronage and BUS loans, was perpetually in debt. The effect of Kendall's method of payment was to eliminate at least some of the time, energy, and money that newspaper editors spent in haggling customers to pay on time.[44]

Partisan enthusiasm reinforced the *Globe* editors' ability to develop a sound business model founded on wise individual choices and public subsidies. *Globe* agents who collected subscription money from new readers were akin to missionaries spreading a sort of political bible. In a nation enraptured by the Second Great Awakening, it is not at all surprising that mass politics sometimes took on a religious tone, particularly since the BUS raised important moral questions relating to fairness, privilege, and economic opportunity. Finis Ewing, a fervent anti-BUS political ally of Jacksonian representative Spencer Pettis and Senator Thomas Hart Benton, was a Presbyterian minister whom Jackson appointed as register of the federal land office in Lexington, Missouri. In between these jobs, Ewing procured new *Globe* converts, sending subscription money back to Blair in Washington.[45] Writing from Hamilton, Ohio, *Globe* agent Robert W. Lewes implored Blair to ensure accurate delivery of the paper in order to defeat "heresy," "prostitutes," and "corruption," all of which were embodied by pro-BUS presses. "Let the people be enlightened," Lewes wrote, "and they will allow justice to themselves and their invaluable, patriotic Chief." It almost seemed as if Jackson, not Christ, was the savior. Emphatic, urgent, and laden with metaphor and religious overtones, Lewes proclaimed: "Let us have the Extra Globe. . . . We want to send it into the dark corners when they have no light and when they love darkness rather than light because they see nothing but Clay papers."[46] Just as spreading the Holy Bible was intended to bring light to darkness, so too was spreading the *Globe* supposed to conquer evil bank presses.

It is striking how many readers abandoned their subscriptions to the *Telegraph* and *Intelligencer* and switched to the *Globe* within eight months of Blair's print debut in Washington. One resident of northern Virginia, Richard Hauton, became a new subscriber to the *Globe* in March 1831 because Duff Green's not-so-veiled attacks on the administration upset him. Ammon Hicks in Monroe County, Missouri, wanted Blair's paper so that he could "have some chance of refuting some of the base charges so frequently put in circulation" by the few remaining anti-Jacksonians in the state. Another correspondent, Tandy Collins of Burtonsville, Virginia, had read the *Intelligencer* for thirteen years. Collins was typical of many new subscribers who wrote, "I have all a long [*sic*] belong[ed] to the true Old Hickory Family and do still adhere to their doctrine. Beleiving [*sic*] you to be one of that family I wish to become a Subscriber to your paper."[47]

Blair's business correspondence shows that the *Globe* penetrated far-flung, rural locations in very remote regions of settlement, including Rawlins, Mississippi; Nellsburgh, Missouri; and Dubuque, in unorganized territory along the Mississippi River that would not enter the union as the state of Iowa until 1846. John Donelson, one of the president's nephews, wrote to Jackson from Fort Smith, in the Arkansas Territory, thanking him for sending the *Globe* westward.[48] That the *Globe* could be delivered to sparsely populated western territories that had not yet become states demonstrates the impressive geographical reach of the Post Office as well as the party-building enthusiasm of Jackson and his followers. This is worth emphasizing since advances in transportation and communications were only beginning to break down long-standing patterns of localism and regionalism.

Stepping back and taking a broader, bird's-eye view of the political economy of the era can help us put many of Blair's letters in appropriate context. The historian Brian Balogh employed the term "out of sight" to characterize the power of government in settling the West during the nineteenth century, which is to say that the state's influence was very real but often imperceptible to ordinary white Americans.[49] Undoubtedly private enterprise, individualism, and voluntary migration were significant parts of the West's settlement and development. Those looking for evidence that the American state was weak and decentralized in the antebellum era might underscore that even the transportation companies, banks, and newspapers that received government subsidies were not directly managed by government employees. The spread of newspapers, moreover, was subsidized mostly by letter writers rather than the general taxpayer. And a private conveyance company that contracted with the Post Office to deliver the mail was not the same as a government managing the company's day-to-day activities.

But in a practical and theoretical sense, these factors could not be divorced from government largesse. Aside from funding the printing contracts and postal subsidies that underpinned editors' businesses, the antebellum state set currency rates, protected patents, removed Indians, and secured property rights. Individual states purchased some or all of the stocks and bonds that capitalized banks and transportation companies—a crucial subsidy given the benefit of spreading risk and allocating funds in areas where investment capital was scarce. We might conceptualize party newspapers in the same way: as hybrid public-private businesses that benefited from the state as a helping hand, rather than a coercive impediment to individual initiative and innovation.[50] In fact, newspapers had an interlocking and mutually reinforcing relationship with other public-private institutions that helped to settle the West, including post offices, internal improvements, and banks. The Post Office Department and the Second Bank might be described as two of the most important institutions providing for a more nationally integrated economy and political culture during these years. All of them were central to what historians have dubbed the transportation and communications revolution. Postmasters delivered newspapers while editors served as postmasters and received public money for publishing postal routes in their papers. Internal improvements allowed for faster delivery of party and commercial presses, which published the increasingly standardized departure and arrival times for steamships and packet lines. Banks, post offices, internal improvements, and newspapers, all of which received at least partial state funding, formed interconnected webs of trade and ideas as part of complex domestic and international economy.

The president continued to ensure that the *Globe* won printing contracts from the various executive departments. Before leaving Washington for a summer break in 1832, Jackson wrote to Secretary of State Edward Livingston expressing pleasure "on hearing that [Livingston] intended giving the job of printing the Diplomatic correspondence to the Editor of the Globe." Jackson was confident that Blair's work "will be done faithfully and *well* and as cheap as it can be by anyone" and added, "It would be mortifying to see his establishment again embarrassed for the want of that support which the work of the Departments afford." This was Jackson's way of insisting to Livingston that if there were printing contracts available, they should go the *Globe*, and that the absence of them might leave impoverished an editor who was willing and able.[51]

Throughout the 1830s, Blair continued to depend on a dedicated group of Jacksonian loyalists who used their power, resources, political connections, and built-in constituencies to find new subscribers. One *Globe* agent, Pierce Van Voorhis of New York City, sent $10 for *Globe* subscriptions back to Blair in November 1833. Van Voorhis predicted confidently, "We think by next week we might send you quite a number more subscribers if their papers come." This was a multiplier effect of sorts. Once a few readers started reading the *Globe*, then, assuming that they were satisfied by the service and content of the paper, they could spread the paper to all of their friends. "We feel, Dear Sir," Van Voorhis continued with optimism, "a large interest in your paper and hope and trust as we have large majority of our friends in the Lower House that you may obtain the printing for Congress instead of N. Biddle."[52] Biddle, of course, was not angling for congressional printing, and Blair would have to wait a few years before obtaining these lucrative contracts, but this letter indicated a widely held belief among Jacksonians that Gales and Seaton, Blair's actual competition, were mere proxies of the BUS.

Estimates of the *Globe*'s subscription list give us a sense of the paper's prominence and reach. A *Globe* column on August 30, 1832, boasted that the *Extra Globe* had a regular subscription list of 11,000. This number was probably too high. Exact subscription numbers can be difficult to determine, especially since editors exaggerated their circulation to obtain advertising and patronage. Another estimate in late 1833 placed the *Globe* subscription list at 6,480, outpacing that of the *Intelligencer*. This was still a remarkable ascendancy since the *Intelligencer* had been in Washington for over three decades.[53] The decision to aggressively win over subscribers from competitors demonstrated Kendall's and Blair's savvy business practices. Their success as businessmen was testimony that political polarization could be profitable.

By 1833 Blair set in motion plans to open up a new *Globe* office in New York City. Busy writing editorials, Blair employed John Cook Rives, a former clerk in the fourth auditor's office of the Treasury Department, to handle the paper's business and accounting concerns.[54] Astute and formidable, Rives ensured that *Globe* customers paid on time. In April, Rives estimated that the *Globe* had paid off all of its debts and that the enterprise was now profiting. A few months later, he negotiated with manufacturers in New York City to obtain rushed delivery of a cutting-edge Napier press for $3,125. Only the nation's leading newspapermen, including James Watson Webb and Gales and Seaton, possessed this technology.[55] In December, Blair created the *Congressional Globe*, a sixteen-page weekly document of legislative proceedings published when Congress was in session. The *Congressional Globe* acquired enough of a reputation that by the late 1830s, congressmen began appropriating public funds to provide subscriptions for themselves. As testament to the *Globe*'s triumph, Blair and Rives became printers to the House in 1835, and when Gales and Seaton concluded their publication of the *Register of Debates* in 1837, the *Congressional Globe* stood alone as the sole account of congressional debates.[56]

Kendall and Blair effectively appropriated public subsidies in founding the *Globe*, which helped cultivate loyalty to Jackson and opposition to the BUS. They turned the paper into an extensive nationwide operation that regularly published anti-BUS editorials well before Jackson handed down his July 1832 veto. When Jackson encountered intense political opposition during his second term and faced legal challenges from the Senate concerning the removal of the bank's public deposits, this communications network was already in place to defend the president. Party mouthpieces had existed before, but as an *administration* press, according to one historian, the *Globe* was wholly new. Every president after Jackson and preceding Lincoln viewed an administration newspaper as essential to political success.[57]

The *Globe* also revealed tensions within Jacksonian ideology. Jackson's followers, soon to be called Democrats, prided themselves on their Jeffersonian heritage of limited government, states' rights, equal opportunity, and local control. They campaigned on rooting out corruption in the federal bureaucracy and making government more efficient, decentralized, and frugal. As such, "the world is governed too much" was the motto that appeared beneath the masthead of every *Globe* issue. But once in power, Jacksonians made no apologies for using state institutions to build a party organization. Previous administrations had access to federal subsidies, but only the Jacksonians possessed the openness to party building to make these subsidies work to the fullest extent. Kendall's career was a case in point. Perhaps few individuals, let alone entire political parties comprised of diverse constituencies, maintain ideological consistency at all times, but it is worth pointing out that harnessing state powers in support of the *Globe* was congruent with later events for which Kendall is well known: the decision to suppress the delivery of abolitionist mailings in the South and to support the Gag Rule in Congress. Ostensibly a defense of states' rights but which also threatened clauses in the First Amendment, Kendall's position showed that the Jacksonians were willing to abandon their penchant for limited government so long as it kept them, and many of the slave owners they represented, entrenched in power.[58]

THREE

The Monster Strikes Back: Nicholas Biddle and the Public Relations Campaign to Recharter the Second Bank, 1828–1832

Some time in November 1828, Gales and Seaton, the two editors of the pro-BUS *National Intelligencer*, applied for a $15,000 loan from the bank's parent branch in Philadelphia and requested placement on the institution's board of directors. Senator Daniel Webster of Massachusetts advised Biddle that funding sympathetic media outlets like the *Intelligencer* would be beneficial to the bank's interests and that without the loan, the newspaper might fall into bankruptcy. In letters to Webster and fellow BUS director John Potter, Biddle explained the bank's rationale for rejecting both requests. Biddle wished to "keep the Bank straight & neutral in this conflict of parties," and since Gales and Seaton had already accumulated debts to the bank in excess of $50,000 and lacked adequate security for the loan, they would have a difficult time paying it back. Biddle made it clear that the bank's relationship with the *Intelligencer* was cordial but had boundaries.[1]

Keeping the BUS separate from politics was a standard line that Biddle repeated to many correspondents in 1828 and 1829, but by the early months of 1831 his attitude and approach toward the press had shifted.[2] In a letter to Gales on March 2, 1831, Biddle, responding to what he viewed as ignorant attacks from Jacksonian demagogues, called for "the free circulation of plain honest truths by means of the press." He asked Gales to send him the *Intelligencer*'s list of subscribers along with their respective addresses "with the additions you propose to make for increased diffusion of your paper" and offered to "defray the expence, if necessary, of copying that list which, for greater convenience, should be divided into States." The more collaborative partnership was to ensure that the *Intelligencer* reached as many readers as possible. By June 1831 Biddle helped finance the production of 25,000 copies of *Intelligencer* "extras" for dissemination in Missouri and New Hampshire.[3] Biddle's work with Gales and Seaton was an integral part of the bank's push for a new twenty-year charter—an extended and intermittent public relations campaign, punctuated by several dramatic climaxes, that took place between 1829 and 1834. The campaign was one of the earliest business lobbies conducted on a nationwide scale in the United States.

Evidence from numerous manuscript collections, bank balance sheets, newspaper editorials, drafts of presidential addresses, minutes of BUS board meetings, correspondence and internal memoranda between bank officers, and records of legislative debates illuminates the multiple ways in which the Second Bank propagated a positive message through space and time. Among the diverse forms of media that functioned as vehicles in the transmission of pro-BUS ideas were articles, essays, pamphlets, philosophical treatises, stockholders' reports, congressional debates, and petitions. Biddle was not the first to employ these campaign techniques, as this chapter shows, but it was the scale and degree to which he used them that proved significant. His campaign achieved a nationwide presence primarily because the bank's vast financial holdings allowed for the deployment of large sums of cash; because it mobilized an impressive array of branch officers, state bankers, lawmakers, intellectuals, voter counters, contacts, and confidential agents; because it standardized a uniform message while simultaneously targeting specific readers in specific geographic locations; and, most interestingly, because advancements in transportation and communication, in combination with the peculiar institutional structure of the BUS in the form of branch offices, enabled one man to reach scores of correspondents separated by hundreds of miles of distance.[4]

To succeed, Biddle had to persuade members of Congress who supported Jackson but remained uncommitted on the bank question. In surreptitious fashion, the BUS president enlisted the services of men like Silas Burrows, Charles Jared Ingersoll, James Watson Webb, and John Norvell, the latter two of whom were newspaper editors. All of these men professed varying degrees of support for Jackson, which gave the campaign an important bipartisan element. Moreover, Biddle dispatched secret agents, equipped with several hundred dollars of bank funds, to infiltrate the New York and

Pennsylvania state legislatures with the intent of persuading undecided law-makers and procuring pro-BUS resolutions. Although these expenditures confirmed the Jacksonian charge of bribery and corruption, Biddle and his fellow directors justified them by invoking the bank's business model, which depended on a positive public image and reputation. The degree to which a mostly private business went to broadcast such an image was, at that point, relatively unprecedented in American history.

Even more important than the dollar amounts involved were the organizational features and geographical reach of Biddle's campaign. After strategizing with the bank's wealthiest stockholders and directors, Biddle issued commands to his branch officers to draw up pro-BUS petitions and citizens' memorials for presentation in Congress. Branch officers, in turn, networked with the presidents and cashiers of state banks across the country and provided Biddle with local assessments of public opinion. From Philadelphia, Biddle supervised the dispersal of large quantities of pro-BUS media to individuals located in Alabama, Missouri, New Hampshire, Kentucky, the Michigan Territory, and countless other locations. The Second Bank's national presence, according to Biddle and his allies, provided an essential public good, but it was this very national presence that provoked visceral hostility from Andrew Jackson and his loyal followers.

Only a few months into his first term, President Jackson started formulating ideas for an alternative to the Second Bank. He solicited feedback from his friends and political allies.[5] The need for a substitute bank became all the more pressing when Jackson learned of alleged misdeeds at several of the bank's branch offices in the run-up to the 1828 election, including the accusation that the bank had actively campaigned against him by supporting his opponent, John Quincy Adams. Anti-BUS Jacksonians charged that the bank had loaned more readily to customers who supported Adams, appointed a disproportionate share of pro-Adams men to the bank's board of directors, and contributed bank funds directly to the Adams campaign, particularly at the branches in Louisville, Lexington, Portsmouth, Boston, and New Orleans. Many of the charges were vague on details, unsubstantiated, and denied even by those who were loyal to the president, but Jackson continued to receive news of the bank's political interference and corruption throughout his first term, which only stiffened his resolve for a protracted fight.[6]

When Biddle met with Jackson to discuss plans to pay off the national debt, the president thanked Biddle for the plan but told him in frank terms that he did not believe that Congress had the constitutional authority to charter a bank outside of the District of Columbia.[7] Jackson's secretary of the Treasury and attorney general at the time recommended a cautious approach toward the bank question, but the president had other ideas. As he later wrote, Jackson "foresaw the powerful effect, produced by this monied aristocracy, upon the purity of elections, and of Legislation; that [the bank] was daily gaining strength . . . by its corrupting influence . . . which I viewed as the death blow to our liberty."[8] Therefore, in his first annual presidential address, delivered to Congress on December 7, 1829, Jackson criticized the Second Bank publicly for the first time. "Both the constitutionality and the expediency of the law creating this Bank," he said, "are well questioned by a large portion of our fellow citizens, and it must be admitted by all that it has failed in the great end of establishing an uniform and sound currency." Included in the address was Jackson's prediction that the bank's stockholders would call for an early renewal of its charter, well before the current one would expire in 1836. Those who had not participated in the drafting of the president's message were surprised since Jackson had not really campaigned on the BUS while running for president in 1828. Jackson concluded by leaving it up to Congress to consider whether a purely public institution founded upon the credit and revenues of the nation—and yet keeping some of the regulatory provisions that Jackson deemed advantageous—would satisfy his objections.[9]

Jackson's address convinced Biddle that a proactive media campaign was in order. He started collaborating with Senator Samuel Smith, a pro-BUS Jacksonian from Maryland who chaired the body's Committee on Finance, which began to examine the veracity of Jackson's claim about the currency. On January 25, 1830, Biddle wrote a report explaining the advantages of the bank's currency and sent it to Smith, who relayed it to the committee without naming Biddle as the author. The final committee report, delivered to the Senate on March 29, concluded that the BUS provided "a currency as safe as silver; more convenient, and more valuable than silver, which . . . is eagerly sought in exchange for silver." To illustrate, the committee explained how in no other country in the world could a merchant deposit silver in a BUS branch office in New Orleans and then travel 1,000 to 1,500 miles to a city in the Northeast and receive an equivalent amount of silver for, at most, a 0.25 percent charge, which was significantly less than the cost, risk, and time it would take to ship silver between the two cities. This was "a state of currency approaching as near perfection as could be de-

CHAPTER THREE

sired."[10] A few weeks after the publication of Smith's report, on April 22, Biddle optimistically informed the senator that the report "has done a vast deal of good" in influencing other members of Congress and that "some thousands will be circulated."[11]

In Congress's other chamber Representative George McDuffie of South Carolina, chairman of the House Committee of Ways and Means, issued a similar report on April 13. Addressing Jackson's criticisms head-on, McDuffie's report proceeded much in the way that Smith's had done, pointing out the superiority of the bank's circulating medium compared to precious metals. Citing price currents and interregional exchange rates during the War of 1812, McDuffie posited that the absence of a national bank had been disastrous for the nation's fiscal operations.[12] A finer point in McDuffie's report praised the uniquely modern financial operations of the bank's branch system, particularly in relation to geographical space. That the bank was required to transfer public money between any two parts of the nation at no cost was impressive given the nation's immense territorial reach. One passage from McDuffie's report extolled the virtues of the bank's innovative financial structure: "The power of annihilating space, of transporting money or any other article to the most distant points, without the loss of time or the application of labor, belongs to no human institution." McDuffie's phrase of "annihilating space" recalled fellow South Carolinian John C. Calhoun's 1815 message to Congress in which he proclaimed, "Let us conquer space," while advancing a nationalistic program of roads and canals.[13]

To give the Smith and McDuffie reports wide readership, Biddle went to the bank's board to ask for approval in using some of the institution's funds for printing and dissemination. The board assented. These printing orders were expenditures, not loans, so Biddle was engaging in interregional corporate lobbying and at the same time taking a decidedly political move that would invite widespread condemnation, and not just from the bank's foes. In contrast to 1829, when the amount the bank paid for printing reports for the entire year was a trifling $105.25, the total for the year 1830 rose to $5,876.67. By no means was Biddle ready to give up on persuading the president that a new charter was in everyone's best interest, but the increased expenditures from this year suggested that Biddle was at least slightly perturbed by Jackson's first annual message and willing to risk blowback in order to shape public opinion. According to legislative records, Biddle spent $256.00 of the bank's funds in sending copies of the Smith and McDuffie reports to the Boston branch office, and $830.11 for the New York office.[14] Biddle thus utilized the bank's preexisting institutional framework in the form of branch offices in order to wage his lobby campaign. A growing interregional transportation and communications network, funded partially by public subsidies, enabled the bank president in Philadelphia to explain to an individual living in distant St. Louis or Natchez how the BUS worked and how it benefited everyone.

In August, the board approved funds for the dispersal of 20,000 copies of McDuffie's report and gave Biddle verbal permission "for widely disseminating their contents through the United States." Three months later, Biddle submitted an article on banking and currency to the board. Written by former secretary of the Treasury Albert Gallatin and published in the *American Quarterly Review* of Philadelphia, it contained a "favorable notice" of the BUS. Biddle suggested that it would be expedient to make "the views of the author more extensively known to the public" and that the bank possessed the means to help the article find a larger audience, beyond the number of people who would normally read the *Review*. The board agreed, giving Biddle wide latitude to "take such measures in regard to the circulation of . . . the said article . . . as he may deem most for the interest of the Bank."[15]

Among the numerous printers spread across several states that Biddle employed in this endeavor were those operating small partnerships, including Garden and Thompson; Gray and Bowen; Carey, Lea, & Co.; Hunt Tardiff & Company in Nashville; James Wilson of Pittsburgh; and his preferred printer, William Fry of Philadelphia. In addition to printing and circulating reports and pamphlets from Smith, McDuffie, and Gallatin, these printers disseminated the bank's triennial stockholder reports. This reflected Biddle's questionable assumption that merely by explaining the bank's operations with empirical facts, rather than resorting to demagogic rhetoric, American citizens would take the presumably rational course of opting for a new BUS charter. Perhaps most alarming to Jacksonian critics were the sums of cash that Biddle appropriated for himself—a full $1,000 of the bank's money in 1830 for printing and circulating Gallatin's report. Biddle could argue that as the bank's president, he bore a special responsibility to BUS shareholders for stability and continued profits, but for Jacksonians this was an unacceptable and unilateral entrance into the political arena.[16]

When Jackson read McDuffie's report, he pushed back strenuously and coordinated with allies. The president called McDuffie's report a "joint effort" between the bank and Congress marking "the first shot" in what would turn out to be a long struggle. He encouraged James A. Hamilton to compose a strongly worded response, which appeared in the *United States Telegraph* as a series of anonymous editorials.[17] Meanwhile, in Massachusetts, David Henshaw, a wholesale druggist and cofounder of the *Boston Statesman* whom Jackson had appointed as the chief customs collector in Boston, wrote and published *Remarks Upon the Bank of the United States* (1831). This was a rejoinder to McDuffie's report. Among his sundry criticisms, Henshaw rejected Congress's implied powers to charter a national bank, the judicial precedent established by Chief Justice John Marshall in *McColluch v. Maryland*, the right of Congress to pass a twenty-year charter that would effectively tie the hands of future congresses, and the special privileges afforded by the bank's monopoly.[18]

By the close of 1830, the *Globe* debut, coinciding with Jackson's second annual message, eliminated the possibility that the administration was being flippant in its attack on the bank, and unsurprisingly, Biddle added new elements to his media campaign. He contacted George Tucker, a professor of political economy at the University of Virginia. Tucker wrote back in January 1831, after having received "two friendly letters" from the bank president, and was "much gratified" to hear that his ruminations on money and currency "proved satisfactory." He then asked Biddle to forward him a copy of the *North American Review*, noted that he agreed "in the main drift" with McDuffie's report, and after a week or so would "endeavor to propose an article" on banking. Several months later Tucker informed Biddle, "The offer that you politely make to have copies of the reprinted article sent to any of my friends is accepted principally because it may possibly be of service." The Virginia professor then told Biddle that he had drawn up a long list "for the purpose of inducing influential individuals to give their attention to the subject, that public opinion may manifest itself in every part of the Union." Tucker concluded by asking if Biddle could send him copies of "Mr. Gallatin's able article." The composition of the list of "influential individuals" and Tucker's use of the phrase "in every part of the Union" suggests that the two men were attempting to promulgate a standardized, nationwide message. Receipts published in a congressional report several years later indicate that for the year 1831 Biddle paid $1,300 to Gales and Seaton for printing and distributing copies of Gallatin's pamphlet to various BUS branch offices and $2,850 to Carey and Lea for the same, with copies of Tucker's article included.[19]

Biddle also turned his attention to the state legislatures of New York and Pennsylvania, two of the most populous and politically important states in the union. Both legislatures were nominally Jacksonian, but there were significant pro-BUS elements and many who were uncommitted on the bank question. Biddle hoped that the passage of pro-BUS resolutions in these bodies would serve as an indicator of public opinion; a barometer that Jackson dare not cross lest he threaten his chances for reelection by losing these states in the Electoral College. Of the two states, New York would certainly be the more difficult challenge as it contained some of the most vociferous anti-BUS critics. Biddle relied on numerous contacts, including Gallatin, to exchange editorial comments, distribute pamphlets, and report on the latest movements in Albany.[20] To move the legislature, Biddle turned to Silas Enoch Burrows, an erratic and elusive merchant from New York City. While serving as the bank's confidential agent in Albany, Burrows went further than what Biddle instructed him to do. According to John I. Mumford, editor of the *New York Standard and Statesman,* Burrows spoke for the bank in offering a $500 bribe to the editor with the implicit understanding that the *Statesman* would cease its attacks on the BUS. Mumford then exposed Burrows's scheme publicly. On April 11, the New York state legislature passed resolutions opposing the renewal of the bank's charter.[21]

In the more favorable confines of the Pennsylvania state legislature, Biddle had at least two proxies. One was Charles Jared Ingersoll, a former district attorney from Philadelphia who was then serving in Pennsylvania's lower chamber. Biddle assisted Ingersoll in drafting the language of resolutions that upheld the bank's utility and constitutionality.[22] The other proxy was John Norvell, a newspaper editor who, like Ingersoll, was a pro-BUS Jacksonian. Under Biddle's instructions, Norvell went to Harrisburg to act as a confidential agent. Biddle asked Norvell in a private letter to obtain "a list of names" with their locations, presumably to send pro-BUS material to members of the legislature who had yet to declare a position on the bank. The editor wrote that he was "very hospitable" to a number of legislators, inviting them to dine at his place, "lending five, ten, and twenty dollars to them," which he never expected to get back. He told Biddle, "Your hundred dollars are pretty well exhausted." Norvell worried that Biddle's plans "would excite a suspicion of my motives" that could not be quelled easily and closed with a stern plea and admonition: "For Heaven's Sake, throw this letter into the fire as soon as you have read it. It contains some things not to be disclosed to the world."[23] Historians have either missed or understated Norvell's presence in Biddle's campaign. This particular incident of bribery did not involve large sums of cash and carried significant risks since anti-BUS Jacksonians were already deeply suspicious about the corruptive powers of the bank. But in March 1831, with Jackson still having yet to declare his unequivocal desire for the bank's destruction in a public setting, many of his followers were still up for grabs. It is unclear whether Biddle's machinations alone shifted any votes, but the Pennsylvania state legislature eventually passed Ingersoll's resolutions.[24]

It helped Biddle to have at his disposal an interregional system of branch offices that he could use not only to respond to local economic conditions but also to transmit pro-BUS media and collect information on public opinion in various parts of the nation. An unnamed officer at the Richmond branch BUS composed a private missive to Biddle on March 17, 1831, that began, "I received lately . . . a private circular, requesting to be furnished with a list of names of the persons in this quarter to whom information may be sent." The officer cautioned that the question of the bank's renewal in his congressional district had become politicized, partly because of rivaling state banks, and partly because of unscrupulous politicians. Lamenting that "the population of this congressional district (except that of the city of Richmond) is the most ignorant and perverse of any in the State," the officer predicted that sending pro-BUS material to the area "can do no good, but—may, probably would do harm." If Biddle sent pro-BUS literature to Richmond and its surrounding areas, the officer predicted, then "certain demagogues in the district" would "indulge in the most shameless misrepresentations, and invectives against the Bank." The "usual slang" about the BUS bribing the press "would not be forgotten."[25]

Although the bank officer advised against sending material to the Richmond office, he left open the possibility that if Biddle wished to have articles published for circulation, then "some of them may be sent here for distribution."[26] Branch offices, then, served multiple functions: on one level, they were like post offices and other public spaces where media could be delivered and read. It was not just money and balance sheets that flowed to and from Philadelphia, but political ideas, too. With twenty-five branches under his command, Biddle had twenty-five proxies staffed with scores of subordinates who could carry out orders issued from Philadelphia. But information also flowed in the other direction. Branch offices evolved into locations of strategic importance, supplying Biddle with critical intelligence about where to best send pro-BUS media. Originally designed to provide credit to cash-starved regions, branches became places where Biddle could periodically assess public opinion.

The letter from the Richmond office expressed one of the most enduring fears among the bank's supporters: anti-BUS Jacksonians were manipulating public opinion with gross exaggerations, outright falsehoods, and demagogic rhetoric. Expenditures and loans to pro-BUS newspapers were therefore justified to properly inform the public about the bank's operations.[27] Shaping public opinion was not just good politics according to this view. It was connected with the bank's business model, and on some level, its very existence. An internal report circulated among the bank's directors and stockholders, published in December 1833 but describing events that took place between 1829 and 1832, is revealing. "The Bank of the United States," the report noted, "derives much of its advantages from its credit, and its general reputation for solvency." Based on this assumption, the authors of the report continued, the bank had the right to defend itself against "those who circulate false statements."[28] In an era in which customers' bank deposits were not protected by insurance, psychological and political factors alone could lead to devastation. A damaging headline in a partisan newspaper might, under the right circumstances, trigger a bank run where customers withdrew their deposits en masse. If left unchecked, one bank run could quickly spiral out of control into a larger financial panic. Implicitly, the report demonstrated how the objective, raw numbers of finance and accounting were inextricably linked with intangible factors like reputation and confidence.[29]

A few months later, Norvell reconnected with Biddle after having recently moved to Detroit, in the Michigan Territory, where he took a job as a postmaster. Moving further away from Biddle had done little to dampen Norvell's spirited defense of the Second Bank. In fact, Norvell saw it as an advantage: "I shall have it in my power to render services to the [BUS] . . . with less risk of suspicions, than if I [was] in Pennsylvania, I feel no hesitation in asking you for an advance of 400–500 dollars," which he planned to pay back at a later date. Norvell offered to travel to New York, Ohio, or any other state not too remote from Michigan "in order to ascertain public or legislative sentiment" so that he could help the bank. He was essentially proposing to act as a paid, itinerant intelligence gatherer for the bank, much in the way he had done for Biddle in Harrisburg. But this was not all. He saw friendly newspaper coverage in Michigan as crucial to the bank's success. "One of our newspapers here," he wrote, "controulled by one or two of the government offices, has commenced an attack upon the bank." Norvell expressed "no doubt" in being able to take charge of this paper "to change its course towards the bank." He later went on to edit the *Democratic Free Press*—symbolizing the ability of pro-BUS media to reach some of the furthest reaches of settlement—and became a U.S. senator when Michigan entered the union in 1837.[30]

CHAPTER THREE

To more fully appreciate the context of Norvell's correspondence with Biddle, it is helpful to examine the era's developments in transportation and communications. Without them, the two would have been unable to write to each other over such vast distances. In a larger sense, advancements in transportation and communication enabled Biddle to reach a national audience in a more timely manner, which distinguished his lobby from political campaigns in the early republic. It was not just that Norvell was an editor and postmaster who eagerly offered to travel through several states as a paid agent in service of the BUS. The celebrated completion of the Erie Canal in 1825 had inaugurated a canal boom that spurred steam travel, reduced shipping costs, stimulated economic growth, and more easily integrated previously disconnected regions of the country into a national market. Americans built 2,000 miles of canals in the 1830s and approximately 5,000 new post offices in roughly the same period, an increase of nearly 70 percent.[31] The transportation and communications revolutions were evidence that public and private capital came together in government policy that framed individual decisions within important boundaries. The point was to ensure the common good and simultaneously nurture a business climate in which innovation could thrive. State governments funded public schools that reduced illiteracy. They capitalized canal and road projects, thus absorbing the risks and jump-starting construction that might have otherwise taken longer with only private investment. At the same time, state authorities left construction, toll collection, and managerial duties to private contractors. What is more, the BUS was a public-private institution that promoted national integration much in the same way that the Post Office and railroads did. In fact, the bank was one of the most frequent users of the Post Office because it was so often transferring large sums of money back and forth between its various branch offices.[32] All of these policies and institutional arrangements, many of them observable only to the keenest eye, established the preconditions for mass political campaigning, including Biddle's recharter effort.[33]

Focusing on transportation and communication gives us one standard for comparing Biddle's lobby with similar efforts. The earliest attempts at organizing political campaigns on an interregional basis over perceived economic injustices may have predated the country's founding. Various non-importation and nonconsumption boycotts of the 1760s and 1770s come to mind.[34] In the 1820s, the Jacksonians started integrating graphics, campaign emblems, handbooks, manuals, and above all, newspapers, into their political campaigns in order to link ordinary voters with elite candidates.

In this way, the bank adopted many of the same practices that political parties had been using for several years.[35] Other major social and political movements in the antebellum era—including temperance, abolitionism, and women's reformers who argued against Indian Removal—organized mass petition drives and lobbied Congress to varying degrees. Yet these movements contained strong grassroots elements spearheaded by ordinary individuals, which, by definition, meant that they were not—and in many cases distinctly opposed—corporations like the Second Bank that tended to integrate elite networks and significant financial resources to project a positive self-image.

A more contemporaneous and structurally similar campaign occurred during the Sixteenth Congress (1819–1821), approximately ten years prior to Biddle's lobby, when the Pennsylvania Society for the Encouragement of Manufacturers and other like-minded voluntary societies launched an interregional petition drive for the passage of the Baldwin tariff bill. Protariff associational societies at this time often contained complex, multilevel organizational structures with several hundred members, published a variety of media, collected signatures for petitions intended to sway members of Congress, dispatched agents into state legislatures, and held regular meetings.[36] Despite its multistate apparatus, however, the protariff lobby was mostly a northern phenomenon whereas Biddle worked with agents on both sides of the Mason-Dixon line. Also missing from the tariff lobby was a key characteristic that defined Biddle's lobby: a singular and hierarchical corporate body that directed operations from above.

The point of these comparisons is to show that Biddle did not invent many of the techniques he used, but it was the corporate form he used and the *scale* to which he implemented these techniques that proved significant. For example, efforts to charter a national bank in 1791 and 1811, and businesses promoting canals, turnpikes, and banks at the state level, preceded Biddle's lobby by many years, were led by corporations, and disseminated similar media. Here the key differences were geographical extent and financial scale. The sums of cash employed by internal improvement companies to influence state legislatures paled in comparison to those of Biddle's lobby. The First Bank operated at a time when most of the country's population of about 4 million people lived close to the Atlantic seaboard and when American politics still contained powerful currents of deference to elites and distrust of the word "democracy." Lobbying campaigns by the Jacksonian era, however, sought to mobilize voters in a country of about 13 million inhabitants who were spread out over a much more geographically expansive territory.[37]

The core of Biddle's lobby emerged in the spring and summer of 1831 in the form of financial assistance to partisan newspaper editors for circulating BUS reports, internal documents, letters, balance sheets, and editorials. Duff Green of the *Telegraph*, James Watson Webb of the *Courier and Enquirer*, and Thomas Ritchie of the *Richmond Enquirer* were some of the most high-profile editors to receive substantial loans from the bank. Other newspaper enterprises that worked with Biddle included the *United States Gazette*, the *Philadelphia Inquirer*, the *National Gazette*, and the *National Journal*. The *Intelligencer*, edited by Gales and Seaton, was Biddle's preferred medium.[38]

Throughout the 1820s, Gales and Seaton regularly published excerpts from the bank's committee meetings, but as Jacksonian attacks on the bank intensified, the two men began to include more pro-BUS opinion pieces. Biddle helped finance and circulate them. In early 1831, Senator Thomas Hart Benton of Missouri launched a vigorous and sustained assault on the bank. Much of Benton's ire was directed toward the bank's so-called branch drafts. Payable for all public duties and virtually identical to standard BUS notes, these drafts circulated in the millions in denominations of $5, $10, and $20 after an 1827 BUS board meeting had authorized their use at the southern and western branch offices. Crucially, though, they did not bear the signatures of the bank's president and cashier as outlined in the original BUS charter, leading Benton to condemn them in Missouri town meetings as "vicious," "illegal," and "fraudulent."[39]

Jacksonian editors began circulating copies of Benton's anti-BUS speeches, which impelled Biddle to start giving consistent printing orders to Gales and Seaton to print *Intelligencer* "extras."[40] According to their arrangement, Gales received payment with drafts drawn on the local BUS branch in Washington. The rate he charged Biddle was $5 for every extra 100 copies produced and distributed, which temporarily doubled the *Intelligencer*'s ordinary circulation of 5,000 to 10,000. While discussing remuneration with Gales in March 1831, Biddle wrote, "If there is any mistake on your part and you are overpaid, it will answer for the next occasion, which may perhaps be shortly, of getting your aid to circulate other papers in regard to the Bank."[41] The financial marriages between banks and newspapers on display in Biddle's correspondence testify to a relationship that was often mutually beneficial: struggling editors received a helping hand while banks acquired a medium of communication to improve their image.[42]

At its peak in 1834, the *Intelligencer* employed 165 workers and its subscription list grew to 7,440, due in no small part to Biddle's help. To reach a mass audience, Gales and Seaton used the latest technology, including a cutting-edge Napier press. Invented by an English manufacturer in 1824, this two-cylinder press could print 2,000 sheets per hour, which was about six to eight times the rate of what a hand press could churn out.[43] The greater production output of the Napier press combined with advances in papermaking to reduce the cost of consuming newspapers, which attracted more readers and contributed to a burgeoning civil society. All of this made Biddle's campaign quantitatively different from political lobbies of the early republic.

Yet Gales and Seaton were not sound businessmen, and despite repeated assurances to Biddle that profitability was just around the corner, indebtedness to the bank was perpetual for the two editors.[44] This has puzzled both contemporaries and historians because the two editors consistently won lucrative congressional printing contracts. Richard Smith, the cashier at the Washington branch BUS, could offer only "circumstances beyond [the two editors'] control" to explain their failure to turn a profit. One of the few historians to write a monograph on the *Intelligencer* cited labor inefficiencies and the two editors' overreliance on printing contracts, but confessed, "The reason why the congressional printing contracts failed to make Gales and Seaton free from debt is not clear."[45] Perhaps attention to the two editors' business practices and consumptive habits may be instructive. The editor of the Jacksonian *Frankfort Argus* accused Gales of using public money to "indulge in princely vices" with "scarcely a cessation" in "gambling, wine, and entertainments."[46] If we assume that there was at least some truth in this characterization, Gales's lifestyle choices were ill-advised for an editor. The newspaper business yielded only a small profit margin in the best of times. As with most businesses, the overwhelming majority of the *Intelligencer*'s gross receipts went to workers' wages. Editor Hezekiah Niles estimated that the *Intelligencer* did more than $100,000 in business per year, "a great part of which is disbursed for labor performed." In 1827, Gales and Seaton stated that they paid $800 each week for the cost of paper and the wages of 100 workers, so if the same rate applied when they employed 165 workers, as they did in 1834, they would have been paying $60,000 per year for wages and paper alone.[47] Repaying loans at the standard rate of 6 percent interest while maintaining a lavish lifestyle would have been challenging indeed.

Moreover, Gales and Seaton sometimes eschewed a bottom-line, profit-driven mentality in their business when they opted to print documents for their political allies free of cost.[48] Whether any amount of shrewdness in business or editorial acuity could have altered the fundamental outcome of the Bank War is difficult to measure, and perhaps even doubtful given the likelihood of Jackson's veto. But the business habits and practices of Gales and Seaton are worth considering insofar as they revealed the agency that editors exercised in influencing Biddle's campaign. It was not *entirely* a top-down campaign dictated from Philadelphia with little input from others. Editors' lifestyle choices and business habits in many cases influenced how effectively they could appropriate public printing contracts and bank loans to run a profitable newspaper enterprise, which in turn shaped the way in which the Bank War unfolded.

Tragedy struck the Biddle family as the summer and pro-BUS media campaign were both heating up. On Friday, August 26, 1831, Thomas Biddle, Nicholas's brother, fought a duel against Jacksonian representative Spencer Darwin Pettis of Missouri.[49] The two men met on an island in the middle of the Mississippi River near St. Louis with an estimated 1,000–3,000 people in attendance. The duel resulted in fatal wounds. Pettis was struck just below his right breast while Biddle suffered a wound just above his hip bone. Both were dead by Monday.[50] A twenty-nine-year-old lawyer-turned-politician, Pettis was a Jacksonian hard-liner who shared Benton's antipathy toward the BUS, criticizing it as a dangerous, unconstitutional, and poorly managed monopoly that threatened the liberties of the people. The younger Biddle, a veteran from the War of 1812 who became a federal pension agent, took offense at Pettis's attacks and resolved to defend his brother. Four months previously, he had penned an anonymous article under the pseudonym "Missouri" where he referred to Pettis as a dish of "skimmed milk" and "a plate of dried herrings." Pettis received word that Thomas was the author.[51]

He called out Biddle publicly in "very caustic and severe terms" and indicated that he would use violence if necessary to defend his honor.[52] The two traded barbs in party newspapers, slowly escalating their affair. What likely inflamed relations beyond repair was Pettis's decision to question Thomas Biddle's manhood when he noted that Ann Mullanphy, Biddle's wife, had not produced any offspring—insinuating that Biddle's reproductive shortcomings were to blame. For two men with personalities predisposed to confrontation, situated in a milieu of southern honor, this was a dangerous line to cross.[53] In July, Biddle launched a premeditated attack. While Pettis was asleep one night at the City Hotel in St. Louis, Biddle walked into Pettis's hotel room, unveiled a cowhide and pistol, and started whipping the congressman. A loud uproar ensued. Pettis defended himself with a sword-cane. Neither man sustained life-threatening injuries. For a while the conflict seemed only to simmer as Pettis, who felt constrained as a member of Congress running for reelection, opted to take the safe route of using the legal system. He had Biddle arrested for assault to kill and brought before a justice of the peace.[54]

But peer pressure brought the simmer to a rolling boil. Pettis's friends and peers found his response weak and inadequate, with one friend recalling that "there was a deep feeling against Pettis in the public mind" and that "the people and press indulged in many remarks towards Mr. Pettis, very unfavorable." They thought Pettis was "cowardly to the extreme" and "should have proceeded immediately to inflict summary punishment" on Biddle. For his part, Biddle initially rebuffed calls to fight Pettis in a duel. Only equals could fight duels according to the code of honor, and Biddle did not consider Pettis his equal. But here too the temptations of friends proved too much to bear. Biddle's friend, colleague, and father-in-law, John Mullanphy, was among many who urged Biddle to fight.[55]

The Biddle-Pettis affair shows how the Bank War played out on the ground as a nationwide phenomenon, intersecting with other major developments in the antebellum era. Public opinion, southern honor, peer pressure, and, most important, partisan newspaper editors acting as individuated historical agents, drove two hot-headed men to an early death over what seems to have been, at least by modern standards, a relatively petty squabble. One contemporary, Jacksonian Lewis F. Linn, reinforced the prevailing assumptions of how men of a certain status, age, and class should behave, praising Pettis for "cool, calm, collected courage" and "perfect propriety" in the face of danger. Biddle won recognition in local papers for his devotion as a husband, his "gentlemanly courtesy," his "honor as a soldier, and his fidelity as a friend."[56] As vehicles for transmitting ideas, values, and beliefs, partisan newspapers played a significant role in shaping the culture of honor, both obscuring and illuminating its most pernicious aspects. On the one hand, newspapers could stave off potential conflicts through the use of pseudonyms—literary devices that allowed political figures and editors to freely voice their opinions without fear of reprisal. On the other hand, one had to walk a fine line in these situations, and even if one followed the appropriate etiquette, disputes could still end badly. Added to this was a notoriously vituperative political discourse that rewarded editors financially for propagating exaggerated rhetoric.[57]

The link between the Biddle-Pettis affair and larger Bank War has been understated in the literature, which is surprising considering that the bank issue formed an important backdrop for the duel and at least partially explained why the duel took place.[58] The initial exchange of insults that escalated the affair of honor originated in a political dispute over the wisdom of maintaining a national bank. The issue hit close to home as Thomas was a director of the BUS branch office in St. Louis. In a letter written to Nicholas a few days after the duel, Mullanphy, who was also a director, posited that Thomas's death was "owing to his active vigilance in the Bank business at this place, it is within my knowledge that he must have saved at least 50,000 [dollars] for this office."[59] Mullanphy did not indicate precisely how Thomas had saved this sum, but for many Missourians, to help this bank was to help an unpopular institution. Opposition to the establishment of a branch BUS in St. Louis had been brewing for several years. Edward Dobyns, a friend of Pettis's and fellow Jacksonian who witnessed the duel and many of the events leading up to it, wrote several decades later that the bank question "was being agitated," and that "the mother bank [in Philadelphia], having established a branch in St. Louis, with the view (it was thought) to control the politics of the state.[60]

As Thomas Biddle was succumbing to gunshot wounds, on the other side of the country, in Philadelphia, his brother, Nicholas, was about to attend an important board meeting with the Second Bank's leading stockholders, directors, and managers. The meeting took place on September 1, 1831— less than a week after the duel. Nicholas would not have known about his brother's death because news between the East Coast and St. Louis traveled at about a two- to three-week delay. The purpose of this gathering of financial higher-ups was to comment on the condition and future of the BUS. Biddle submitted a report to the stockholders detailing the bank's assets and liabilities, and the bank paid for its printing and dispersal. One section stated, "[The bank's] circulation is in all respects equal, and in most respects superior, in value, to any metallic currency of the same amount" and went on to say that never had there been any paper currency, spread out over such an extensive country, that was comparable to the bank's bills and notes in its security, convertibility, and uniformity of value. This was strikingly similar in tone and language to the Smith and McDuffie reports. One likely explanation is that Biddle had authored all three.[61]

Per the bank's charter, this type of meeting happened only every three years, which meant that the next meeting would not convene until September 1834. If one assumed that procuring a bill to recharter the bank, and then passing it through Congress, would take several months, then waiting until the next triennial meeting to authorize an application to recharter would fall perilously close to the bank's expiration in March 1836. Most businessmen dread uncertainty, and for an institution as economically influential as the BUS, it was not unreasonable to wonder if the bank, once discontinued, might have to wind up its affairs and call in all of its obligations with potentially disruptive consequences. Put another way, if the bank wanted to apply without unsettling risks, it needed to apply now. The power that the stockholders invested in the bank's president and directors was broad and elastic: "If at any time before the next triennial meeting . . . it shall be deemed expedient by the president and directors to apply . . . for a renewal of the charter . . . they are hereby authorised to make such application." The Jacksonians' suspicion that the bank's stockholders would initiate an early application for recharter, which the president outlined in his first message to Congress, proved accurate.[62]

Having received the go-ahead from the board, Biddle needed to find the right time to submit his application for recharter to Congress, which involved delicate political considerations and a range of options. If Congress passed a bill to recharter and Jackson vetoed it, there was some hope that pro-BUS forces could secure a two-thirds majority to override the president. This was only a remote possibility. Party discipline was already a key attribute among Jacksonian politicians, and enough congressmen would rally to the president's aid under almost any circumstance. Perhaps, then, Biddle could reach an agreement with Jackson over a significantly modified bill to recharter with the likes of Secretary of the Treasury Louis McLane, William Berkeley Lewis, and Secretary of State Edward Livingston acting as intermediaries. McLane had authored a report praising the bank's functions and recommending recharter "at the proper time" while the president had refrained from criticizing the bank in his third annual message, feeding rumors that Jackson might be softening his stance.[63] The most intimate of Jackson's correspondents knew otherwise. As a somewhat irritated Jackson wrote to John Randolph, "You have done me no more than justice when you repelled with indignation that I had changed my views of the Bank of the United States." The president declared emphatically, "I have uniformly on all proper occasions held the same language in regard to that institution."[64] The unfortunate reality for Biddle was that he almost never corresponded with Jackson directly, and the intermediaries he used may have overestimated their ability to persuade the president. When viewed in combination with Jackson's call for

CHAPTER THREE

a substitute national bank in 1829 upon entering office, Jackson's letter to Randolph illustrates that, contrary to what some scholars have speculated, the president was rather consistent in opposing the BUS even if many of his cabinet members were open to a modified recharter.[65]

But even those who were not privy to the president's personal views and yet still hoped for compromise cautioned Biddle not to provoke Jackson until after the presidential election. This contingent included Edward Shippen, Senator Samuel Smith, and McLane. Jackson, they said, would interpret an early application as a hostile act and would place the bank question at the center of the upcoming election. Then, finally, there was a group of men who assumed that while an early application carried risks and Jackson's future behavior was unpredictable, the president would have almost no incentive to compromise with Biddle during a second presidential term. Submitting early could potentially corner Jackson into taking an unpopular stance, which would weaken his support before the fall elections. Representatives Mercer and McDuffie in the House and Senators Clay and Webster were in this camp. Clay stated, "My own belief is that, if *now* called upon [Jackson] would not negative the bill; but that if he should be re-elected the event might and probably would be different." Biddle informed Clay a week later that "nothing is yet decided."[66]

In the face of such conflicting recommendations stemming from diverse interests, Biddle dispatched Thomas Cadwalader to Washington to count votes in Congress and meet with prominent members of the Senate and Jackson's cabinet. A senior BUS officer and director, Cadwalader was connected to Biddle through marriage and served as the bank's acting president when Biddle was absent. Excerpts from a series of letters written between the two men testified to the degree to which Biddle trusted Cadwalader's opinion. "With you I have no reserves," Biddle wrote in one letter, and in another, he confided, "I have not said this to anybody except yourself." On December 25, 1831, the ever cautious Cadwalader stated to Biddle, "I do not yet *decide*—but *incline* to *suppose* that after the council at the Treasury, I shall advise the Comee to start the memorial." A few days later, Biddle firmed up his decision. In a letter to Smith explaining why the bank was moving forward at this time, Biddle underscored, first and foremost, the desires of the bank's stockholders and the need to avoid uncertainty.[67]

The conventional view of the recharter controversy holds that Senators Clay and Webster prodded Biddle into submitting to Congress an early application for the bank's renewal. There was risk in confronting the president by applying four years before the current charter expired, but for their own political ends, Clay and Webster wished to weaken Jackson's popularity. Some scholars have argued that this conflict, which brought about the bank's eventual destruction, could have been avoided.[68] The interpretation presented in this chapter, however, which is based on close attention to the bank's board meetings and Biddle's correspondence, suggests that the conventional view downplays or ignores some key facts. There is very little likelihood that Jackson and Biddle could have agreed on a new BUS charter.

In terms of how most historians have conceptualized the Bank War, the personalities of Jackson and Biddle have often loomed large. While most accounts explore party formation, competing constitutional interpretations, and disruptive economic events, at their core they are narrated as a boxing match between two powerful individuals, each with flawed personalities. Indeed, one famous lithographer of this era, Anthony Imbert, employed the boxing metaphor in his depiction of the Bank War. The limitation of this individual-driven narrative is that it fails to take into account the instances in which BUS-related issues captivated entire communities that were far removed from Washington politics.[69] Partisan newspaper editors, who shaped public opinion in their editorials and published the personal attacks that sometimes culminated in violent duels, exerted considerable clout in transforming the Bank War from a primarily elite-driven political issue confined to the power corridors of Washington and Philadelphia to one that played out on the ground level in locations that were 1,000 miles away from the East Coast. Attention to events like the Biddle-Pettis duel and the bank president's letters with John Norvell and the Richmond bank officer suggest a multisided Bank War; one that interacted with and revealed important developments in transportation, communications, southern honor, and the business model of partisan newspapers. Biddle orchestrated an interregional public relations campaign and corporate lobby as a response to Jacksonian attacks, but once set in motion, the Bank War phenomenon unfolded at the national level in ways that even the powerful bank president could not control.

FOUR

⌀

Monster News! Veto and
Reelection

Congress became the main theater of action in the Bank War during the
first six months of 1832. At Biddle's behest, the House and Senate debated
passage of a new bank charter, four years before the present one was due
to expire. Citizens and financiers flooded the legislative body with petitions
expressing their support or opposition to the BUS. Congressional committees investigated the bank's financial statements under charges of bribery
and corruption while Jackson's allies pulled out all the stops in an attempt
to erode the bank's base of support. All of this came to a dramatic conclusion with Jackson's veto and reelection.

On January 11, 1832, the Senate directed Jackson's secretary of the Trea-
sury, Louis McLane, to make public the names and titles of all of the Second
Bank's foreign stockholders, including the number of shares held by each.
Anti-BUS Jacksonians repeatedly used these numbers to castigate the bank
as a foreign entity that concentrated large sums of capital in a few hands and
prioritized the interests of European aristocrats over ordinary Americans.[1]
Similar arguments were presented in the Senate on January 26 by William
L. Marcy of New York in the form of an anti-BUS citizens' memorial signed
by 139 people and corporations. Topping the list of signatories was David
Henshaw, one of Boston's foremost merchants and customs collectors, who
had published a response to McDuffie's pro-BUS House report on the state

67

of the bank's currency the previous year. Like most anti-BUS Jacksonians, Henshaw and his fellow memorialists argued that the Second Bank, as a monopoly with exclusive privileges, violated the quintessentially American ideal of economic opportunity for all. The memorial cited statistics showing that only a small number of domestic and foreign stockholders owned most of the bank's capital stock, leaving few opportunities for shareholding among the middling classes of society.[2]

But in general, friends of the bank maintained the advantage of numbers in Congress. On January 9, Senator George Mifflin Dallas of Pennsylvania entered into the Senate the formal application for recharter. The language of the application was based on resolutions that had been approved by two BUS board meetings in Philadelphia. A few weeks later, Dallas sold shares of the BUS stock he owned, anticipating "ad hominem" attacks from Senator Thomas Hart Benton of Missouri for having a financial stake in the very institution he was promoting in Congress. These attacks, Dallas believed, would not only cause the bank's stock price to fall and therefore eat into his own profits but also illustrated the relationship between reputation and solvency that economists know well.[3] The memorial that Dallas presented was written by Biddle and the directors, underscoring the bank's importance as a national institution: "Its own immediate operations are connected intimately with the local business of almost every section of the United States, with the commercial interchanges between the several States." Among other key provisions were arguments that the BUS "facilitated all the productive industries of the country," that it gave "stability to all the rewards of labor," that it provided sufficient capital for transportation projects, and that it propagated a stable currency. These points formed the foundation of citizens' memorials and petitions signed by state bankers, state lawmakers, and bank advocates in the coming months—documents that would, in turn, be sent back to Congress in the early months of 1832 in hopes of renewing the bank's charter.[4]

This chapter, which narrates Biddle's lobby as it continued to unfold in the spring, summer, and fall of 1832, presents a detailed account of how much the bank spent and lent in its effort to secure a new charter. From the beginning of Biddle's media campaign to Jackson's veto, the BUS spent somewhere between $50,000 and $100,000 in printing orders for circulating reports, treatises, editorials, and in small payments to confidential agents. The subscription lists for these orders typically ranged from 5,000 to 25,000 copies. In the same period, the bank loaned perhaps as much as $150,000 to $200,000 to members of Congress and about $100,000 to editors. Most of the loans to editors went to James Watson Webb, Duff Green, and Gales and Seaton; in other words, the editors of large newspaper enterprises with nationwide subscription lists. These figures exceed—and add greater detail to—historians' previous estimates and provide at least one measure of the scope and scale of Biddle's lobby.

Yet just as meaningfully, this chapter also explores the manner in which the Bank War played out on the ground level in the various states. By the end of 1832, it was clear that the issue had taken on a life of its own, related to—and yet geographically and qualitatively distinct from—the more elite-driven tussle between Jackson, Biddle, and their immediate allies. If the traditional Bank War known to many historians consisted of backroom wheeling and dealing and a war of words hurled at one another through the political institutions that dotted the East Coast, this "Second Bank War" so to speak had a more violent and unsettling character. It involved more semi-elite and ordinary Americans expressing their views through duels, public meetings, acts of arson, politically motivated bank runs, and, most troubling of all, assassination attempts that were both real and imagined. Only a broader view of this defining chapter of Jackson's presidency, and one that elevates editors as major political actors and communicators of information, can link these two Bank Wars.

During his recharter campaign, Biddle continued to appropriate previously existing communication networks between the branch offices and the bank's Philadelphia headquarters. Since its inception, the BUS had sent regular statements of its financial condition to the Treasury secretary, who then issued orders to the bank president about what to do with the public deposits.[5] The cashier at the bank's parent branch, meanwhile, would dispatch instructions regarding preferred lending practices to the various branch offices. In turn, the branches sent weekly statements of their assets and liabilities back to Philadelphia, allowing the bank's senior officers to continue to make adjustments if necessary. Between late 1831 and early 1832, William McIlvaine, the cashier of the parent branch, advised the branch offices in the South and West to ease up on their long-term discounts so as to gradually beef up the monetary reserves of the East Coast branches for impending payments on the public debt. While this was going on, Biddle worked behind the scenes on his lobby. In effect, he delegated the bank's monetary policy to McIlvaine while communicating political matters with the branch officers.[6]

By looking at the timing of Biddle's meetings with the bank's board and the presentation of pro-BUS memorials in Congress, historians can see the relationship between those who organized the media campaign from above in Philadelphia and those throughout the nation who expressed support for the bank at the grassroots level. The bank's board of directors made preparations for its renewal application at meetings on December 16, 1831, and January 5, 1832. Only afterward did Congress receive the first memorials and resolutions signed by state bankers and groups of pro-BUS advocates. Biddle, in fact, penned several of his branch officers across the country on January 16, asking them to solicit state bankers to draw up memorials and petitions for Congress.[7] One of the few surviving memorials contained in Biddle's various manuscript collections, dated January 28 and sent from Kentucky to Congress, demonstrated the campaign's interregional reach. The memorial praised the BUS for promoting a sound currency, sustaining state banks, and invigorating agriculture, commerce, and manufactures. It added that failing to recharter the bank would halt internal improvement projects, devalue property, and immediately "paralyze industry and destroy confidence."[8] Its ideas and reasoning were noticeably similar to those contained in the original memorial in Philadelphia, almost as if Biddle himself had instructed branch officers and state bankers across the country to craft the memorials as he saw fit. Bank advocates signed a total of 118 citizens' memorials and seventy state bank memorials to Congress while Jacksonians forwarded to Congress only eight anti-BUS citizens' memorials and no state bank memorials. In today's language, we might call this an "Astroturf" political campaign led by Biddle.[9]

Letters sent into the *Globe* office in Washington suggested that Kentucky's Jacksonians had gotten word of what they saw as Biddle's artificially engineered ploy to gin up support for the bank, and they were livid. An unknown *Globe* correspondent, writing from Louisville, Kentucky, on February 4, 1832, composed a letter to Blair laden with literary allusions, biblical references, and nods to classical mythology. The letter lambasted the bank as two sinister Shakespearean characters, Shylock and Molock, and asserted that "there have been two orders sent forth, from the [w]hore of Babel, the Mother Bank of the U.S. to the branch" in Louisville. The first order was "to send out her idol worshippers, with petitions . . . for signature, their names . . . to inforce and require of Congress the renewal of the charter." The author of this highly gendered and inflammatory letter conveyed the view that efforts to gather pro-BUS petitions for Congress resulted from Biddle's meddling. The "idol worshippers" were Biddle's political subordinates. And yet, not only did this letter evince an interregional quality

CHAPTER FOUR

to Biddle's campaign but also it demonstrated the ways in which Biddle's behind-the-scenes lobby could provoke angry reactions and counterefforts across the nation.[10]

As the bank's application slowly worked its way through Congress, anti-BUS Jacksonians mounted their own campaign of negative publicity and obstruction.[11] Representative Augustin Clayton of Georgia introduced a resolution to form a committee that would investigate the bank on the charges of mismanagement and violation of its charter. Although most of the House was pro-BUS, Speaker of the House Andrew Stevenson of Virginia ensured that this committee would be led by the bank's enemies. Formed on March 14, 1832, and composed of seven members, the select committee would travel to Philadelphia to examine the bank's account books, gather extracts from minutes of the bank's board meetings and correspondence between bank officers, and conduct interviews with written testimony from the principal actors involved.[12]

Clayton's majority report, released on April 30, pummeled Biddle's relationship with the press, claiming that the bank had abused its powers because it issued loans of unusually long duration to editors and loaned without adequate security. One loan that aroused suspicion was for $20,000, issued to Duff Green in February 1831. Bank advocates countered with written letters documenting how both Green and Biddle explicitly agreed that the *Telegraph* would continue to maintain its editorial independence on the bank question in the spirit of free expression. More damaging to the reputation of the bank were loans from Biddle to Webb with Silas Burrows acting as intermediary. Burrows had approached Biddle to discount some commercial paper, and Biddle gave him $15,000 worth of BUS notes. Burrows lent this sum to Webb and Mordecai Manuel Noah, who were coediting the *New York Courier and Enquirer* at the time. Since the *Courier* started publishing editorials that were more favorable to the bank after receiving the $15,000 loan from Burrows, according to Clayton's report, it was reasonable to conclude that the bank bribed Webb. Biddle had taken this sum out of his own personal funds and did not record this transaction in the bank's account books until the beginning of the new year, seven to eight months after he had approved the loan. What looked especially suspicious for the bank's adversaries was that Biddle had approved the loan on his own accord without formally bringing it before the board. He had asked only for personal security rather than the more standard requirement of collateral security, and he had finalized the loan outside of the bank's normal lending hours prescribed in the bank's charter.[13]

At least one of Biddle's colleagues and closest allies disapproved of these types of unilateral and underhanded lending practices. Before they were approved, all applications for loan discounts were supposed to go before the bank's exchange committee. But in day-to-day practice, this was often a formality. The bank president handpicked members of the committee and often made the final call on important decisions.[14] Testimony from Clayton's report showed that Biddle sometimes discounted without the board's approval, ostensibly because each board member had worked with Biddle long enough to understand the business principles and integrity with which he operated.[15] When Cadwalader left Philadelphia on business in early 1832, Biddle single-handedly expedited loans to some of his preferred editors. Cadwalader returned to the bank in March to serve as acting president as Biddle traveled to Washington to negotiate with McLane about a postponement of payments on the public debt. It was then that Cadwalader informed Biddle that he was surprised at the "great amount" of these loans. One was "an accommodation to Gales and Seaton, of several years standing," indicating that Biddle probably renewed the loan on a continual basis when it fell due. Particularly alarming to Cadwalader was Biddle's secrecy. Cadwalader contemplated resignation. While he recognized that Biddle's behavior stemmed from his "zeal for the interests of the Bank," Cadwalader said to the bank president in no uncertain terms, "Do me the justice to acquit me of all knowledge of, or participation in [these] transactions." One of the most influential men in pushing Biddle toward recharter a few months earlier, Cadwalader was now castigating the bank president's tactics and strategies.[16]

The bank's allies in Congress pushed back hard against Clayton, not only for his conclusions but also for the manner in which he conducted the investigation. Representative John Quincy Adams, serving on the pro-BUS minority committee, issued a rare and lengthy supplementary report that chastised the investigation for being one-sided and overstepping its authority in examining the bank's confidential business transactions.[17] Corporations, Adams held, were entitled to trial by jury under a court of law, not a prejudiced, partisan, and predetermined vendetta designed explicitly to ruin peoples' reputations. He compared the majority committee's tactics to a religious inquisition, pointed out that subsidizing the press was not a crime, and proclaimed that impugning the motives of those who lawfully discounted commercial paper was "not only pregnant with injustice to individuals, but utterly beneath the dignity of the Legislature."[18]

CHAPTER FOUR

As the congressional hearings began to wrap up, Adams requested an amendment to publish "the names and amounts of payments to members of Congress in anticipation of their pay as members, before passage of the general appropriation bill." The results appeared in the concluding pages of Clayton's report as a list of "advancements" extended by the BUS branch in Washington to individual members of Congress. Political scientist James Morrison aggregated the advancements to a total sum of $125,000. He then compared each congressman's vote on the bill to recharter the bank to whether they received advancements, concluding that all but three of the Jacksonian House members who supported recharter had taken BUS loans. If these "advancements" were, in fact, loans meant to corral pro-BUS votes, this would mean that a total of 201 members of the House took loans from the BUS. However, an 1834 Senate report showed that in 1832 all of the BUS branches had lent to only forty-four members of Congress.

In addition, Morrison's analysis implied that Biddle was advancing money to curry favors, but closer inspection shows that the advancements were probably just standard payments to members of Congress for their salary. The BUS, as the Treasury Department's fiscal agent, facilitated the collection and distribution of all public moneys, including payments to public officials. Congress and the Treasury Department were both located in the nation's capital, and so the BUS branch there would have provided the most convenient credit facilities. In other words, the bank was paying members of Congress before their summer recess began under the assumption that Congress would later vote on an appropriations bill to fund government expenditures, thereby replenishing the bank with funds from the Treasury. This interpretation is supported by a written statement from Speaker Stevens, who explained that the numerical value of each advancement differed for each congressional member because of attendance record and mileage. It may have been understandable to assume that every bank payment to members of Congress had a nefarious purpose, especially given the revelations of Biddle's secret loans. But this particular case was different, and it suggests the need for a careful and complex portrayal of the bank president.[19]

Representative George McDuffie's minority report, released on May 11, contained the most vigorous defense of Biddle's actions. Burrows, the report explained, had repaid the bank on March 2, 1832; Webb had only endorsed the notes and never communicated directly with Biddle in this particular instance; and the transactions could not have been an act of bribery because the *Courier* had already professed support for the bank prior to the loan. The report also noted that Biddle had loaned thousands of dollars to

Jacksonian editors, many of whom opposed the BUS. According to Biddle's written testimony before the committee, hard-line Jacksonians had turned the bank question into a highly politicized issue and would find fault with Biddle no matter how he dealt with Webb's loan application. If the bank granted the loan, Biddle held, it would be accused of bribery; if it rejected the loan, Jacksonians would claim that the bank was politically motivated in its lending practices—an accusation they had aired consistently since the 1828 election. From Biddle's point of view, this was a self-fulfilling prophecy of sorts: the Jacksonians would concoct a misleading charge against the bank, and the bank would spend its own money in defending its reputation, only to see Jacksonians turn around and claim that the bank's spending subverted democracy, thereby confirming their initial charges! Stuck between Scylla and Charybdis, Biddle agreed to Webb's application because New York state banks had denied credit to Webb given the editor's position on the BUS; because the *Courier*, as a profitable business, possessed the means to repay the loan; and because Walter Bowne, the mayor of New York City and former BUS director, had spoken highly of Webb.[20]

As a major media outlet with 6,000–9,000 subscribers and nearly $70,000 per year in gross receipts, the *Courier and Enquirer* seemed like a promising loan applicant.[21] Like Gales and Seaton, Webb and Noah employed the latest technology and communications methods. They owned a Napier press and secured a $20,000 loan from the BUS in early 1831 to purchase boats, presses, and types. About half the loan went to two "news schooners," the *Courier and Enquirer* and the *Eclipse*. In the era before trans-Atlantic telegraph lines, news from Europe arrived by ship, so the thinking was that if an editor could send his own ship into the ocean to intercept the American-bound ships, he might gain an advantage over his competitors by being the first to report on foreign news. These methods gave Biddle's campaign a modern flavor.

But if Webb, like Gales and Seaton, managed a premier nationwide newspaper establishment equipped with the latest technology, several thousand subscribers, and tens of thousands of dollars of revenue per year, generous loans from the BUS, and lucrative printing contracts, he also shared their spendthrift ways. According to an 1844 statement by Webb's brother-in-law, Lispenard Stewart, Webb, a highly combative and abrasive individual prone to physical fights and even dueling, had spent the 1830s living "in a style unsurpassed by any gentleman of the city." The editor's personal possessions included a "magnificent dwelling" and a summer residence "surrounded by all the appointments and appliances of wealth and luxury."

Webb lost thousands of dollars through ill-advised personal bets and stock market schemes that went bust. And yet he kept a cellar of expensive wines, maintained lush gardens, bred horses, "wore only the best clothes," stayed at the "finest suites" in the City Hotel, and "regularly dined at New York's finest establishments." Unsurprisingly, Webb had an enormous list of creditors who became frustrated by the editor's delinquency and ostentatious lifestyle. Bankruptcy greeted the New York editor during the panic of 1837. That Biddle continued to lend to an untrustworthy borrower testifies to the premium he placed on favorable media coverage.[22]

Several years later, the evidence of Biddle's clandestine financial entanglements with Webb uncovered by Clayton's report reverberated with violent consequences. On February 9, 1838, Matthew Livingston Davis, a congressional correspondent who worked in Washington for Webb's *Courier and Enquirer*, anonymously accused an unnamed congressman of corrupt ties with the executive branch. This caused an "angry and excited debate in Congress."[23] Three days later, Representative Henry Wise of Virginia, presuming that Webb was the author, called for a House investigation. In response, Representative Jonathan Cilley, a Maine Democrat and former editor, replied that if Webb was the source, then the accusation was not worthy of serious consideration, particularly since the congressman was unnamed and Webb, according to Clayton's report, had taken bribes from Biddle.[24] Upon reading Cilley's comments in the *Globe*, an angry Webb traveled to the nation's capital. He solicited his friend, Whig representative William J. Graves of Kentucky, to demand clarification from Cilley. When Cilley refused to accept Webb's letter from Graves, Cilley and Graves exchanged words through letters. Graves, egged on by fellow southerners like Wise, then submitted a note to Cilley, part of which stated: "I am left no other alternative but to ask that satisfaction which is recognised among gentlemen."[25]

Cilley and Graves gathered their rifles (an unusual choice for a duel), ammunition, their seconds, and a few witnesses and met near the Anacostia Bridge in Washington on February 24. On the third exchange of shots, Cilley fell mortally wounded. Graves survived unscathed.[26] A House committee condemned the affair as barbarous, noted that it violated the deliberative character of the House, reprimanded Webb for a breach of House privileges, and underscored that dueling was illegal, but it did little substantively to punish the affair's participants.[27] Historians have viewed the Cilley-Graves affair as a prime example of the complex set of rules and behaviors known as southern honor, but as with the Biddle-Pettis duel, they have not linked it to the Bank War in any meaningful way.[28] For both duels, the bank was a—and perhaps *the*—underlying issue of contention. A significant part of what precipitated the duel was a disagreement over Webb's reputation; a reputation that had been, according to Jacksonians, permanently stained because of the bank's bribes. We might then interpret the duel as a nasty aftershock of a political fight that had taken place six years earlier and had continued to fester in the public mind, which was likely because in 1838, the country was experiencing a major financial panic and the BUS was constantly in the news. Newspaper editors, wielding vicious attacks while hiding behind anonymity, immersed in an honor-based culture, could take seemingly arcane disagreements over finance and transform them into violent confrontations. The Bank *War* is typically conceptualized as a *political* war of words and deeds, as opposed to an actual armed conflict. But a broader and deeper view of the Bank War shows that the political crossfire could and did lead to deadly, weaponized crossfire, including the loss of human life.[29]

Compared to Clayton's majority report, the text of McDuffie's minority report demonstrated a much more sophisticated understanding of finance. It accurately stated that a bank's deposits, which enabled more lending, were more than just liabilities and would never be withdrawn from a bank in one fell swoop. Repeating the sentiments expressed during the Second Bank's stockholder meeting the previous September, McDuffie's report admonished members of Congress: "The uncertainty which prevails on this subject, is calculated to exert a pernicious influence over the industry, enterprise, and trade of the country."[30] In large part because of Biddle's concerted efforts, the wishes of the bank's most senior officeholders and investors materialized into a position that was subsequently adopted by a majority of the House. The tone of Clayton's report, in contrast, was emotionally charged and moralistic. It posited an older theory of economic development based on the assumption that the amount of gold in a country determined its prosperity, regardless of its balance of trade. Without much evidence, it claimed that the bank had set up too many branches, had created an unsustainable credit bubble, and was about to repeat the same mistakes of 1819.[31]

But however weak the majority report was in its argumentation, its practical effect was to underscore that the bank's allies did not have the votes for a veto-proof majority. This was critical because it meant that Jackson held the future of the bank in his hands. Steadfast as ever, he showed almost no willingness to compromise. To fellow southerner and military officer John

CHAPTER FOUR

Coffee, Jackson emphasized, "My friends need not fear my energy—should the Bank question come to me, unless the corrupting monster should be shoaren of its illgotten power, my veto will meet frankly & fearlessly."[32] The contents of the Clayton report also convinced anti-BUS Jacksonians of their worst suspicions: that the bank was willing to buy off the press and subvert the republic to maintain its power.[33] In a letter to Allan Ditchfield Campbell, a friend and Presbyterian minister, Jackson proclaimed:

> The Bank report did nothing more than confirm what I had always thought, that it was, as at present constituted, one of the greatest Mamoths of corruption ever created, winding its way into all the ramifications of our Government, and endeavoring to corrupt, & corrupting every branch of it—we have seen its effects upon the Press—it is yet to be seen how far it has operated upon the pure streams of Legislation. This monster, as it stands, & as administered, must be put down, or it destroys the virtue & morality of our country, and with that, our present happy form of Government.[34]

Jackson appropriated classical republicanism in casting the Bank War as an epic high-stakes struggle with liberty and virtue on the line. Unless Biddle and his allies in Congress could put together a bank bill that radically restructured the bank's functions and reduced its power beyond all recognition, Jackson would almost certainly veto. That Biddle and Clay clung to the slim possibility of Jackson's acquiescence seems to have arisen from the fact that the president expressed his true feelings to a group of close friends that included Coffee, Campbell, Randolph, Hamilton, and Kendall. The key point to emphasize here is that none of these men communicated consistently with Biddle, whose chief contacts on this matter were Livingston, McLane, Clay, Webster, and Cadwalader.

Unaware of the president's intentions, or at least convinced that a veto would prove damaging to Jackson politically, Biddle pushed ahead with the recharter effort in Congress. There was some concern that the tariff, an explosive issue that warranted serious consideration, might consume valuable debate time, thereby delaying the recharter bill until the next session of Congress, after the presidential election. But Biddle had cultivated multiple relationships in Congress, beyond the outspoken and highly visible Clay and Webster. The modern phrase "revolving door" might best describe the porous boundaries between the BUS and Congress. Some congressmen had worked previously as BUS branch officers and directors. This was the case with Missourians William Henry Ashley and John Bull, and John Sergeant, a member of Pennsylvania's congressional delegation who had also been a prominent shareholder and director of the parent branch. Sergeant, who shared lobbying and vote counting responsibilities for the bank with his brother-in-law, anti-Jacksonian representative John Goddard Watmough, and fellow Philadelphian Horace Binney, ran for vice president on Clay's ticket in 1832.[35]

By the summer, Biddle's multipronged and multiyear effort came to a head. The House and Senate passed bills to recharter the bank by relatively comfortable margins. The Senate bill, spearheaded by Dallas, passed on June 11 by a total of 28 to 20. McDuffie guided a bill through the House on July 3 by a vote of 107 to 85.[36] The next day, Independence Day, saw Biddle "openly canvassing" for support in the nation's capital according to Postmaster General William Barry. Because it was Jackson, the war hero, who would decide the bank's fate, and because it was July 4, the meaning of Jackson's response would forever be imbued with patriotic fervor.[37] The final bills sent to Jackson's desk contained modifications of the original bank charter that were intended to assuage many of the president's objections. The bank would have a new fifteen-year charter; would not issue notes in denominations of less than $20; would report to the Treasury Department the names of all of the bank's foreign stockholders, including the amount of shares they owned; and would face stiff penalties if it held onto property for longer than five years.[38]

None of this mattered in the end. Jackson issued a momentous veto that sent shockwaves throughout the nation. That Jackson vetoed the bill in spite of these modifications testifies to his stubborn character and commitment to what he regarded as nonnegotiable constitutional principles. The authorship of the veto message was a collective effort, drawing input from Andrew Jackson Jr., the president himself, two of his private secretaries (Andrew Jackson Donelson and George Breathitt), and Roger Taney, then serving as attorney general and the only anti-BUS member of Jackson's official cabinet. But more than any other figure in Jackson's circle of advisers, it was Kendall who crafted most of the arguments and language that appeared in the final product. Some of its most prominent themes—antimonopolism, sectionalism, the constitutionality of chartering a federal bank, states' rights, foreign stockholders, the bonus paid to the Treasury, bribery of the press and Congress—had been around for many years, even going back to the panic of 1819 and before. Then there was the recurring Jacksonian warning that mixing the private, for-profit interests of stockholders with the public trust of the Treasury constituted corruption and endangered liberty. Kendall's unique contribution was to add a certain class animus toward wealthy businessmen and a radical interpretation of the president's constitutional authority.[39]

The veto was thus packed with significance in terms of political institutions for it not only rejected the legal precedent established in *McColluch v. Maryland* (1819), in which the Supreme Court upheld the constitutionality of the BUS, but also inserted the president into the legislative process. The balance among the three branches of government would never be the same again. The founders, who erected institutions that narrowed the range of possibilities for Jackson (he could not just declare himself emperor despite what his political opponents said), created three branches with coequal authority. Prior to Jackson, presidents had exercised the veto sparingly, only with bills that raised clear constitutional issues. But Jackson's veto showed that institutional paths were not set in stone; in certain cases powerful individuals could shift them. Through his own volition, Jackson showed that a president could veto legislation merely if he did not like it. This position was based on Jackson's assumption that as president, he and *he alone* represented all of the American people, whereas members of Congress represented only their local districts. After Jackson's veto, Congress would have to consider the wishes of the president before they sent bills to his desk. It is because of decisions like the bank veto that historians have often credited Jackson with inaugurating the modern presidency—one that was coequal with Congress on paper but superior in practice.[40]

"The veto has just been read," Senator Dallas wrote to his friend and U.S. attorney Henry Dilworth Gilpin from inside the Senate on July 10. Perhaps because Dallas knew that so many of the president's most stalwart champions were southerners, he concluded that the veto "irreparably [threw] the Government into the arms of the South."[41] Attitudes toward the BUS in most parts of the South were ambivalent at best and deeply hostile at worst, despite pockets of pro-BUS sentiment in the region's scattered commercial centers.[42] Most of the votes against the bank's 1832 recharter bill came from southern congressmen. The irony was that Jackson, ever the proud and defiant southerner, had, with most of the South's blessing, vetoed and effectively destroyed a financial institution that brought many economic benefits to the South. This became clear when state-chartered banks in the old Southwest began adopting risky, highly leveraged lending practices in the bank's absence. When panic struck in 1837, the regions where state banks had taken the most risks were also the ones that experienced the most hardship.[43]

All of this begs us to ask: If the bank was so valuable to the South, then why did so many southerners oppose it? Perhaps historians need to take seriously southerners' constitutional scruples about a federally chartered corporation. Perhaps what seems like a fairly clear case of rational, economic self-interest to modern readers—a southerner supporting the bank—may not have been so rational for people living in a different cultural milieu, operating with different assumptions. Rationality is ultimately subjective, constructed, and changes over time. Opposition to the BUS in the South might be an apt illustration of how personality, psychology, identity, nostalgia, and nationalism so often seem to triumph over pure pocketbook politics. Or perhaps the Jeffersonian suspicion of concentrated financial power may have had true staying power in the South. If the testimony presented in Clayton's investigation is any indication, even political elites with formal educations, let alone laypersons, could find it difficult to grasp the complex workings of the BUS. The bank's regulatory and financial benefits may have also been so hidden from plain sight that only their absence could reveal them. Any and all of these issues could be true.

The politicians and constituencies who joined Jackson in defeating the Second Bank, the regions they inhabited, the occupations they held, and their reasons for opposing the bank have been the subject of lengthy historiographical debates that go back decades. While the full extent of these debates lies outside the scope of this chapter, there are some essential and often misunderstood characterizations about the bank's popularity that are worth clarifying. First, it is difficult, if not impossible, to partition public support and opposition to the bank along the neatly bifurcated lines of rural versus urban, farmers versus merchants, northerners versus southerners, slave owners versus free laborers, easterners versus westerners, and creditors versus debtors. Generalizations may suffice for the purposes of broad-based knowledge, but there are important exceptions. One assertion that appears frequently in the historiographical literature is that state bankers were jealous of—and even angry about—the Second Bank's public deposits, vast specie holdings, monopolistic relationship with the federal government, regulatory powers, and ability to lend at low rates.[44] While this may have been true in Georgia, the numerous state banks linked with New York's Albany Regency, and a few other areas, there is also substantial countervailing evidence. The BUS, by rescuing state banks from ruin in a handful of cases and by preventing them from lending excessively, served the interests of state banks in the long run. In fact, the BUS deliberately maintained large specie reserves and kept its own lending practices under a tight leash so that it could safely carry out its fiscal responsibilities, preserve the reputation and confidence of its own notes, and restrain state banks from imprudent loans. In some circumstances, Biddle instructed branch officers to adopt a more lenient policy with state banks rather than immediately demanding that they repay all of their debts to the BUS in specie. As the cholera epidemic raged in New York City in 1832, the BUS extended its accommodations to the state banks. Had the BUS not been flexible in this situation, Biddle firmly believed that the city's merchants, who borrowed frequently from the state banks, would have been unable to pay import duties.[45]

In addition, BUS branches and state banks need not have been oppositional forces. Many individual financiers worked for both BUS branches and state banks at different times in their careers, and the two types of intermediaries were often not in direct competition. BUS branches in the South and West, for example, were more likely to lend by purchasing bills of exchange rather than discounting notes on personal security, a method best left to the state banks in the minds of senior BUS management. To discount on personal security effectively, one needed to know the reputation and credit of the borrower. This was more difficult for BUS branch officers serving in the South and West because they had been trained in Philadelphia.[46]

Adding up all of the money spent in Biddle's campaign lobby prior to Jackson's veto presents several challenges for historians, primarily because the relevant financial statements are scattered and contain incomplete information. Sorting out the difference between loans that clearly had a corrupt intent and those that were merely providing convenient credit facilities, moreover, can be more of an art form than science. Sometimes loans could serve both functions. To complicate matters further, financial terminology was not standardized (see Appendix 1), and Biddle did not record some of his more clandestine maneuvers in the bank's account books. In addition to Clayton's 1832 House report, a Senate report published in 1834 has proved useful insofar as it divided most of the money involved in Biddle's lobby according to three different types of financial transactions: the loans to members of Congress; the loans to newspaper editors; and the instances in which the BUS spent its own money in circulating reports, speeches, pamphlets, treatises, and other publications.

Aside from the secret loans to editors, which warranted criticism and evinced bribery, most loans to editors and members of Congress did not constitute a grievous threat to democratic institutions in the way that Jacksonians claimed. The bank's loans to congressmen started before Jackson's election (and thus before the Bank War) and stayed relatively consistent at $200,000–$300,000 for the years 1826 to 1834.[47] Since the BUS had a branch in Washington and functioned as the Treasury Department's chief fiscal agent, it was not at all surprising for members of Congress, and other public officials for that matter, to maintain accounts with the BUS. Defenders of the bank insisted that as long as editors and congressmen offered ample security for a loan, were not delinquent in their payments, and did not receive special deals on the terms of a loan, they had as much right as any loan applicant to borrow from the bank. After all, one of the bank's chief purposes was to operate a profitable business that could return dividends to stockholders.[48]

If the 1834 Senate report gave the bank a bit of a free pass when it came to loans to members of Congress and the press, it pulled few punches when it came to the bank *spending* its own money on circulating reports, speeches, pamphlets, treatises, and other publications. For the Senate committee, this type of spending was unnecessary and counterproductive. It would have been more judicious and wise, the committee stated, for the bank to have used the standard practice of lending to newspaper organs.[49] After spending only $105.25 on printing orders unrelated to the daily operations of the bank for the entire year of 1829, Biddle's bank spent $18,490.79 during the election year of 1832. This made the bank vulnerable to the charge "of a direct interference in elections, from which it should most cautiously have abstained, even in appearance."[50] Here was an important distinction between lending—a legitimate and necessary practice for a bank—and spending its own money in an attempt to shape the public sphere. In addition, the Senate Finance Committee admitted that the BUS had every right to defend itself against injurious attacks and to explain its operations, which aligned closely with the position of the bank's stockholders and board members in 1831. But the committee criticized the bank for the way in which it went about this mission; namely, in concentrating so much discretionary and unilateral power in the hands of the bank president. A March 1831 board resolution, which invested the bank president with the authority "to cause to be prepared and circulated such documents and papers as may communicate to the people information in regard to the nature and operations of the bank," was vague enough to invite suspicion, particularly since Biddle had spent a few thousand dollars each year on "unspecified objects."[51] Indeed, if we consider the small bribes to confidential agents like John Norvell, then at least some of the Jacksonian charges of corruption were valid.

To summarize, the best available evidence gathered from multiple sources suggests that the bank spent somewhere between $50,000 and $100,000 of its own money from the start of Jackson's first term to the veto. This sum included payments to various agents (confidential and otherwise) and orders for the printing and dissemination of sundry reports, articles, treatises, pamphlets, editorials, and other documents. In the same period, the bank loaned about $150,000 to $200,000 to members of Congress and perhaps $100,000 to editors.[52] Few, if any, historians have attempted to calculate the amount of money that Biddle spent and loaned in this period in a systematic way.[53] One hundred thousand dollars in 1832 would be equivalent to several million dollars today, though there are many caveats to any estimate ranging over such a long period of time. For comparison, $1,000 might have paid for a male "prime field hand" slave or the annual salary for a mid-level public official working in Washington. To make further sense of these amounts, we might consider that the size of the U.S. economy in 1830, as measured by gross domestic product (GDP), was approximately $1 billion.[54] The U.S. federal budget for 1832 was $34.6 million, which was about the same amount as the bank's paid-in capital stock. The bank averaged about $9 million in specie and around $16 million in deposits for the month of August over a period between 1828 and 1834.[55]

It appears from the calm wisdom of hindsight that the veto dealt a significant, if not fatal, blow to the recharter effort. But in the minds of historical actors living in real time, the battle was far from over. Jackson still had to run for reelection. He was so concerned about the Second Bank's powers leading up to the veto that he seems to have genuinely believed "that not only our State Legislatures might be dispensed with, but congress dissolved, & the Bank left to Legislate, and the Supreme court to execute its mandates."[56] As he had done previously, Jackson continued to make suggestions to Kendall about what to publish in the *Globe*. The president wanted *Globe* readers to know the extent of the bank's corruption. Though their preferred methods of subsidy differed, the Jacksonians, just as much as the bank's allies, knew that newspapers were key to persuading voters. One of Jackson's Connecticut allies believed that the friends of the bank "[would] redouble their exertion to deceive the people" and that it was imperative to disseminate "correct information [t]o the honest yeomanry of the country." Accordingly, Jacksonians in Connecticut established two newspapers in the state, with plans for another.[57]

Outside of Washington, a different Bank War was already under way.

In the aftermath of the veto, citizens from Philadelphia to St. Louis, and numerous places in between, gathered at public meetings to express their opinions on the bank.[58] News of the veto arrived in St. Louis a little less than two weeks after Jackson had issued it, leading to calls for competing pro- and anti-BUS gatherings. Observers speculated that about 500 Jackson men attended an anti-BUS meeting at a "Town-house" adjoining the "public Market Square," with slightly above half of this amount attending the pro-BUS meeting that convened at the St. Louis Courthouse on July 23. Both meetings resulted in the passage of resolutions and the nomination of candidates. On August 9 the *Globe* copied excerpts from St. Louis newspapers, completing the circle of information flowing back and forth between the East Coast and Mississippi River Valley.[59]

Public meetings were permissible and even laudable forms of political protest, but from time to time anti-BUS resistance went far beyond the bounds of legal and acceptable behavior. On July 26 an unidentified person(s) set fire to a building owned by the bank in an alleged case of arson. According to a letter written to Biddle by Herman Cope, head of the bank's Cincinnati Commercial Agency, a fire burned through the third floor and roof of the Broadway Hotel, then owned by the bank, leading to an estimated $5,000–$6,000 of property damage. Cope concluded that "there [was] little or no doubt that this has been the work of an Incendiary (an inmate of the house at the time) for the purpose of plunder" since the fire started at 4 o'clock in the morning in a part of the hotel that was inaccessible to most. While there were no fatalities or serious injuries reported, Cope notified Biddle that he was willing to advertise a suitable monetary reward in the "Public prints" if he believed that it would induce someone to come forward with information leading to the arrest and conviction of the alleged arsonist.[60]

If Cope was correct that the fire was deliberate and not accidental, it is worth thinking about the immediate and long-term context. The immediate context was that Jackson's veto provoked strong reactions. It seems too coincidental to ignore the issue of timing—a fire at a building owned by the bank occurred less than two weeks after news of Jackson's veto would have arrived in Cincinnati. The long-term and broader context was that the bank had acquired large tracts of land in western areas such as Cincinnati, Louisville, and Lexington through the process of foreclosure during the economic convulsions of 1819–1821. This was always a sore spot for Jacksonians, who contended that the bank did not legally possess the ability to own property beyond the small amounts needed to build branch offices. If Cope's conjectures were true, the Cincinnati fire was one manifestation of how the Bank War, conceived in the elite corridors of Washington and Philadelphia, could be transmitted to various parts of the country with destructive consequences.[61]

Just south of the Ohio River, in Kentucky, post-veto skirmishes played out in the lead-up to the president's reelection campaign. Since many Jacksonians viewed the bank, just as much as Henry Clay, as their chief adversary in November's election, they attempted to embarrass and potentially cripple the institution by propagating rumors that some of its branches in the South and West were insolvent. A coordinated attack on the Lexington, Kentucky, branch BUS was a case in point. During the summer months of 1832, the branch had to pay out $23,000 in specie to customers who were not regular depositors at the bank and who "were not part of the commercial class." This was followed in September by repeated calls for specie on the order of about $1,000–$1,500 per day. When these demands led to a partial suspension of specie payments, Jacksonians argued that the BUS was curtailing credit in order to influence the upcoming presidential election. In effect, they were trying to manufacture a self-fulfilling prophecy. After receiving an urgent request for more specie, Samuel Jaudon, the cashier at the bank's parent branch in Philadelphia, dispatched two clerks with $50,000 in gold coin to Lexington. Intimately aware that psychology, reputation, anxiety, and attitudes mattered just as much as raw numbers and accounting principles when it came to the survivability of a bank, Jaudon advised the Lexington cashier that the best way to prevent further calls for specie was to "pay it out to all applicants with the utmost readiness and cheerfulness, and if any fears should have been excited by such newspaper paragraphs as you allude to, they will soon be quieted."[62]

Partisan newspapers were major players in this unfolding drama, underscoring the ability of editorialists to affect bank balance sheets through rumor and intrigue. The Jacksonian *Kentucky Gazette* published daily attacks to create the impression that the branch was insolvent. There was also evidence to suggest that newspapers, by republishing congressional reports first printed in Washington, helped to transmit and amplify a Bank War that originated on the East Coast to places like Kentucky. Joseph Towler, the cashier of the Lexington branch BUS, spoke to several delegates at a Jacksonian convention in Harrodsburg (a town southwest of Lexington) in which "resolutions were unanimously adopted; the object of which is, to produce upon the public mind, that the institution is insolvent, and unable to redeem its notes." The resolutions, Towler told Biddle, were "chiefly taken from Clayton's [House] report" that had come out a few months earlier.[63]

To ward off this attack, the bank's board in Philadelphia proceeded much in the way as it had done the previous year: by conceptualizing the various branch offices as individual instruments working in concert. The Lexington office was fortified with $275,000 in specie shipped from other branch offices in St. Louis, Louisville, Cincinnati, New Orleans, and Philadelphia. Viewing each branch office as an integral member of a team, Jaudon assured the Lexington cashier, "Your office, then, and those at Louisville, St. Louis, and Cincinnati, must stand ready to assist and support each other at any moment. Your united strength is so great that no combination need be feared."[64] Like a military leader quickly transferring his troops from one side of the battlefield to another in order to prevent a catastrophic breach in his wall, Jaudon understood that a bank run at any of the branch offices might imperil the entire network. Individuals seldom get the credit they deserve for averting disaster, partly because it is difficult to prove the counterfactual that things may have turned out much worse. But by quickly sending communications and financial resources to any point in the institution's interregional network of branches, Biddle and other board members like Jaudon could prevent politically motivated attacks. As a result, the pronounced withdrawals of specie from the Lexington branch did not produce a damaging bank run.

Unfortunately for the branch officers in Lexington, this was not the end of Jacksonian mischief. Two men, David Thomas and Lewis Wilson, walked into the branch and applied for a $1,000 loan. The bank's board rejected the application but approved a smaller one for $400. Thomas and another Jacksonian, William T. Buckner, complained in the *Kentucky Gazette*, a Jacksonian paper, that the bank would only approve high-value loans for self-professed Clay acolytes. Members of the Lexington branch board of directors, at least three of whom were self-identified Jackson supporters, rejected these charges with published statements in two rival publications, the *Lexington Observer and Reporter* and the *Paris Citizen Extra*. The directors declared in unequivocal terms that the charges of partisan lending practices were "utterly at variance with the truth" and "false in every respect."[65] Interestingly, the scuffles at the Lexington branch prior to the 1832 presidential election were similar to the ones that took place four year previously. Then, as now, Jacksonians complained bitterly of politically motivated lending practices while the bank's officers, many of them Jacksonians, vehemently denied the charges.[66]

The bank's cashier at the Lexington branch office notified Jaudon in Philadelphia "on high authority" that a gentleman he met was certain that the attempted bank run was manufactured "in pursuance of instructions from Washington."[67] The Jacksonian effort to weaken the BUS by attacking its most vulnerable branches might plausibly be viewed as an understudied dimension to the Bank War and more specifically, as a precursor to Jackson's later decision to remove the bank's federal deposits. For his part, Biddle, on September 26, 1832, only a few weeks before the election, sent a copy of Senator Daniel Webster's response to Jackson's veto to John Tilford, the president of the Lexington branch. "It is desirable that [Webster's speech] should be circulated," Biddle wrote, "so as to counteract the injurious impressions" of the veto. So long as the speeches circulated by Tilford were "explanatory of the operations and conduct of the bank" and avoided an overtly political stance, Biddle took a top-down approach to his campaign while leaving some flexibility and autonomy for Tilford's judgment: "You may cause to be printed and circulated any amount of such papers as you may consider necessary for vindication of the bank, and give me an account of the expense."[68]

Kentucky, the home of Clay, Kendall, several members of Jackson's administration, and a politically divided state characterized by close elections, had become a political hot spot in the Bank War between the veto and the fall elections. More than a merely a war of words between competing newspapers, what transpired in the Bluegrass State might be depicted as a "mini Bank War" or part of a "Second Bank War"—underemphasized or ignored entirely by historians and yet shaped, often imperceptibly, by an ever-growing interregional network of transportation and communication financed by various mixtures of public and private capital. This Second Bank War took a while to unfold and occurred on the ground level, geographically removed from the elite corridors of Washington, Philadelphia, and New York. It involved semielite and ordinary individuals participating in riots, politically orchestrated bank runs, arson, political meetings, duels, assassination attempts, and other disturbances. Newspapers connected these two Bank Wars because they communicated information and because editors had roles to play in both. In this way, both sides in the conflict communicated key talking points from the East Coast to Kentucky, where the Bank War took on its own distinct character.

Going into the fall elections, the tariff and the bank topped the list of the most pressing controversies. Kendall and Blair were tasked with coordinating Jackson's reelection campaign. This was partly because Jackson spent much of the summer attending to personal matters and recuperating from long-standing health problems at his home, the Hermitage, outside Nashville. Kendall, acting as a de facto national party chairman, gave the campaign an element of centralized control. From his headquarters in Washington he worked with a small army of campaign organizers from all parts of the country, sending out and receiving a daily flow of correspondence and campaign propaganda.[69] As they had done in the previous three years, Kendall and Blair framed the bank question as one of a privileged monopoly against a popular war hero, which was an effective strategy since Jackson's personal popularity remained strong.

Jacksonians doubled down on their denunciations of the bank, which ranged from the legitimate to the hyperbolic. Blair charged that "the citadel of the aristocracy" and "the NOBILITY SYSTEM" were buying off members of the press, including Philadelphia editor Robert Walsh.[70] Pro-BUS editors had their rejoinders ready. The *National Gazette* directed the contents of one of its publications of a BUS stockholder meeting "to the attentive consideration of the sober classes of the community."[71] Gales and Seaton referred to Jacksonian editors as "hirelings" who warned "the people against British influence. . . . In this way they may delude fools, but men of sense" would conclude that British gold was just as good as any gold to promote economic development.[72]

At issue here were two contrasting visions of nationalism related to the desirability of the bank's global character. Biddle's nationalism, like Hamilton's, called for a robust and self-sufficient financial system that utilized global commerce. The Jacksonian position, showcased in the veto and explicitly linked to the American Revolution, put forth a tangible concern among millions of Americans that European aristocrats wished to tamper with democratic elections and a free press. As the election results came in, there was no question which kind of nationalism carried the day. Jackson defeated Clay in the Electoral College in a landslide, 219 to 49.[73] At least on the question of foreign influence in the economy, the Jacksonian nationalism showed that perception often mattered more than reality. Section 11 of the original BUS charter of 1816 stipulated that "stockholders actually resident within the United States, and none other, may vote in elections by proxy" and "none but a stockholder, resident citizen of the United States, shall be a director."[74] The British stockholders so often derided by Jacksonian hardliners had no legal say over the makeup of the bank's management. Jackson's Anglophobia is perhaps understandable given his experiences fighting British soldiers during the American Revolution and War of 1812, but foreign

CHAPTER FOUR

investors in Jackson's time never owned more than 30 percent of the bank's stock, which was less than half the percentage that foreign stockholders subscribed to during the First Bank's tenure in 1803.[75]

Jackson's reelection was potentially a knockout blow for the bank, and there was some concern among the president's supporters that if the bank could not achieve its objectives through the electoral process and a peaceful transition of power, something worse might be in the works. On November 6, 1832, a few days after election results in Pennsylvania had become known, a Philadelphia shipyard worker named Henry Selden Crabb wrote to Jackson in regards to a potential assassination attempt.[76] Crabb had just attended a local Hickory Club meeting and stopped into an oyster bar in the Southwark neighborhood where he heard two men talking in animated and energetic terms about the future of the country. One of the men then lowered his voice to a whisper and declared that "two men of high standing in this place" had promised a sum of $50,000 or greater "*to reward the man, or set of men, who would remove your Excellency out of the way—Or in other words, ASSASSINATE You!!!*" Crabb attempted to follow the two men but lost track of them in the darkness of night. While recognizing that this scheme lacked hard proof and may have been unworthy of the president's attention, Crabb cautioned, "For God's sake Sir be not too secure in the idea of yr safety nor trust too much to the virtue of man. The malignant & fiendish venom of the partisans of the Bank: is almost beyond the reach of probability and I solemnly believe that they would stop at nothing."[77] Duly noting all of the caveats associated with this letter, here was potentially some of the first bits of evidence that the energies unleashed by Biddle's lobby, the veto, and the tumultuous election were getting out of hand and developing in ways that neither Jackson nor Biddle could control. What started out as a war of words over abstract constitutional and philosophical principles was now turning into an urgent life-or-death scenario. Indeed, there was a sense that the violent rhetoric of the Bank War, broadcast in newspapers and other forms of print culture, could mutate into violent action. The Biddle-Pettis duel had already made this clear. And as later events would show, this would not be the only time that Jackson would hear about assassination attempts, both real and imagined, that were framed by contemporaries in the context of the Bank War.

The election results of 1832 revealed a fair degree of continuity with the previous two presidential contests, particularly when one looks for the geographic, occupational, economic, psychological, and ethnocultural factors that tended to influence voter behavior. Voter turnout continued to be high (though slightly less compared to 1828) and would remain so throughout the rest of the nineteenth century. Specialists of nineteenth-century political history will note that the Second Party System was no repeat of the first one. The Jacksonian coalition, for example, included some old Federalists who appreciated Old Hickory's penchant for a strong executive. Conversely, many National Republicans and later, Whigs, grew out of the more economically nationalistic wing of the Jeffersonians.[78] In northern states like Ohio, Pennsylvania, and New York, Americans of German, Dutch, Scots-Irish, and Irish Catholic ancestry, and even recent immigrants, tended to vote for Jacksonian candidates. A good many of these voters adored Jackson's personality and applauded his military heroism and record of fighting the British. Masculinity, honor, and a sense that Jackson stood for restoring the once-cherished virtues of the founders reinforced these sentiments. Included in Jackson's coalition were many artisans, radicals, and industrial workers clustered in northeastern urban centers like Philadelphia and New York City. White southerners, meanwhile, had been overwhelmingly supportive of Jackson since at least the mid-1820s, and perhaps longer. They reaffirmed the president's commitment to Indian Removal, the extension of slavery, and the destruction of the BUS. Jackson won 69.5 percent of the popular vote in the slave states, or 87 percent if one chooses to exclude the four Border South states that did not secede from the union.[79]

In 1832, as in 1824 and 1828, candidates issued policy statements in friendly newspapers and campaigned actively on their own behalf. National conventions gradually replaced caucuses. Campaign biographies were published. "Hickory Clubs" throughout the nation supplemented the work of local and state Jacksonian committees.[80] Candidates and voters continued to broadcast their views through various forms of print media that included newspapers, books, advertisements, circulars, broadsides, pamphlets, and political cartoons; they took symbolic stands through hickory poles, songs, buttons, ribbons, and other campaign paraphernalia; and they attended barbecues, rallies, banquets, and parades.[81] It is tempting to look at the lopsided election results from 1832 and affirm the traditional view that the Jacksonians possessed the superior organizational skills and campaign techniques. But this may be only partially correct. It is probably more accurate to say that National Republicans, especially in New England, embraced partisan campaigning, if only reluctantly and belatedly. Adams and Clay supporters may not have welcomed partisanship in an ideal world, but they recognized it was essential to winning elections. Where a compelling case can be made of differentiating the Jacksonians from their opponents lies in editorial style. On average, anti-BUS Jacksonian editors possessed more of a propensity for mudslinging and vitriol compared to their more subdued pro-BUS opponents, best exemplified by Gales and Seaton. In this sense it was not so much the number of newspapers that mattered but the intensity and enthusiasm that editors on each side of the Bank War brought to the table.[82]

What made the 1832 presidential election unique was that it was quite possibly the first time that a major legislative issue—the renewal of the bank's charter—came before the voters for a referendum during a presidential election year. At least one historian has observed that Jackson's margin of victory in the popular vote, measured as a percentage, declined between 1832 and 1828, and surmises that Jackson's stance on the bank question was at least partially responsible for this decline.[83] Before Barack Obama's reelection in 2012, Jackson had been the only two-term president in U.S. history whose popular vote margin in his reelection campaign fell short of the margin that initially put him in office. Indeed, the Jacksonians lost support in urban centers compared to 1828, while still performing well in the areas immediately surrounding urban cores and making inroads in non-commercial areas. Many Jacksonian editors quickly fell into line under the pressure of party leaders and a readership that approved of Jackson's stand. Later congressional elections, moreover, brought to power a 23rd Congress (December 1833 to March 1835) comprised of Jacksonian House members who were more fervently anti-BUS. This may have stemmed from the fact that those who supported the president's bank position, either out of loyalty or conviction, were more likely to receive financial and organizational assistance from elite party members, thereby boosting their chances of securing a party nomination.[84]

That Jackson won a resounding victory in 1832 need not necessarily diminish the efforts of Biddle, who assembled an impressive amount of resources, both human and financial, into a hierarchical and interregional corporate lobby designed to secure a new bank charter. Donations and favorable media coverage *in and of themselves*, whether in 1832 or in the twenty-first century, do not guarantee any particular outcome, even if they shape political behavior in powerful ways. This suggests the need for considering multiple variables. In a two-party system, moreover, it is exceedingly difficult to overcome a presidential veto, especially when an issue like the bank's recharter becomes polarized along party lines. And for their part, the Jacksonians, because they used partisanship and patronage networks effectively in their management of the federal bureaucracy, possessed powerful tools to counter the bank's prowess.

At least one larger implication of Biddle's lobby is the immense challenge of constructing monetary policy that is independent of political pressures, whether they be fickle voters or an overbearing president. Since the earliest days of the republic up until the present, independent monetary policy has been a chief concern of economic policymakers. Biddle's campaign shows us that even the brightest and most talented bankers, despite their best efforts to remain neutral, are still very much partial actors with a deep interest in preserving their institutions through political means. The Jacksonian-induced politicization of Biddle's activities came into clearer focus during Jackson's second term, much to the detriment of the Second Bank's future prospects.

FIVE

⌒

Two Sides of the Same Coin: The Panic of 1833–1834 and the Loss of Public Support

Reelection gave the Jacksonians momentum and an opportunity to destroy the "Monster Bank" once and for all. They continued to appropriate the political and financial institutions under their control—House committees, numerous state banks, Post Office patronage, and partisan newspapers—to chip away at the bank's power. The most consequential attack on the BUS during Jackson's second term was the president's decision in late 1833 to order the Treasury Department to remove the bank's public (or "federal") deposits. This added turmoil to Biddle's already packed schedule. Not only did he have to consider the loss of $10 million in public deposits and the payment of $15 million in public debt within a one-year time frame, both of which would strain the bank's resources, but there were ongoing congressional investigations, infighting at the bank's board meetings, expectations that the BUS would continue to lend to commercial houses in order to keep them afloat, the desire among the bank's stockholders for consistent dividends, and even unpredictable events like cholera outbreaks and bad harvests.

By focusing on the ways in which Biddle confronted these challenges, as this chapter does, we are able to make sense of the complex financial system of the antebellum era. In the process, we can uncover insights about both the institutional structure of the bank and the leadership style of the brilliant yet rash Philadelphian who managed it. The bank president communicated monetary policy with his branch officers in a way that resembled his inter-actions with newspaper editors. Both utilized interregional communications networks that were shaped by powerful economic, political, and institu-tional forces. Yet within these boundaries, unpredictable events merged with the individual decisions of branch officers and editors to complicate and even subvert Biddle's well-laid plans. The culmination of Biddle's response to the removal of the bank's public deposits was an injurious miscalculation: a manufactured economic crisis that cost him crucial public support.

During the same months that Biddle was trying to save the bank from ruin, the Second Bank War continued to unfold. Bank-infused public meet-ings, bank-related riots, and even numerous assassination attempts of a sitting U.S. president, both real and imagined, and framed in newspapers as consequences of the Bank War's violent rhetoric, suggest that the Bank War had become absorbed through the public consciousness. The issue had taken on a life of its own, beyond what Biddle intended. Newspaper busi-nesses, as public-private institutions, and newspaper editors, as transmitters of information and as shapers of public opinion, linked the traditional and Second Bank Wars.

In December 1832, for the third time in four years, Jackson singled out the BUS for criticism in his annual message to Congress. Having learned of Biddle's plans to delay payments on the public debt earlier that year, Jackson called for additional investigations of the bank in Congress. Biddle's attempt at flexibility violated the bank's charter and Jackson's goal of retiring the public debt (or what we would call "the national debt" in today's language) by January 1833. The president was now convinced that the public deposits could not be safely entrusted in Biddle's hands and that the recent elec-tion results had validated his position. The overwhelming election victory, Jackson thought, had given him a popular mandate to remove the deposits. Kendall developed these points in a draft of the president's message, which Jackson softened and pared down before delivering the final product.[1] Soon afterward, Jackson told one of his young protégés, fellow Tennessean James Knox Polk, who was nicknamed "Young Hickory," that "the hydra of cor-ruption is only *scotched, not dead*" and expressed confidently that "an in-vestigation [would kill the bank] and its supporters *dead*."[2] Accordingly, the House Committee of Ways and Means and Senate Finance Committee launched investigations that addressed Jackson's concerns, issuing reports in March 1833 and December 1834, respectively.

CHAPTER FIVE

On the question of the safety of the public deposits, anti-BUS Jacksonians did not have much of a case. Secretary of the Treasury Louis McLane had asked Henry Toland, a prominent Philadelphia merchant, to examine the bank's account books. A former BUS director who had, oddly enough, sold chinaware and other goods to Jackson using the bank's credit facilities, Toland found the ratio between the bank's assets and liabilities to be sound and concluded that the institution could safely meet all of its obligations. Pro-BUS Jacksonian representative Gulian Verplanck of New York, chairman of the House Ways and Means Committee, issued a report that reinforced Toland's assessment, including a resolution stating that "the Government deposites may . . . be safely continued in the Bank of the United States." If the Jacksonians planned to continue attacking the bank based on the assumption that it was mismanaging the public money or taking perilous financial risks, this was a strategy grounded more in party politics and less in any dispassionate reading of the empirical facts.[3]

Few outside of the business community understood the intricacies of finance, so the Jacksonians might be forgiven for possessing only a basic understanding of how the bank's public deposits actually worked. To the Jacksonians, the storage of the public deposits in the bank's vaults signified a dubious appropriation of the people's money for private gain in the form of stock dividends and risky speculative ventures. More ominously, they seemed to strengthen the bank's ability to bribe members of Congress and the press, and to coerce the state banks. Leaving aside the likelihood that the Jacksonians derived political gain from their exaggerated rhetoric, their characterizations of how the public deposits functioned were overdrawn. It is true that Biddle cited deposit removal as a main reason to curb lending from the fall of 1833 to the summer of 1834. And while most banks generally sought customers' deposits to enable more lending, when one looks at some of the BUS balance sheets published in congressional reports, it is clear that the Second Bank differentiated between its public deposits and its private deposits. Its public deposits would have been used, per Treasury Department instructions, to pay pensioners and the salaries of public officials, or to pay down the public debt. But Biddle would not have used these specific deposits to bribe editors and politicians.[4] Theoretically the bank's *private* deposits might enable more lending to editors and congressmen, but Jackson had no control over them. Indeed, Biddle continued to make such loans well after the removal of the public deposits. Furthermore, there were counterintuitive elements to banking that Jacksonians missed or ignored. Much like bank notes in circulation, deposits were categorized for accounting purposes as liabilities. Specie (monetary reserves) and capital stock were arguably more important than deposits in determining the extent to which a bank could lend.[5]

The second part of Jackson's criticism—that of the public debt—amounted in substance to a miscommunication between Biddle and Thomas Cadwalader that was quickly rectified. But it revealed the extent to which Biddle was willing to act unilaterally on matters of significant financial consequence. In March 1832 the bank's board passed a resolution authorizing its three-member exchange committee to find a way of fulfilling Jackson's desire to pay off the remaining $15 million in the nation's public debt while at the same time continuing unabated its accommodations for members of the commercial community.[6] The result was a plan in which Biddle would dispatch Cadwalader to Great Britain in July to negotiate a deal with Baring Brothers, the international merchant banking house and BUS partner and creditor primarily responsible for marketing U.S. securities to overseas investors. Cadwalader was instructed to postpone for approximately one year the payment of $5 million worth of the "three percent stocks"—U.S. Treasury bonds issued during the early republic bearing 3 percent interest (U.S. 3's for short). The bondholders, over half of whom were foreigners, would hold onto the U.S. 3's until October 1833 with the bank paying interest on the bonds in the meantime. As part of this agreement, the BUS would pay a one-half percent commission to Barings. Cadwalader, operating on his own accord, included a provision in which the bank would purchase some of the bonds on a temporary basis, but he had forgotten that the bank's charter forbid any purchasing of public debt. When Biddle discovered this, he disavowed the contract and instructed Cadwalader to negotiate a new one.[7]

As for why Biddle believed that delaying payments on the public debt would serve the greater good in spite of Jackson's desire to pay it off completely by January 1833, Biddle cited several temporary and unforeseen factors: the outbreak of cholera in the summer of 1832, a shortage of specie emanating from a trade deficit, the bank veto, and a desire to avoid inconveniencing the mercantile community. In a letter to Jacksonian representative Charles A. Wickliffe of Kentucky, Biddle explained that the arrangement with Barings enabled the bank "to enlarge its facilities in Kentucky."[8] From Biddle's point of view, holding onto specie that would have otherwise been shipped to Europe for bond payments was critical for the BUS, and by extension, the business community and the nation at large. Unlike American investors who had purchased U.S. Treasury bonds, foreign bondholders would not accept BUS notes. They demanded specie or specie equivalents

Figure 1. Foreign Bill of Exchange in £500, drawn by the Second Bank of the United States (drawer), on Baring Brothers in London (drawee), dated August 27, 1836. The bill is drawn in favor of the payee, N. Robinson, who was the Second Bank's agent in Great Britain. The bank's president and cashier, Nicholas Biddle and Samuel Jaudon, respectively, provided endorsements (signatures). Personal Photograph. Catalog Number INDE 2257. Collection of Independence National Historical Park, Philadelphia.

such as foreign bills of exchange in pounds sterling (see Figure 1 and Figure 2).[9] Polk, speaking for a minority of the House committee, pointed to the chronology of some of the bank's financial statements to dispute the legitimacy of Biddle's claims. As Jackson had done in his veto message, Polk referenced the bank's rapid expansion and contraction of loans over short periods of time as evidence that the "Monster" was trying to make or break the fortunes of small communities at will for political gain. What they missed, or chose to downplay, was that the bank's loans had a natural variation according to region and season (see Figure 3). If the bank's loans in the South had decreased between crop harvests and because most bills of exchange had come to maturity, then any reduction in business would not have been malicious.[10]

The bank, the minority committee contended, was delaying debt payments because it wanted to hold onto the public deposits as long as possible and because it had loaned excessively in the South and West. Just as Clayton had insisted in his 1832 anti-BUS report, Polk assumed that more lending automatically entailed more risk. This seemed like common sense, but it was also somewhat misleading. When a bank issued a loan, it was indeed taking a risk, but it was also purchasing an asset that earned a rate of interest commensurate with that risk. Moreover, the BUS had a responsibility to return dividends to its private stockholders, who pledged four-fifths of the bank's capital. The BUS could only return dividends if it profited, and it could only profit if it lent. The rapid expansion of cotton, slavery, and land sales then occurring in the American Southwest required credit, and the bank, like any for-profit institution, saw a valuable investment opportunity. Polk backtracked a bit, clarifying that he was not arguing that the BUS was insolvent—only that it was mismanaged—and that this mismanagement could cause a reasonable person to doubt the safety of the public deposits. Jacksonian hard-liners accepted this view.[11]

The more compelling line of argument in Polk's report concerned the relative secrecy under which Biddle operated. The bank's exchange committee, which Biddle supervised along with two other close-knit colleagues, sent Cadwalader to Great Britain without permission from the Treasury Department and without notifying the bank's government directors until after the negotiation with Barings had been completed. Recall that Biddle had taken this approach before when he issued secret loans to Gales and Seaton that even Cadwalader found objectionable. In this case, loud protestations emanated from the government directors, who had been left out of the process. Their concerns were valid. The three-member exchange committee made some of the bank's most important business decisions, but without any input from the government directors, anti-BUS Jacksonians believed, Biddle's bank was unaccountable to the public.[12] The bank's government directors, unlike its private directors, were supposed to speak primarily for the public interest and have a say over the manner in which the BUS handled the public's money. According to this reasoning, the Treasury Department, whose chief purpose was to oversee matters of public revenue and spending, including payments on the public debt, should have also been informed of Cadwalader's actions. That some of the bank's private directors had been evasive and given minimalist answers in response to Polk's questioning lent credence to Jacksonian claims. Even the anti-Jacksonian Senate, made up of many of Biddle's political allies, did not condone the contract with Barings and could offer only lukewarm support for the bank when it, too, looked into this matter.[13]

A key issue, then, exposed by the House and Senate investigations was the discordant relationship between the public directors appointed by Jackson and the private directors elected by the bank's stockholders, a majority of whom were allied with Biddle and almost always outvoted the former on key policy questions. Part of this acrimony can be explained by the bank's corporate organizational structure, which delegated a great deal of power to the bank president. Biddle served on all but one of the bank's numerous committees, controlled over 30 percent of all of the votes allocated to the bank's stockholders for electing directors, and personally selected members of the all-important exchange committee. Unsurprisingly, this distribution of power resulted in decisions that confirmed Biddle's predilections.[14]

Biddle was secretive—perhaps unnecessarily so—but Jackson, too, can be faulted for antagonistically sowing divisions at the bank's board. In August 1833, without permission, Jackson ordered the government directors to examine the bank's expense account over concerns that the BUS was still interfering in elections. The government directors found that the tens of thousands of dollars of printing orders to editors like Gales and Seaton, categorized under the heading "stationary [sic] and printing," justified Jackson's suspicions.[15] In response, on September 24, 1833, the bank's directors passed resolutions on a 12 to 3 vote authorizing the production of 5,000 copies of a stockholders' report that rebutted many of these charges. This was the same report pointing out that the bank's business model rested on a positive reputation, which led Biddle and most other board members to believe that spending some of the bank's funds on the printing and dissemination of pro-BUS reports was justified (see Chapter 3). The report stressed that "in no part of the charter of the Bank, in no law of this country is there found any power in the President [of the United States] to interfere in the internal concerns of the [BUS], or to direct secret investigations" and affirmed Biddle's discretionary power to spend money on behalf of the bank as he saw fit.[16]

If congressional investigations and the appointment of government directors yielded only mixed results for Jackson's goal of eviscerating the dreaded "Monster," the removal of the bank's public deposits proved to be much more consequential. Kendall and Taney posited that the bank would continue to marshal its vast financial resources to obstruct Jackson's vision of fiscal reform. The only way to enact Jackson's reforms, they insisted, was to remove the approximately $10 million in public deposits stored in the bank's vaults. But there were obstacles. According to the bank's charter, the only person who possessed the authority to remove the deposits was the secretary of the Treasury, who had to report to Congress his reasons for removal. Jackson hoped that his new appointee, Philadelphia printer William John Duane, the third man to occupy the post in four years, would demonstrate his loyalty through dutiful compliance. The president, after all, had specifically selected Duane because of his constitutional scruples, loyalty to the administration, and financial knowledge. He also wanted to appoint someone from vote-rich Pennsylvania, which had backed the Jacksonian ticket twice in the Electoral College. To boot, Duane had a long record opposing the BUS as a member of the Pennsylvania state legislature and Working Man's Party, so Jackson reasonably assumed he would go along. But go along he did not. Duane refused to remove the deposits! Jackson, in turn, summarily dismissed Duane and appointed Taney, then serving as attorney general, to replace him. As an interim Treasury secretary (he never received Senate confirmation), Taney ordered the removal of deposits to take place on October 1, 1833, spread out over four quarterly installments. Intentionally, the process would start when Congress was out of session.[17]

Biddle responded with measures that were both precautionary and vindictive. Monetary expansion had prevailed over the previous five years, especially in 1831, when the bank's loans bulged from $41 million to $63 million.[18] But with deposit removal proceeding and the hopes for recharter dimming with each day, Biddle now curbed lending. At least partially, this was a sensible response to the public and private responsibilities that Biddle had to consider: his duty to protect the institutions from political attacks as the attempted bank run at the Lexington branch demonstrated; the goal of managing a (mostly) for-profit institution that would return dividends to its shareholders; the need to honor the nation's credit and reputation through consistent payments on the public debt; and the responsibility of maintaining a stable and uniform currency, which had always been the bank's greatest asset (pun intended). Yet there was also a more punitive motivation for these loan restrictions; that is, he wanted to manufacture a recession in order to convince Americans that a national bank was indispensable to a thriving, well-regulated economy.

One of the first orders of business for Biddle under this new paradigm was to minimize the bank's risks by building up its liquidity. On October 8, 1833, Biddle ordered a $5.83 million reduction in the bank's purchase of earning assets, which was financial speak for curtailing credit. An additional reduction of $3.32 million followed in January, bringing the total to about $9.15 million. This meant that the total reduction in loans was nearly the same amount as the total public deposits that Taney was in the process of removing.[19] The bank's discount rate—the interest rate the bank charged when it purchased commercial paper from customers in exchange for lending out its own notes—rose sharply. In addition, Biddle ceased renewing long-term accommodations and recalled (or called in) many of the bank's loans. Borrowers would have to repay the bank immediately. As current

Figure 2. Reverse Side of Bill of Exchange. The phrase "Pay Malcolm & Co. or order," followed by the endorsement of an agent, indicates that the BUS was most likely drawing on funds in its foreign account with Barings to pay for goods produced by Malcolm & Co. that would be shipped to the United States. Personal Photograph. Catalog Number INDE 2257. Collection of Independence National Historical Park, Philadelphia.

loans were repaid and the bank scaled back the number of new loans it issued, specie accumulated in the bank's vaults.[20]

To carry out his proposed reductions, Biddle, as he had done in his lobbying campaign, relied on the bank's interregional network of branches. As early as the spring of 1832, when it became clear to the bank's officers that the Treasury Department would be demanding full repayment of the public debt in less than one year, the parent branch began calling for stricter lending practices. In particular, Biddle ordered the branch officers in the South and West to purchase only short-term bills of exchange (ninety days or less) that were payable in the Atlantic cities.[21] The branches in Boston, New York, Philadelphia, and Baltimore would be making payments on the public debt. These were the same branches that Jacksonians would most likely target for deposit removal. So by instructing the southern and western branches to purchase bills payable in the mid-Atlantic and New England regions, the bank was transferring a great deal of its assets to meet these challenges. Moreover, Biddle remembered how Jacksonians tried to instigate bank runs at several of the bank's offices, especially in Lexington, so there was an additional rationale for minimizing risks in the West. In August 1833, with deposit removal soon to go into effect, the bank recommitted to this policy by passing resolutions. Biddle and his colleagues in Philadelphia then disseminated copies of these resolutions to the presidents and cashiers

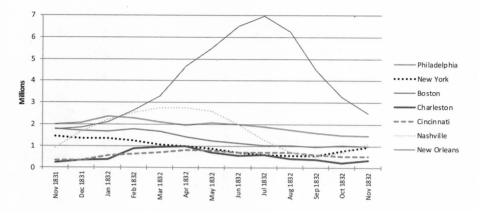

Figure 3. Graph of Bills of Exchange Purchased by BUS Branch Offices, 1832. This graph shows the importance of the branch BUS in New Orleans, which served as the agent for all other western branches, as well as the seasonal nature of bills purchased in the South and West. *Source*: House Document 8, 22nd Congress, 2nd Session, Serial Volume 233, 4; 13–25.

of each branch office, along with instructions particularized to each locale. This was an effort to synchronize both monetary policy and political strategy between Philadelphia and the South and West.[22]

In a letter written to Joseph Johnson, the president of the Charleston branch, Biddle described how purchasing bills of exchange drawn on northern mercantile houses "naturally throw into circulation large masses of your notes, which soon find their way to the north, and being immediately paid, create a charge upon the bank and the northern offices," which Biddle wanted to avoid. If BUS notes accumulated in northern cities, merchants, factors, and state bankers could take these notes to a BUS branch office and redeem them for specie, which Biddle needed for payments on the public debt.[23] Similar sentiments were communicated to the presidents of branches in Buffalo, Boston, New York, New Orleans, and other cities. In each letter Biddle maintained a polite, courteous tone that gently conveyed the board's wishes while at the same time allowing for some flexibility and autonomy so that the branches could respond to local conditions.[24]

It was not an easy task for the branch officers to implement Biddle's instructions. Letters sent from the cashiers and presidents of the branch offices in the South and West to Philadelphia, transcribed, excerpted, and presented in congressional debate, show that the branch officers had to juggle multiple responsibilities and variables, many of which were unpredictable. If crop harvests were delayed or insufficiently abundant, for example, branch offices would be forced to renew many of their loans, thereby delaying Biddle's plans for reductions. P. Benson, the cashier at the bank's Cincinnati office, began one letter thusly: "Our discount line does not go down as fast, I am afraid, as the parent board wish." The cholera "raged here so violently . . . that the business of the place has been thrown into a confusion that it will not recover from for some time." Benson was doing everything he could to reduce his bill purchases, but lamented, "the demand for money for the winter operations in produce, as well as for eastern acceptances, is enormous; and we shall have a severe struggle for some time to resist it." He hoped to fulfill the parent board's wishes by the close of winter.[25]

Similarly, Edward Shippen, the Louisville office's cashier, wrote to Philadelphia on the topic of loan reductions, illustrating the complex set of variables through which antebellum-era financiers had to navigate. It was difficult to reduce loans, Shippen said, because the BUS had to prop up commercial houses, whose merchants needed the bank's credit instruments to purchase merchandise and groceries, especially flour, pork, hemp, and tobacco. Because merchants in the Northeast had imported excessively in 1832, Shippen observed, merchants in the Louisville area had also overextended themselves. This was an imbalance "from which nothing but the indulgence of the bank, and the aid of one full year's products of the country, can relieve them."[26] Kentuckians could only pay for finished goods from the Northeast by exporting local crops, and if the precise timing of crop exports did not align with the imports—perhaps because of late or bad harvests— then they would have to rely on some type of financial intermediary to keep them afloat as they waited. This was one of many areas where the BUS proved useful. The statement, "We do not ask to be made an exception to any general rule, but only that you will give us as much latitude as circumstances will justify" was Shippen's way of intimating that there needed to be some give-and-take even if the parent branch ultimately called the shots.[27]

No magic wand could make Biddle's loan restrictions go exactly according to plan. The branch officers seemed to have taken seriously their duty for the public interest, being reluctant to leave their customers hanging out to dry. As the cashier at the Pittsburg office informed the parent branch, the amount of bills of exchange purchased "could not be lessened, at this time, without inconvenience to our customers."[28] At the same time, there were many merchants whose economic interests did not align with those of the bank. Commenting on his efforts to reduce lending according to the wishes of the parent board, the cashier at Nashville wrote, "I have not been so successful as I could wish, because it is in the interest of the merchants to counteract this policy."[29] If there was demand for credit in the area of Nashville, mercantile houses would pick up the slack in the event that the BUS scaled back. The result could be reduced profits for the bank.

A financial statement presented in a December 1834 Senate report gave an empirical basis to the notion that local factors and unforeseen circumstances prevented Biddle from enacting a one-size-fits-all loan reduction. While the parent branch had ordered a reduction of $9.15 million between October 1833 and July 1834, what actually took place was a reduction of $7.51 million.[30] The disparity can be attributed not only to larger structural and economic forces but, just as interestingly, to the individual agency of branch officers negotiating with Biddle for leniency. This was a back-and-forth that resembled Biddle's relationship with partisan newspaper editors. In a larger sense, the communications between the branch officers and the parent branch in Philadelphia show us that banking in the antebellum era was often more of an art form than science.

The main effect of Biddle's monetary policies was a mild economic contraction. Individuals and financial institutions that relied directly or indirectly on the BUS for credit, especially state banks and merchants, had to adjust by tightening their own credit. During boom times, merchants could easily offer their own commercial paper to the bank for discount, accepting the bank's notes in return. If the bank was consistently renewing long-term loans and issuing more notes, it was implicitly taking on more risk, which was permissible and even expected during times of economic stasis or expansion. But as concerns over risk mounted and credit conditions tightened, the bank became more stringent in its acceptance of commercial paper. It charged a higher interest rate when it discounted.[31] If merchants could no longer borrow from the BUS as before, then the manufacturers and farmers who relied on them would have to adjust accordingly, either by paying up their debts immediately or by scaling back production, or both. Inevitably consumers would feel the pinch. "Biddle's Panic," as some historians have called it, was the BUS-induced slump that lasted from the fall of 1833 to the summer of 1834, characterized by falling prices, declining wages, weakened investor confidence, widespread loan delinquencies, numerous business failures, and higher unemployment.[32]

From the first quarter of 1832 to November 1834, the number of bank notes in circulation decreased by 25 percent. With a shrinking money supply and weakened confidence stunting consumer demand, crop prices fell.[33] This was menacing for farmers who counted on rising—or at least stable— crop prices to pay back the loans that financed their operations. Falling crop prices forced farmers to default on their loans, wrecking bank balance sheets in the process and, in turn, imperiling the entire financial sector. To protect their cash reserves, banks suspended specie payments, which meant that they refused to honor credit instruments at full face value in specie. While suspension was supposed to prevent bankruptcy and allow more flexibility for creditors, it soon contributed to an atmosphere of fear and anxiety. Customers worried that their hard-earned dollars were not secure in banks' vaults, so they moved quickly to withdraw their deposits in a rush to liquidity.

Economists today understand this phenomenon as a self-reinforcing feedback loop—something only the most attuned, financially savvy, and perceptive of antebellum Americans could see playing out in real time. While no feedback loop lasts forever, the damage caused at least partially by the collective folly of panicky borrowers during Biddle's Panic was considerable. Bankruptcies spread. Wages and property values plummeted. Bank notes in money markets traded well below face value. Tens of thousands of laborers, mechanics, artisans, and factory workers, particularly in the Northeast, lost their jobs. Brokerage houses failed. Bank and railroad stocks went down. With stock prices declining, investors could no longer pledge stock as collateral for future lines of credit or other business ventures, which crippled highly leveraged investment schemes.[34] Increased interest rates depressed interregional trade. Particularly hard hit were slave trading firms like Franklin & Armfield, which relied on long-term credit to transport slaves hundreds of miles over a several-month period as part of the infamous domestic slave trade.[35] Related to this was the 31 percent drop in the price of upland cotton selling in New York City between September 1833 and May 1834. While less calamitous than the declines of 55 percent for the period of 1839–1840 and 60 percent for the period of 1818–1820, the price decline during Biddle's Panic injured numerous segments of the population.[36]

That contemporaries used the term "panic" to describe these phenomena indicates antebellum Americans' sense that psychological factors like fear, uncertainty, rumors, and anxiety explained the origins, severity, and duration of the contraction. One meeting of prominent New York business leaders and merchants in March 1834, according to the *New York Spectator*, described a "state of public excitement and apprehension" where "the slightest incidents may produce fatal effects." Referencing bank balance sheets and appropriating the writings of former secretary of the Treasury Albert Gallatin, the merchants noted that "the alarm became a panic, not dependent upon, or to be explained as a matter of ordinary reason." Just as the bank's September 1831 stockholders report had suggested, peoples' intangible emotions had the power to dramatically alter the tangible, objective numbers of finance.[37]

There were some signs that Jackson's opponents would benefit politically from the deposit removal controversy and accompanying panic. In the summer of 1834, many states' rights southerners, rejecting on principle what they saw as executive usurpation, joined anti-Masons, evangelical reformers, merchants, National Republicans, lawyers, and other members of the northern middle class to gather in Rochester, New York, for the inaugural convention of a new political party. They called themselves "Whigs" after the British political party of the same name. British Whigs had opposed the Catholic absolutist monarchy, and so too did American Whigs reject "King Andrew." As a somewhat disparate collection of voting blocs, the Whigs did not agree on every issue—especially slavery, as later events would show—but what tended to unite them, at least in the North, was a belief in "improvement" in an economic, nationalistic, and moral sense. And, of course, a mutual dislike of Andrew Jackson, whose followers were now more commonly calling themselves "Democrats." To varying degrees, Whigs opposed the president's positions on federal support for internal improvements, tariffs, public land sales, Indian Removal, and, especially, the BUS. As one of the Whigs' chief spokesmen, Clay capitalized on opposition to deposit removal to corral the Senate into passing the only censure of an American president in history.[38]

While the coalition of voters that supported the Whig Party in northern states largely resembled those that had supported John Quincy Adams in 1824 and 1828, the economic crisis of 1833–1834 tilted party allegiances away from sectionalism and more toward interregional cooperation. In the words of political historian Donald J. Ratcliffe, "Suddenly, as never before, American voters were being asked to approve or disapprove stands taken by national and state leaders on policies relating to economic growth and its concomitant social effects, and these issues related directly to the immediate personal experience of voters."[39] Related to this, the purge of moderate, pro-BUS Democrats that had started in 1832 continued. The White House put pressure on Democratic members of Congress and state legislatures across the country to support Senator Thomas Hart Benton's effort to expunge Clay's censure from the Senate—something that eventually succeeded in 1837. Many commercially oriented Democrats in major cities joined the Whigs, leaving the politicians that remained in the Democratic Party more ideologically opposed to any type of national bank.[40]

For Whigs, basing their political prospects at least partially on the economic pain and disruption generated by Biddle's monetary policies was risky. The pressure of a multiyear political fight with the Jacksonians seemed to be taking its toll on the bank president. To the president of the branch BUS in Boston, Biddle argued that "nothing but the evidence of suffering abroad" would save the bank. To Representative Watmough, Biddle emphasized, "all the other Banks and all the merchants may break, but the Bank of the United States shall not break." The *Globe* accurately surmised that the bank had restricted loans "in the hope of producing from the general distress a reaction of public sentiment in its favor."[41]

The tone and tenor of Biddle's correspondence had changed noticeably, with letters in the early part of 1834 expressing more confrontation and selfishness. Biddle defied congressional inquiry and boldly asserted that the bank's profit motives and obligations to its private stockholders trumped any concern for the public good. With the Jacksonians having violated the bank's charter by removing the public deposits, Biddle and most of his fellow board members reasoned, the bank would forfeit its public duties. In essence, Biddle was abdicating his role as a central banker.[42] When a Senate committee demanded to see the bank's quarterly financial statements, Biddle provided the material but urged the committees not to publish the information since "the private accounts of individuals with the bank, as with all similar institutions, [were] regarded as confidential."[43] To a House committee run by Jacksonians, Biddle was uncooperative. He maintained that the House did not have the right to examine the books of what he now regarded as a purely private corporation. Biddle may have been correct in a legal sense, but Jacksonians saw confirmation of their worst fears. If the bank had not violated its charter, they asked, why was Biddle stonewalling? In April 1834 the full House, whose ranks of anti-BUS Jacksonians had grown since the 1832 elections, struck a body blow to the BUS, voting 132 to 82 that the bank "ought not to be rechartered" and 113 to 103 that the "public deposits ought not to be restored."[44]

For his needlessly stubborn behavior, Biddle lost crucial support among stalwart allies and fellow members of the bank's board of directors.[45] Anti-Jacksonian representative Horace Binney of Pennsylvania communicated to Biddle that Webster, the long-time ally, seemed to think that "the Bank ought to reduce slowly & moderately as they can—& occasionally to ease off—where it is requisite to prevent extreme suffering." Webster feared that Jacksonians were capitalizing on Biddle's loan restrictions to steer public opinion against the bank.[46] Biddle's misfortunes were also evident in the shifting statements of the moderate Jacksonian governor of Pennsylvania, George Wolf. In his annual message to the Pennsylvania state legislature in December 1832, Wolf recognized that the bank had "established a circulating medium in which the people have confidence" and that it "greatly facilitated the operations of the general government, so far as its pecuniary transactions were concerned." He hoped that strict constructionists on the one hand and the bank's zealous advocates on the other would not obstruct the passage of a new bank charter that was "sufficiently restricted, checked and guarded."[47] But on February 26, 1834, Wolf noted that although the bank had publicly pronounced that the panic stemmed from deposit removal, "Many of the friends of that institution admit, that a restoration of the deposites is not necessary to the relief of the money market."[48] Wolf was no fire-breathing ideologue. He stopped short of calling on Biddle to relax credit, but his hedge indicated which ways the winds were blowing. New York governor William L. Marcy joined Wolf in breaking from Biddle. These were impactful losses not only because they signaled the defection of moderate, pro-BUS Jacksonians in northern states that Biddle had once courted successfully but also because Wolf and Marcy headed the two most populous and politically powerful states in the union.

Since Congress adjourned in the summer of 1834 without having passed a new charter, the bank's board convened to reevaluate the political and economic implications of their loan reductions. On June 27 a seven-member committee moved to revoke its previous order of curtailment. It would be a while before Congress came back into session, and the bank did not want to prolong any misery. Henceforth the bank would again lend at normal rates and give permission to its branches to increase discounts to relieve any commercial pressures they felt in their communities.[49] Because this was an internal deliberation at the bank's board, the wider public would not learn of the relaxation of credit for a few more weeks. Meanwhile, it was clear that not just elite politicians, but merchants and farmers, too, were abandoning the bank president. Redwood Fisher, editor of the *New York American Advocate and Journal*, wrote to Biddle that there was "much dissatisfaction" in New York "among a very large portion of the friends of the Bank, and those of influence in the Whig Party." Fisher attributed the increased anti-

BUS hostility among New York farmers to "the [Albany] Regency presses" who induced New York farmers to "believe that their suffering is owing to" Biddle's policies.[50]

On July 10 leading merchants in New York City wrote a letter to the bank's board of directors, pleading for a resumption of regular lending practices. As long as there was hope of a recharter, the merchants were willing to accommodate the bank by extending their own credit. But with Congress adjourned without any relief measures or a new bill to recharter the bank, continued loan curtailments seemed counterproductive. The merchants declared that "the system of restriction adopted by the Bank . . . should now be *entirely abandoned*" and that the BUS "ought to come forward to the relief and support of the commercial interests of this country."[51] The following day, the *National Intelligencer* informed readers of the bank's decision to resume lending. This was capitulation: a proud banker admitting defeat.[52]

Throughout the spring and summer of 1834, Whig politicians and newspaper editors became frustrated with Biddle's inconsistent behavior. Periodic adjustments in monetary policy, including a temporary loosening of credit in the spring, were undermining Whig arguments. In March, editor James Watson Webb relayed the concerns of a number of pro-BUS politicians in New York. "I must say in the spirit of frankness," Webb wrote to Biddle, "that your friends in New York & in Congress loudly complain that you are continually putting them in the wrong by granting relief and thereby rendering their prediction perfectly futile." Although Biddle was Webb's lifeline in terms of credit, in this case the New York editor was exercising independence of thought. Whigs had welcomed economic distress to make the case for a new BUS charter, but now Biddle himself was standing in the way. Many representatives from New York felt "very sore" on this subject and urged Biddle to be more consistent in his monetary policy.[53]

Other Whig politicians and newspaper editors openly admitted to exaggerating the negative effects of the panic for political gain but lamented that public opinion was turning decidedly against the BUS—so much so, in fact, that Whigs started running anti-BUS candidates in New York. Albert Tracy, an agent working for Thurlow Weed's *Albany Evening Journal*, declared in unequivocal terms that "the Bank is unpopular and every day is becoming more so—It is managed so far as political purposes are concerned, in the most wretched and contemptible manner." Although he was a brilliant financial mind, Biddle repeatedly demonstrated poor political instincts. Tracy pummeled Biddle's "inconsistency" and worried that the bank's relaxation of credit would "falsify that our panic makers have predicted the horrible distress." Tracy's letter was an internal communication sent between two employees working for the same business, but it validated the Jacksonian accusation that Whigs were deliberately trying to hype the panic.[54]

The bank's decision to resume normal lending in mid-1834 transformed a steady drip of Whig infighting into a stream. George Washington Lay, a New York Whig congressman and political ally of Weed, predicted, "We shall surely be beat, if we consent to carry on our shoulders the Bank of the United States." "The Bank itself is unpopular," Lay grieved, and "a recharter is impracticable."[55] The *Globe* gleefully reported in September that New York Whigs were increasingly disassociating themselves from Biddle and the Second Bank. A county meeting of "*young* Whigs of West Chester, New York" in September resolved to "disclaim any connexion with the United States Bank."[56]

What had become apparent in the Biddle-Pettis duel, the post-veto public meetings, the attempted bank runs in Kentucky, and the Crabb letter describing a potential assassination attempt of the president—in other words, a "Second Bank War"—continued to evolve during the same months that Biddle and the Whigs were attempting to restore the bank's public deposits. Partisan newspapers, with their ability to transmit hyperbolic political rhetoric, linked both Bank Wars and helped unleash energies that political bigwigs could neither predict nor control. Some of these energies were genuinely democratic in the small "d" sense of the term. In the spring and summer, a large number of pro- and anti-BUS public meetings sprang up throughout the country. Reprinting columns from newspapers in many other states, the *Globe* notified its subscribers of these meetings on an almost daily basis.[57] However, there were other elements to the Bank War phenomenon in 1834 that were dark, disturbing, and relatively unprecedented. On February 14 the *Globe* published two anonymous letters, allegedly addressed to President Jackson, and one to the president's nephew and private secretary, Andrew Jackson Donelson, warning that the president would be assassinated unless he restored the public deposits and rechartered the bank. The column attributed the letters to pro-BUS scheming. Two of the letters, both of which predicted that Jackson would be struck down by the Ides of March, were similar in tone and substance. Duff Green, editor of the *United States Telegraph*, who republished the *Globe*'s column the following day, was skeptical. He admitted that the president received assassination letters but believed it was not the bank's friends who concocted them, but Van Buren loyalists. The anti-Jacksonian *Cincinnati Gazette* dismissed the letters as a fabrication of Amos Kendall and seared him for resorting to deception.[58]

In publishing anonymous letters, partisan newspapers made it difficult to divine fact from fiction, and while anti-Jacksonian skepticism may have been warranted in this particular instance, the president did, in fact, receive multiple death threats from authentic sources around this time. On February 17 a resident of Cincinnati, Ohio, wrote an anonymous assassination letter to Jackson. The letter began: "Sir, Damn your old soul remove them Deposits back again, and recharter the Bank or you will sertainly be shot in less than two weeks; and that by myself!!!!!!" Noting the economic distress in Cincinnati, the author claimed there were "about 900 Mechanics who about 2 years ago were in good circumstances [but] who ha[ve] not now one dollar in their pockets." He added that 1,000 journeymen were recently fired, a local manufacturing company had gone bankrupt, money had declined in value, and "Merchants are failing every day."[59]

No attempt on Jackson's life came from the anonymous Cincinnatian, whose letter was not reported widely in the press, but it was clear that something noticeable had changed in the environment wrought by Biddle's loan restrictions. The economic and political anxiety unleashed by the Bank War was forcing Americans to choose sides and to attribute many of their own personal grievances to Jackson or Biddle. In January 1835, less than a year after receiving the letter from Cincinnati, Jackson encountered a real-life assassination attempt—the first of any sitting U.S. president. He was attending a memorial service for a former colleague in Washington when an unassuming man emerged from the crowd and fired a pistol at the president from a distance of less than ten feet. The pistol fired, but the bullet did not discharge. The assailant tried a second pistol with the same result. Soon members of the president's cabinet, military officers, and bystanders seized the man and took him away to custody. Under interrogation, the would-be assassin, Richard Lawrence, an unemployed painter from England, replied that Jackson's destruction of the BUS was responsible for his misfortunes. Lawrence, who blamed the damp weather in Washington that day for the unfathomably low chance that both of his pistols failed to ignite, hoped that Jackson's death would free up more money from the national bank so that mechanics would have plenty of work and recover their liberty.[60] Jackson initially claimed that Lawrence's actions were the result of an elaborate bank plot involving Senator George Poindexter of Mississippi, a prominent BUS supporter. Although two physicians and a Senate investigation concluded that Lawrence was mentally deranged and therefore could not be convicted in court, the *Globe* and Senator Benton held that pro-BUS forces had manufactured such a hostile climate that the previously unthinkable was now a potential reality.[61]

Assassination attempts, both real and imagined, suggested that ordinary individuals were interpreting the bank controversy in their own ways; ways that were deeply personal, unanticipated, and expressive of an overall environment of uncertainty, anxiety, and tumult. Newspaper editorialists, and historians since then, often underscored the potential for violent rhetoric to turn into violent action. In April 1834 a crowd of Jackson supporters rioted outside the Portsmouth, New Hampshire, branch of the BUS. According to the *Boston Courier*, the crowd destroyed property, set fire to tar barrels, kindled a bonfire, and burned Clay and Webster in effigy. The mob then occupied the building of the branch bank and "tore down the sign and the eagle, which they bore off in triumph and burnt." Peace officers tried to stop the crowd "but were driven off, as the mob was armed with bludgeons, cutlasses, &c."[62]

It seemed that more Americans were turning to riots as ways to vent their pent-up anger. One historian characterized 1834 as "the great riot year."[63] The violence and panic unearthed by the Bank War, amplified by an economic contraction and transmitted nationally by partisan newspaper editors, resurfaced in October during a preliminary election to choose candidates who would run for Congress.[64] It was symbolic that the election riot occurred in Philadelphia—Biddle's hometown, the location of the bank's most powerful branch, and along with Washington, ground zero for the Bank War. In some cases subscribers to a Jacksonian press learned of a different version of events, accompanied by a slightly different set of facts, in comparison to those who read Whig newspapers. But the basic storyline is this: during the evening of October 3, 1834, a group of Jacksonian Party activists, in celebration of their electoral victories that day, formed a mob in the Moyamensing township of Philadelphia. Inebriated by "strong drink" and armed with banners, lanterns, clubs, and dirks in hand, the Jackson men confronted their Whig opponents outside the Whig headquarters. The Jackson men threw stones and shouted at the Whigs, broke their lanterns, tore away the Whigs' electioneering ring bills, and started physically assaulting them. The Whigs, who were greater in number at this point, forced the Jacksonians to retreat and cut down the Jacksonians' "hickory pole" in the street. After gathering reinforcements in the Southwark district of the city, the Jacksonians returned to the scene. They burned the Whigs' "liberty pole" and trapped the Whigs inside a tavern.[65]

According to one Whig account, the Jacksonians "destroyed the furniture in those which were tenanted—threw out the beds and the bedding, & c., and piled them up in the street, and set the mass on fire." The mob also tore off the window shutters and doors of the Whig tavern and "ransacked the lower rooms . . . threw out the furniture upon the blazing pile in the street, and grossly assaulted all upon whom they could lay their hands."[66] Jacksonian presses noted how Whigs, confined to the tavern, started firing at the Jacksonians in the street with muskets. The Jacksonians again retreated, allowing the Whigs to escape. When it was all said and done, some fourteen to twenty persons were injured, and because of the fire, five housing structures burned. The rioters prevented the fire company from arriving in enough time to save the structures, leading to several thousands of dollars of property damage. But what made the Moyamensing election riots a semi-infamous nationwide event was the death of one bystander, William Perry. A carpenter by trade, Perry had been chatting with a friend across the street from the Whig headquarters. He had nothing to do with the riot, but the riot overtook him. According to a coroner's report, Perry died from a stabbing in the upper thigh, which caused him to bleed to death. John Swift, the mayor of Philadelphia, offered a $500 reward to find and apprehend the killer. Perry's killer was never identified publicly, but the malaise and grief unleashed by the election riots prompted Governor Wolf to call on the state's legislature to "provide an effectual remedy against a recurrence of such disgraceful senses of lawless atrocity and unjustifiable violence."[67]

Both parties claimed Perry as their own, which makes sense if one is trying to delegitimize one's political opponents as savage brutes who are willing to murder and destroy property in order to achieve their goals. Just as they would do with the Lawrence assassination attempt, the *Globe* and other Jacksonian presses blamed Perry's death on an alleged assassin hired by the BUS. To use the word "assassin" was to ascribe a premeditated, political motive to the killer, but it is most likely that Perry's death, as some presses reported, was accidental. On November 7 the *Indiana Journal* republished an article on the election riot from the *United States Gazette* of Philadelphia, and the following day the *Jeffersonian Republican* of Jefferson City, Missouri, offered its own commentary on the subject. Calvin Gunn, the editor of the *Republican*, embodied the typical Jacksonian analysis that Democratic Party candidates running for Congress were not so much battling the Whigs, but the BUS.[68] Unseen from most eyes, the combination of public and private money that financed roads, canals, and railroads came together with Americans' individual initiatives to enable newspaper subscribers in the West to read about bank-related events approximately 1,000 miles away on the East Coast.[69] Operating within a political economy in which state powers were influential but not always perceptible, the editors of the *Indiana Journal* and *Jeffersonian Republican* gave the Moyamensing election riots—and, by extension, the Bank War itself—a nationwide, on-the-ground presence.

Biddle's response to the deposit removal controversy had been disastrous, if not fatal, for the bank. The Whigs hoped that voter frustration over economic dislocation would force Jackson to restore the bank's public deposits. In fact, however, the U.S. economy, owing to domestic and international conditions that were beyond Biddle's control, accelerated into overdrive. The British continued to invest significant amounts of money in the United States, especially by purchasing the bonds that capitalized banks and transportation projects. In spite of temporary price declines, land and cotton sales remained strong. A favorable trade surplus and higher interest rates attracted specie from abroad, which encouraged American banks to print more paper money. An inflationary boom resulted.[70] Having staked their political fortunes on the expectations of a more convulsive depression that did not come to pass, Biddle and the Whigs were pilloried by Jacksonians as incessant fear-mongers. Whigs would try valiantly over the next ten to twenty years to procure a new BUS charter, but Biddle's mercurial and confrontational behavior relegated the BUS to a ghost of its former self. For the rest of his life and beyond, Biddle was saddled with a semi-infamous reputation. In 1841 the bank he once managed, now reconstituted as a private financial institution with a charter from the state of Pennsylvania, died an unceremonious death.[71]

The first eight months of 1834 were pivotal for the Bank War. After previously demonstrating strong support, Webster, Webb, and Governors Wolf and Marcy distanced themselves from Biddle. In this period, the House voted not to recharter the BUS, and in New York, newspaper editors helped turn farmers and merchants against the bank. Far from acting as passive recipients of Biddle's orders, editors played a major role in transforming Biddle's public relations campaign, waged primarily through elite power corridors, to a more grassroots phenomenon with nationwide implications. This grassroots element marked an important difference between Jackson's first and second terms. Energized by the uncertainty of financial panic, ordinary Americans began to express their approval or condemnation of the bank in ways that neither Jackson nor Biddle could have predicted. The increasing incidents of public meetings, riots, and assassination letters written to the president—all of which were framed in the press as manifestations of the Bank War—made this clear.

Historians have often concluded their accounts of the Bank War in 1832 (the bank veto), 1837 (the start of a multiyear financial panic), or 1841 (the collapse of the bank). The narrative shown here suggests that it makes just as much—if not more—sense to conclude the bank's push for recharter in 1834. There is an additional reason why 1834 deserves our consideration: it was then that Americans learned for the first time through congressional proceedings that another public-private institution, the Post Office, wielded its vast resources to shape public opinion for partisan purposes. Like the BUS, the Post Office had a nationwide presence and maintained an incestuous relationship with state bankers, newspaper editors, and members of Congress that might be best characterized as a revolving door.

◆◇◆

SIX

An Unholy Trinity: Banks, Newspapers, and Postmasters during the Post Office Scandal, 1834–1835

On March 29, 1834, Whig senator John Tyler of Virginia read a memo-rial signed by 300 "concerned citizens" of Culpeper County in his home state. The memorial protested Jackson's decision to remove the Second Bank's public deposits. Calling themselves the "sons of the Whigs of the Revolution," the memorialists characterized Jackson's behavior as tyran-nical and unconstitutional. When Tyler finished, his Virginia counterpart, Senator Benjamin W. Leigh, rose to add that the memorial evoked "some considerations of a more general character." Quoting official government documents, Leigh described egregious abuses in the executive branch, par-ticularly the large sums of "extra allowances" paid to private contractors who delivered mail for the Post Office. The Post Office Department ostensi-bly handed out these allowances for expedited mail delivery, but in practice these allowances were exorbitantly high payments for subpar service. Leigh alleged that these allowances were widespread in Virginia and blew gaping holes in the Post Office's budget.[1]

Jacksonian senator Felix Grundy of Tennessee interjected, wondering aloud why Leigh had broached the topic of Post Office allowances during a seemingly unrelated discussion of deposit removal. Leigh retorted that the two issues *were* related. In a protracted speech that followed, Leigh opined,

"We hear much, sir, of the power of the Bank in debate here. But the power of [the Post Office] over the elections of the country, is greater than that of [the bank] and of all the other departments in this Government combined." Leigh called the Post Office a "vast political corporation" that maintained "an intimate association with the public press." Much of its $2 million per year budget, Leigh claimed, subsidized newspaper editors. Shielded from congressional oversight, senior Post Office functionaries served at the whims of the president, who was, as Whigs saw it, Napoleon incarnate.[2]

Leigh was onto something when he linked deposit removal with the abuses going on in the Post Office Department. Both controversies revealed larger patronage networks that linked newspaper editors, financiers, and postmasters in ways that leveraged public money for private gains and partisan interests. Students of the Bank War, informed by a vast historiographical literature, can easily recite Jackson's criticisms of the BUS. They are aware of these criticisms, at least partly, because the Jacksonians were victorious. Yet the role of the Post Office in Jackson's victory is rarely discussed. While some historians have written at length about the links between partisan newspapers and the Post Office, there have not been any sustained efforts to link these studies to the Bank War.[3] As this chapter makes clear, the Jacksonians had powerful institutional, political, and monetary resources at their disposal; resources they used to shape public opinion and build a mass political party. Among these resources were the franking privilege, printing contracts, and subsidies for the delivery of partisan newspapers. Had the Post Office not become a strong, thriving institution prior to Jackson's election, the president would have found it much more difficult to defeat the Second Bank.

By exploring the specific ways in which members of the Jacksonian-led Post Office Department interacted with Jacksonian newspaper editors and Jacksonian-affiliated state banks, this chapter sheds light on the opportunities for social advancement through the federal bureaucracy. The Jackson administration encouraged social advancement for some in the middling rungs of society (see Chapter 1), but this advancement was based less on merit and more on family connections, friendship, financial ties, corruption, and other political alliances. Kendall and Taney were prime examples. The two men took leading roles in transferring the public deposits from the BUS to Jacksonian-affiliated state banks, sometimes called deposit banks or "pet banks." In the process they funded their own land deals and stock speculations and furthered the political interests of the Democratic Party. Many

Jacksonian and Whig politicians accurately characterized the pet bank system as an incestuous revolving door designed to facilitate Post Office expenditures and finance Democratic Party newspapers.

In July 1834, the release of an exhaustive Senate committee report exposed this incestuous relationship, which proved damning for Postmaster General William Barry and his subordinates. The report amplified the Whig fear that the Post Office and deposit banks, with their ability to control newspaper delivery, monetary policy, and employment within the federal bureaucracy, could unduly shape public opinion and enhance the political power of the Democratic Party. Senior Post Office functionaries rewarded private conveyance firms with extravagantly large bonuses for substandard service and then called on these very same firms to fund their own personal expenses. In rewarding their friends with lucrative mail contracts without properly advertising them in public newspapers, Barry and his subordinates violated congressional statute and accepted norms. Along the way, the Post Office accumulated large deficits with some of the deposit banks acting as willing accomplices.[4]

The Post Office Department was one of the largest and most important government agencies during the early republic and antebellum periods. Along with the General Land Office, the Post Office was one of the few federal agencies that engaged directly and consistently with the general public.[5] Created by the Post Office Act of 1792, the agency expanded rapidly as the American population grew and moved westward. By 1829 it maintained 115,000 miles of post roads and employed almost 27,000 people, mostly as postmasters, assistant postmasters, clerks, and contractors engaged in transporting the mail. This figure accounted for roughly three-quarters of all civilian officers in the federal government. Between 1817 and 1828 the number of post offices in the nation more than doubled, from 3,459 to 7,651. In 1839 Amos Kendall, then serving as postmaster general, estimated that there were about 13,000 offices nationwide.[6]

According to the lawmakers who crafted the Post Office Act, the department was designed to be financially self-sufficient, generating all of its revenue from postage. It was not allowed to run a permanent deficit by borrowing from outside sources. Only an act of Congress could increase the Post Office budget, and any surpluses it accumulated were to be returned to the U.S. Treasury. Postage collected from mailing newspapers and letters comprised the bulk of the department's source of revenue.[7] Crucially, the

Post Office used the revenue it collected to subsidize newspaper consumption: the amount of postage it charged for sending newspapers through the mail was less than what it cost to transport them. Part of this loss was offset by charging a higher postage rate for mailing letters. At a time when it cost an ordinary citizen as much as twenty-five cents to send a one-sheet letter through the mail, a newspaper could be sent for less than two cents. By taxing letter writers—especially lawyers, merchants, and others engaged in commerce—the original authors of the Post Office Act seemed to prioritize a certain sense of social equity.[8]

In other important ways, politicians of the founding generation demonstrated through policy their fundamental conviction that enduring republics required informed citizens—a priority so important that they were willing to appropriate the vast powers and resources of the federal government to achieve it. Members of Congress who wished to keep their constituents apprised of up-to-date information could frank newspapers and other forms of political propaganda (broadsides, books, pamphlets, etc.) through the mail for free. Newspaper editors could also exchange their products with one another at no cost. Indeed, the pervasive practice of reposting articles from other newspapers saved editors time and money and allowed readers in one part of the country to stay attuned to events occurring hundreds of miles away.[9] Even when westward expansion raised traveling costs and strained the Post Office's budget, these subsidies continued. The consequences were far-reaching. By subsidizing the circulation and consumption of newspapers and other media, the Post Office played a critical role in market integration, a shared political culture, and the formation of the Democratic and Whig Parties. Readers in geographically dispersed regions, whether in Illinois, Louisiana, Georgia, or Maine, could more easily keep up on major political events like the Bank War by virtue of these subsidies. And although Jacksonians and Whigs differed on what segments of society should pay for subsidized newspaper delivery—the former preferring that only newspaper readers should pay the tax with the latter opting for a tax on every American—both parties agreed that subsidizing the press was a priority.[10]

There were other important financial links between newspapers and the Post Office. The Post Office Department paid editors for advertising postal routes in their papers. When a new postal route came into operation, the department had to inform the public about the requirements for delivering mail along this route, including stipulations that it might reward certain contractors who provided superior service. The department paid editors for the print space of advertising this information, typically for a twelve-week

period. Private conveyance companies would then compete with one another, and the Post Office was required by law to award the contract to
the lowest bidder.[11] The advertising revenue from the Post Office was significant. On the one hand, in order to publish these advertisements, editors
had to purchase special paper, buy more ink, pay printers and pressmen
for additional hours of work, and spend more time folding the advertisements into envelopes before mailing them to subscribers. They also had to
advertise hundreds of routes in their papers, which limited the amount of
space they could devote to news content, editorials, and other advertising.
On the other hand, nongovernmental advertising rates paled in comparison
to those offered by the Post Office. Individuals or firms wishing to advertise
in antebellum newspapers usually paid editors $1 for approximately twelve
to fourteen lines of print space on a one-time basis and a discounted rate if
they paid for longer periods.[12]

Newspaper editors actively sought Post Office advertising contracts in
many cases because they provided financial sustenance in an otherwise uncertain business. In September 1835 Jacksonian editor Daniel Bradford of
the *Kentucky Gazette*, who had helped to draft anti-BUS resolutions at a
political meeting the previous year, wrote to Assistant Postmaster General
Charles Kitchel Gardner, enclosing a bill with the rates he normally charged
the Post Office for advertising routes. "If there is any point," Bradford
wrote, "when government patronage is necessary to *keep up* an administration paper, perhaps this is that point." In Lexington, where he worked,
Bradford bemoaned, "Private patronage is not so extensive to induce anyone *for the profit*." Therefore, he told Gardner he would be "thankful for
small favours" and warned him not to tell anyone except Kendall and to
throw his letter into the fire after reading it.[13] Some went so far as to suggest
that those who controlled Post Office contracts were in a unique position to
influence public opinion. Duff Green, editor of the *United States Telegraph*,
wrote: "The 'powers that be' rely on the post office contracts, as one of the
most efficient means of operating on public sentiment."[14]

Under Andrew Jackson's presidency, the practice of employing newspaper editors as contractors to deliver the mail for the Post Office increased
markedly. Editors often carried the mail to make ends meet. If they were
lucky, they might be appointed by high-ranking department officials to
serve as postmasters or clerks.[15] With mail delivery tied to partisan politics,
complaints of irregular or failed delivery of the news grew in volume and
frequency. Several of Blair's subordinates complained of the "irregularity"
of receiving the *Globe* in distant rural locales such as Sommersville, Tennes-

see; Northampton County, Virginia; and Vernon, Mississippi, all because of Whig postmasters.[16] Editors of the pro-BUS *National Journal* complained that they had received so many complaints of nondelivery from customers that they concluded that the Post Office was engaged in either the "most gross and unprecedented negligence, or equally wanton and unexampled hostility." The *National Union* similarly expressed that Jacksonian papers arrived consistently but that its own subscribers "do not get the Union once in a month." Only a "systemic conspiracy" among Jacksonian postmasters, it posited, could explain this discrepancy.[17] Accusations of Jacksonian postmasters suppressing the delivery of Whig newspapers were common. "To guard against the treachery of the P. Office," Henry Clay once advised Daniel Webster, "if you write me, put your letters under cover to James Harper," the cashier of the Lexington branch BUS. Clay's letter confirmed that BUS branch offices performed functions similar to those of post offices. Although their original purpose was to provide the country with valuable fiscal and monetary services, branches evolved into centers for relaying and communicating political information, too.[18]

Anti-Jacksonians frequently charged that in addition to suppressing delivery of their papers, Jacksonian postmasters abused the franking privilege in delivering the *Globe* for free. This was because the franking privilege was virtually unlimited at this time. All that a congressman had to do was affix his signature to an item, and off it went.[19] Leading up to the presidential election of 1832, the pro-BUS *Cincinnati Daily Gazette* published a lengthy op-ed, authored anonymously by "Q in a Corner," which directed a litany of rhetorical questions toward Blair: "1st. Did not the mail contain . . . 56 lbs. or thereabouts, of EXTRA GLOBES . . . ? 2d. If yes, did not the said packet . . . come free of postage? 3d. If yes—Who FRANKED said Extra Globes?" Continuing emphatically, "Q" pointed out that the law prohibited postmasters from using the franking privilege; that the Post Office should serve the "GENERAL GOOD" and not "THE PARTY."[20] The *New York Courier and Enquirer*, another pro-BUS press, picked up this story. Blair purportedly confessed to franking 100 papers to Cincinnati, but Blair's agents maintained that it was only twenty.[21]

While some Jacksonian editors complained of pro-BUS editors who abused the franking privilege, complaints levied against the *Globe* for the manipulation of newspaper delivery for partisan gain were numerous. Hezekiah Niles complained that people who had never met Kendall were forging Kendall's signature to send the *Globe* to other editors.[22] Pro-BUS editor James Watson Webb agreed. He objected vehemently to the use of public money for partisan gain: "While other papers are charged with postage, [Blair's papers] go 'scot free;' and the People are made to pay for the forging of the very chains intended to degrade them."[23] What might be considered a mundane or quotidian activity in today's world—the delivery of the mail—was highly politicized in the 1830s. Even the building of a new postal route or post office was inseparable from party considerations. In April 1832 the Post Office was planning to build a new office in Chariton, Missouri, but a *Globe* agent, J. P. Morris, urged Blair to tell Postmaster General Barry to cancel this project because Chariton was filled with residents who were, according to Morris, "the most violent political enemies of the administration."[24] Morris did not want Whig voters to receive the mail on convenient terms. Rapid advancements in transportation, communications, and state-building were theoretically supposed to benefit everyone, but they were even better for men like Morris if they benefited Jacksonians and not Whigs.

The deposit removal controversy and establishment of the "pet" banking system showed how Jacksonian Party stalwarts developed and carried out plans to entrench their own partisan interests by coordinating three interrelated institutions: partisan newspapers, state banks, and the Post Office.[25] In March 1833 Kendall, now a leading voice in administration policy, warned Jackson that tariff issues threatened to divide the party. In response, Kendall recommended a renewed assault against the BUS. The president therefore instructed Kendall to locate state banks that could manage the nation's public money and perform the same regulatory functions as the BUS. Kendall sent out memos to numerous state banks across the country, inquiring about their creditworthiness and political affiliation.[26]

Kendall essentially handpicked the state banks that would receive the public deposits that Jackson was in the process of removing from the BUS. After spending several months visiting prospective banks in numerous cities, Kendall gave Jackson an initial list of seven financial institutions, all of which were located in major commercial centers on the East Coast.[27] By 1836 the number of deposit banks in the country had increased to thirty-five. Like BUS branch offices, the deposit banks acted as miniature fiscal agents, so it made sense that they were located in areas where public revenue accumulated; that is, near customs houses, public land offices, and major financial centers. While the removal of the public deposits effectively ended the nation's experiment in central banking at the federal level, it would be misleading to characterize the deposit banking system as an enactment of laissez-faire economic policy. Embedded within the new system were a number of regulations. The secretary of the Treasury could examine the account books of these banks and remove the deposits as he saw fit. The deposit banks had minimum reserve requirements and were to deliver monthly statements to the secretary, who was then supposed to report to Congress.[28]

Despite these safeguards, however, the deposit banking system shifted regulatory oversight from Congress to the executive branch, opening the door for the types of corrupt practices often associated with political patronage. As Duane's experience demonstrated, the Treasury secretary was expected to follow the president's dictates. Partisan concerns prevailed in the selection of state banks: five of the initial seven had elite officers who professed support for the Democratic Party.[29] Even after receiving the deposits, which were effectively the sum of moneys drawn from the vast majority of Americans who paid public duties, the deposit banks approved loans to many members of Jackson's Kitchen Cabinet, who then used the money to engage in speculative ventures, or "pet projects." It is because of these dealings that Whigs derisively named these institutions "pet banks," a label that has stuck to this day.[30] In one noteworthy example, Taney revealed under Senate testimony that he owned $5,000 worth of stock in the Union Bank of Maryland, a Baltimore institution that was scheduled to receive some of the public deposits. Taney's friends at the Bank of Maryland had previously purchased 6,000 shares of stock in the Union Bank, all before news became public that it would become a deposit bank. The assumption was that the bank's stock price would go up once it obtained the federal deposits. In addition, Kendall later took out a $10,000 loan from the Girard Bank of Philadelphia, a deposit bank, to buy land in Kentucky.[31]

When Kendall set up the deposit bank system, he tried his best to disguise the outward appearance of corruption and partisanship. The Post Office was already under investigation by the Senate in 1833, and Kendall knew that there were allegations that the pet banks had loaned to the Post Office, which was illegal. Kendall demanded a pledge from members of the Post Office that they would not borrow from any of the new deposit banks.[32] But Kendall's friends and colleagues in the administration could not help themselves. One Post Office agent went to the Manhattan Bank and the Commonwealth Bank in Boston to apply for loans, informing the banks that the Treasury secretary had requested the loans. The secretary had *not*, in fact, made the request, but the banks approved the loans to the Post Office anyway.[33]

These illegal loans stained the deposit banks' reputation. A Senate investigation revealed that the Post Office had borrowed some $400,000 from five different state banks—$200,000 from the Manhattan Bank; $50,000 from the Western Bank of Philadelphia; $50,000 from the Bank of Maryland; $50,000 from the Bank of Boston; and $50,000 from the Patriotic Bank of Washington, which was quickly repaid. Barry hoped that borrowing from these banks would conceal the fact that the Post Office was deeply in debt.[34] Only the Manhattan Bank was a "pet," but it was also the bank with the largest loan to the Post Office, and half of this loan—$100,000—was approved after the first series of deposit removals had taken place. This was an abuse of public money on two levels: one, because these state banks stored the public deposits, and two, because the Post Office managed revenues collected from postage fees, which the public paid for. Furthermore, it was illegal for the Post Office to borrow on its own credit from the U.S. Treasury because the Constitution specified that only Congress had this power.[35]

The loan from the Bank of Maryland tied the Post Office to a sordid scandal. During the time in which this loan had taken place, the bank's directors had been engaging in shady financial schemes, organizing a "club" that could embezzle customers' deposits to pay for Bank of Maryland stock at inflated rates. The club then leveraged this stock as collateral to invest in an insurance company, opened up new branches of their bank in several states, and speculated in $500,000 worth of Tennessee state bonds. This type of leveraging worked so long as the underlying capital continued to appreciate. But when the BUS restricted credit in late 1833, forcing smaller banks to call in loans, the Bank of Maryland quickly became insolvent.[36]

Meanwhile, as Kendall and Taney were setting up the deposit banking system, the Treasury supplied the deposit banks with $2.3 million in drafts drawn on the BUS. The Treasury Department wrote these drafts as a precaution in the event that Biddle either restricted credit abruptly or demanded the immediate settlement of state bank debts owed to the BUS.[37] Thomas Ellicott, Taney's friend and president of the Union Bank of Maryland, submitted a $100,000 draft to the parent branch in Philadelphia and another to the Baltimore branch BUS. Ellicott needed the quick infusion of cash to cover the Bank of Maryland's overextended liabilities. Although it is likely that Taney privately supported Ellicott's move and was only scarcely removed from the scandals at the Bank of Maryland, Taney publicly repudiated Ellicott and had him removed as head of the Union Bank. In the spring of 1834 the Bank of Maryland collapsed, and by August 1835, when Baltimoreans learned of the scandal, they engulfed the city in a tumultuous and convulsive riot that lasted for three days—an event that should be included in what I have called the "Second Bank War."[38]

The deposit banking system put into practice a Jacksonian belief that the chartering of financial institutions, lubricated by a well-oiled patronage system, could capitalize partisan newspaper enterprises that shaped public opinion in ways that were beneficial to the interests of the Democratic Party. As early as 1832, South Carolina representative George McDuffie, in a House report defending the BUS, had warned of the dangers of state banks that were using their monetary resources to fund favorable media coverage. McDuffie argued that local banks were "buying up newspapers to puff them as specie-paying banks, in order to delude the public, and after getting their bills in circulation, blowing up, and leaving the unsuspecting planter and farmer victims of fraud."[39]

Two years later, in March 1834, anti-Jacksonians in New York similarly claimed that Democrats were chartering new state banks not to supply credit and capital to aid economic growth, but to entrench party interests. The Empire State, home to the Albany Regency and Tammany Hall, was ground zero for the type of politicized banking system the Jacksonians admired and replicated. "To the victor belong the spoils" was the famous phrase, often attributed to New York governor William L. Marcy, that became a pejorative characterization of the Jacksonian philosophy behind rotation of office and political patronage. Richard Davis, an agent working for the anti-Jacksonian *Albany Evening Journal*, had this phrasing in mind when he posited that the creation of several state banks near Poughkeepsie were "at once political . . . tending to strengthen the Van Buren force." If anti-Jacksonians had any chance of beating Van Buren, Davis told the paper's editor, Thurlow Weed, "you must prevent that new Bank from passing." As evidence, Davis cited seven banks within a fifty-mile radius and noted that New York was "abundantly supplied with Bank capital . . . beyond the wants of the community." The only logical explanation was that "the Bank is got up to increase the power of the [Albany] Regency . . . and to let some have a handful of the spoils."[40]

Letters between Jacksonian Party leaders indicate that Davis's concerns had a strong basis in fact. Richard M. Johnson, a congressman and former U.S. senator from Kentucky who later became Van Buren's vice president, requested that Blair ask Secretary of the Treasury Levi Woodbury to transfer the pension fund from the BUS branch in Lexington to the Northern Bank of Kentucky, a deposit bank. Johnson wanted to "revolutionize Fayette County." "It is very important," Johnson wrote, "that something should be done for this Bank and will have a most happy influence."[41] Arthur Lee Campbell, a wealthy Kentucky planter with property in several states who had previously edited the pro-Jackson *Louisville Gazette*, asked Barry in 1833 to appeal to Van Buren for stock subscriptions in the Louisville Savings Institution, a deposit bank. Campbell wrote that with Van Buren's stock subscriptions, "I can, *unseen*, revolutionize the political aspect of our state, from being the *dupes and sport of aristocratic and nullifying* demagogues, to that of steady liberal republican principles, measure, and men."[42] The emphasized word "unseen" lent a duplicitous tone to Campbell's letter.

In an 1836 letter Campbell noted that Kendall, then serving as postmaster general, had appointed his son, James, as a postmaster in Louisville. The younger Campbell also worked at a bank. He received a salary of $800 per year working as cashier of the Louisville Savings Institution and $400 per year "for morning and evening services at the Post Office." One of Jackson's longtime friends and earliest supporters, the elder Campbell had multiple connections to the most senior members of the party.[43] These letters demonstrated a growing trend of chartering corporations with the expressed purpose of influencing public opinion, winning elections, and securing political power. This was certainly not a new use of the corporate form; nor was manipulating public money for private interests, profit, and partisan advantage a novelty. But by Jackson's presidency, both the partisan energy and number of state banks reached new heights.[44]

The nature of Jacksonian-era politics and workings of the federal government were such that newspaper editors, mail contractors, and bankers were sometimes the same people, and if they weren't, they were often connected in an incestuous revolving door. On February 19, 1834, the *New York Spectator* reported that Senator Isaac Hill of New Hampshire allegedly sent a letter to a local bank in Concord, New Hampshire, asking for money to relieve an indebted Post Office. Hill pledged the "word" of Postmaster General Barry as security for the loan. The bank denied Hill's request. A former mail contractor and editor of the *New Hampshire Patriot*, Hill had to have been close to Barry to speak on his behalf.[45] Asa Clapp, who managed the Marine Bank of Portland, was the father-in-law of Levi Woodbury, who succeeded Taney as Treasury secretary. William Johnson, cashier of the Northern Bank of Kentucky, was Woodbury's nephew. Johnson worked at this bank as it acquired assets from the BUS branch in Lexington. The president of the Louisville Savings Institution, a deposit bank, was George Meriwether, a postmaster and Kendall's former partner at the *Argus of Western America* in Frankfort. Jacksonians sought to provide economic opportunities for underprivileged white men through governmental patronage networks, but the evidence suggests that many who climbed the social ladder were already well connected. This was no meritocracy. It helped to have friends, family, political allies, or business partners, or all of the above, occupying powerful positions.[46]

In July 1834 the U.S. Senate issued a report documenting a long list of corrupt abuses and excessive spending practices in the Post Office Department. The Committee on the Post Office and Post Roads had spent more than two sessions of Congress compiling one of the longest and most detailed congressional reports of its time. At the core of the report was the evidence that Barry had borrowed from state banks to dole out special allowances to his preferred private conveyance firms, including Stockton & Stokes and E. Porter & Co.

The issues raised in the Senate report went back to the beginning of Jackson's first term, when the president appointed Barry as postmaster general. Barry helped to carry out Jackson's dismissals of highly competent civil service officers who had worked under previous administrations, giving the Post Office a more politicized atmosphere. On September 12, 1829, Barry, who inherited a budget surplus from his predecessor, John McLean, issued new regulations directing postmasters to deposit their proceeds in banks, rather than forwarding them to the assistant postmaster general, which had been the previous practice. The department also discontinued the thirty-year practice of issuing contracts to the *National Intelligencer* for advertising mail routes for public bidding, electing only to print these advertisements in the *United States Telegraph*, which it called "the Official Government Newspaper at the Seat of Government."[47]

From the beginning of Jackson's first term, the most consistent complaints levied at Barry concerned the awarding of mail delivery contracts to a few favored postal carriers at inflated rates, which cost the department (and therefore the public) more money. These firms transported both passengers and mail mostly by horseback and stagecoach, though increasingly by steamboats and railroads, too. So loud were these outcries that a group of southern mail contractors petitioned the president for a redress of grievances. Their chief concern was the contract given to Reeside Porter & Company, totaling nearly $68,000, for delivery routes running from

Washington to Fort Mitchell, Alabama.[48] The petitioners accused the Post Office Department of "fostering a system of favouritersm, by bestowing its favors & emoluments on such of its friends & favorites" because they had submitted a lower bid to Barry for one southern route. This was not only a violation of congressional laws stating that contracts should go to the lowest bidder, but it involved "a clear loss to the government of a very large amount of the public money." The petitioners asserted that only a handful of individuals—including mail contractors, James Reeside, Edwin Porter, and their friends—were monopolizing practically all of the southern mail routes, getting rich off the public dime in the process.[49]

Jackson took the petitions seriously enough to follow up, but he exhibited a great deal of leniency in taking Barry and his subordinates at their word. With Barry conveniently out of town, Assistant Postmaster General Gardner explained to Jackson that the Post Office Department granted the contract to Reeside Porter because its bid consolidated several routes and contained "a number of improvements," beyond the minimum requirements outlined in the advertisement. Among these supposed improvements were "faster and more frequent service, an armed guard at company expense whenever needed, free carriage of government expresses, and use of four-horse coaches instead of two-horse stages," all of which would save the department "several times" the nearly $5,000 difference between the Reeside Porter bid and those of its competitors. Any reasonable person looking at Gardner's explanation—including the amount of $5,000—would maintain a healthy dose of skepticism. In spite of several sworn affidavits on the part of the petitioners testifying to collusion between Barry, Reeside, and Post Office chief clerk Obadiah Bruen Brown, Jackson again took his appointees and their friends at their word. To the petitioners, Jackson replied that Barry was "bound to . . . render impartial justice to all" and had "faithfully performed his duty." In 1831 the president and the *Globe* continued to defend Barry against accusations, particularly the ones emanating from some members of the U.S. Senate who wanted a more formal investigation.[50]

But by 1834 it had become impossible for even the most die-hard Jacksonians to continue to defend Barry. In just a few years, Barry turned a surplus into a sizeable deficit, with the department owing $488,000 to state banks and $635,000 to private contractors.[51] As postmaster general, Barry had the authority to demand more accountability from the contractors. The Post Office could penalize them for sums of up to several hundred dollars if, because of negligence or incompetence, the mail did not arrive on time.

This happened in a few instances, but more often than not, Barry rewarded his friends with large sums of money for substandard service.[52] While administration insiders initially defended Barry and blamed factors outside of Barry's control—including abuse of the franking privilege, the extension of postal routes, road improvements, and winter weather—the Jacksonians on the Senate committee eventually denounced Barry once the mounting evidence became too hard to ignore.[53]

The full Senate report, released on July 9, 1834, linked the Post Office with the deposit removal controversy and exposed the revolving door of bankers, postmasters, and newspaper editors, all of whom collaborated with public money in an attempt to shape public opinion for partisan ends. One section of the report cited Blair's employment with the Post Office. As a member of the Kitchen Cabinet and editor of the *Globe*, Blair lobbied hard for deposit removal. The Whig-dominated Senate, empowered with examining the account books of the Post Office, tried to uncover evidence that the department overpaid Blair as it had done to private contractors carrying the mail. Unfortunately for the Whigs, a fire in the Treasury building destroyed roughly three-quarters of the relevant financial records related to the Post Office.[54] What the committee *did* find was that between December 1831 and October 1833, Blair earned over $14,300 for advertising mail routes, a sum the committee labeled "enormous." Defending himself in a statement to Congress, Blair argued that this sum was consistent with advertising rates paid to other printers employed by the Post Office, including Duff Green. The *Globe* had to advertise hundreds of mail routes, Blair emphasized, meaning that his payment from the Post Office would necessarily be large.[55]

Blair escaped relatively unscathed, but the Senate committee was more damning of Barry, his subordinates, and their ties to printers, state banks, and private contractors. Whig senator Thomas Ewing of Ohio, the committee chairman, found the Post Office guilty of favoritism and corruption in circumventing the legally prescribed competitive bidding process by rewarding a few close allies with advertising contracts. Because of Barry's gross mismanagement and spendthrift ways, the department was deeply in debt. Not only had Barry paid extravagantly high sums of cash to contractors who performed only regular services (and sometimes not even this much), but he had also exaggerated the department's revenues, minimized its debts, and lied to Congress about the number of miles that postal carriers had to travel. The intent was to make it seem that the department was overdrawn because of westward expansion, and thus to minimize Barry's culpability. To sustain the department's operations and ballooning allowances, the Post

Office borrowed from two main sources: the aforementioned state banks and the U.S. Treasury—both of which were illegal.[56]

Senior officers in the Post Office, according to the committee, maintained a reciprocal financial relationship with private contractors, with certain state banks acting as intermediaries. In other words, men like Barry and Brown gave generous contracts to private firms and then called on these very same firms to support their own *personal* expenses. Politically friendly state banks were the middlemen. In the spring or summer of 1831, the committee reported, Barry asked Reeside "to assist him in negotiating an acceptance for $1,000 to raise some money for his, (Mr. Barry's,) individual use." There is some dispute as to whether this loan actually took place. But in another instance, Reeside drew up a draft for $6,000, negotiated the draft at the Western Bank in Philadelphia, and then arranged for the Post Office, through a postmaster in New York, to obtain $10,000.[57] Reeside was acting as both a borrower and lender for the department. In a certain way, then, the Post Office, aided and abetted by state banks, had become its own financial intermediary—something far outside the parameters established by the original creators of the Post Office.

In addition, Brown obtained a secret $300 loan from the contractor Samuel R. Slaymaker of the firm Reeside and Tomlinson. In January 1833 Brown asked for a $3,000 loan from Slaymaker with Reeside acting as an endorser. None of the three men recorded the transaction, but a witness before the Senate committee testified that Brown intended to use this money to buy property. Brown raised this money from Slaymaker and Reeside by means of several drafts that were eventually redeemed for cash at the Western Bank of Philadelphia, the Patriotic Bank in Washington, and the Bank of Maryland.[58] We will recall that each of these banks lent $50,000 to the Post Office Department. It was normal for postmasters to collect postage revenue and then deposit it as cash in state banks. But borrowing from state banks for personal use (i.e., buying property) went far beyond the legitimate functions of the Post Office and made the deposit bank system seem like a cabal designed to enrich civil servants and elite members of the Democratic Party.

To the alarm and dismay of Whigs on the Senate committee, the Post Office, through its lending and borrowing schemes, appropriated public money for private gain without any accountability. Edwin Porter of the firm E. Porter & Co. testified that Brown lent him "very large sums of money . . . on interest."[59] Porter ran a mail route between New Orleans and Mobile, and in one year there were 150 reported instances of failure to deliver the mail on this route. The Post Office should have fined Porter $6,800 but elected not to do so. Instead, Porter drew up a draft on the Post Office department for $20,000, which was accepted by Barry. By November 1833, moreover, Porter had borrowed $8,000 from Brown. The Senate committee castigated Brown and Porter for numerous transgressions, and Brown eventually resigned as chief clerk of the Post Office.[60]

Newspaper editors, the committee noted, were part of the Post Office's shady spending practices, and Senate Whigs wanted to ensure that editors would not exert an undue influence over public opinion in the future. The Senate committee found that among other examples, William Smith, who managed "an efficient party press in Culpeper county, Virginia," received a substantial allowance of $11,129 per year from the Post Office. In reprimanding Jacksonian newspaper editors, Senate Whigs invoked Thomas Jefferson, who posited, in the words of the committee report, that no printer should be employed by the Post Office because it might exert a "corrupting influence over the community."[61] In other revelations, the Senate committee reported that the Post Office paid printers thousands of dollars for blank sheets of paper, twine, wrapping paper, and for a few miscellaneous articles. Either through incompetent accounting methods or, more likely, intentional obfuscation, the department recorded these payments under the vague heading "incidental expenses." As with postmasters and private contracting firms that carried the mail, there was no real competition or open bidding. Elite functionaries in the Post Office Department consistently picked their preferred editors to print documents. These practices violated an 1832 resolution passed by Congress mandating that a published "Blue Book" would list all of the printers employed by the Post Office, including their compensation, in order to "arrest the abuse of official patronage to printers." If someone worked as both a public printer and mail contractor, the Blue Book was supposed to publish this information so that "the public might judge of the extent and influence of the Executive patronage over the press."[62]

In wrapping up their lengthy committee report, Whigs voiced unqualified objections to practices that had transpired for several years in the Post Office under Barry's leadership. From a fiscal point of view, Whigs argued that the Post Office's indebted condition stemmed principally from excessive payments to printers and private contractors, which was particularly alarming because they occurred at public expense.[63] Only stringent reforms, according to the committee report, would bring the department's budget back to health. The committee passed a number of resolutions, the first of which stated that "large sums of money have been borrowed at different banks by the Postmaster General . . . without authority given by any law of Congress." Subsequent resolutions touched upon the extra allowances paid to mail contractors, the absence of any correlation between the payments and the service provided, and the lack of competition in advertising these contracts. Jackson had stayed loyal to Barry throughout much of these allegations, which went back as far as 1829, but by 1834 the outcry and public scrutiny were too much to bear. The president removed Barry as postmaster general and reassigned him to the position of special envoy to Spain.[64]

The interrelated deposit removal controversy and Post Office scandal show us how Jacksonians in the 1830s erected three interlocking mechanisms designed to promote the Democratic Party: partisan newspapers that shaped public opinion, a partisan Post Office that both employed editors and subsidized the delivery of newspapers, and partisan banks whose capital set everything in motion. This patronage network opened up opportunities for social advancement among ordinary white men, but rather than merit and open competition determining promotion, it was more often family ties, friendship, and party loyalty that carried the day. As much as the Jacksonians inveighed against the BUS as an exclusive monopoly, they were content to monopolize mail routes with their friends and political allies.

After becoming postmaster general in 1829, Barry and his subordinates transformed the Post Office into a highly partisan patronage network engaged in financially dubious practices. Indeed, Barry may have been the quintessential Jacksonian spoilsman, embodying all of the negative connotations of rotation of office. The Post Office not only borrowed from the deposit banks but in some cases acted as its own financial intermediary, which was a clear violation of the constitutional provision that only Congress could borrow from the U.S. Treasury. That Jacksonian newspaper editors and postmasters could appropriate public money in the form of printing contracts to advocate for deposit removal—and then call on the pet banks for their own personal expenses—suggests that they had intended to design a system of patronage that could reinforce itself over time.

As the speeches and writings from the likes of Senator Benjamin W. Leigh and many others attest, Whigs contended that the Post Office exerted a far greater influence over public opinion and party development than the BUS ever could. This perspective may have stemmed from self-interest, but historians should not be quick to dismiss it. With thousands of employees; control over a vast, interregional patronage network; and the ability to de-

CHAPTER SIX

termine how quickly the news arrived (and whether the news arrived at all), the Post Office was a formidable force in American politics. If Jacksonians argued that the BUS was an unfair monopoly that appropriated public money to steal elections and buy off the press, Whigs essentially made the same claims about the Post Office. What is surprising, however, is how little the Post Office is discussed in traditional accounts of the Bank War—an issue that helped to define American politics in the 1830s. As we contemplate new ways of narrating the Bank War, placing the Post Office in a prominent position is one useful place to start.

CONCLUSION

✧

1835 and Beyond

When Barry left Washington, the Post Office's finances were in shambles. Not all of this was due to poor management. The public subsidies established by the Post Office Act of 1792 continued during the antebellum era, even as the country's volume of trade, population, and western boundaries expanded. All of this contributed to persistent deficits and made the department unmanageable. To rectify this situation, the president turned again to Kendall, a man whom he had always trusted for advice and who had stood by him through virtually every major political struggle of his administration. On May 1, 1835, Kendall succeeded Barry as postmaster general.[1]

Signaling a break with his predecessor, Kendall enacted a number of administrative reforms that built upon the skills and experience he had acquired while managing naval accounts in the Treasury Department. On July 7, he outlined a fifty-six-point plan that brought about the removal of incompetent officers, improved recordkeeping and auditing, greater discipline of postmasters to prevent abuses of the franking privilege, the direct payment of postmasters to contractors, and notices to new departmental employees that favoritism and nepotism would not influence promotion.[2] Extra allowances and inflated contracts would be curbed. It was clear that the new postmaster general was responding, in part, to the 1834 Senate report detailing the unholy trinity that came to light in the Post Office scandal. One provision stated: "The deposite banks will be instructed to pay no drafts, (other than those drawn by the treasurer, to close accounts up to the 1st July, 1835), which are not drawn by the postmaster general, and certified as being charged by the accountant." Instead of collecting and spending revenue within the department, the Post Office would now receive a congressional appropriation, supervised by Treasury Department clerks. Kendall also worked to reorganize the department into four offices and moved to appropriate new railroad lines into mail delivery. According to political scientist and historian Matthew A. Crenson, Kendall's reforms effectively transformed the federal bureaucracy away from the spoils system that had prevailed earlier in Jackson's presidency to one in which "government administration became considerably more formal and impersonal." The earlier spoils system, Crenson argued, largely reflected the personal characteristics and quirks of department heads. The hope was that dispersing authority with more formalized rules would ensure that no single leader could corrupt an agency. Only one year into Kendall's term, the Post Office deficit disappeared.[3]

Legal disputes emanating from the termination of one particularly large contract between the Post Office and the stagecoach firm Stockton & Stokes occupied much of Kendall's time over the next ten years, but for the most part he could look back on his time served in Jackson's two terms with a feeling of triumph.[4] He continued to serve as postmaster general in the Van Buren administration, and in 1839, when writing to an unnamed office seeker and friend, Kendall recalled some of the major successes and travails of his own life, as well as the sense of progress that attended the nation's rapid westward expansion. The position of postmaster general came with a salary of $6,000 per year, which enabled Kendall to "greet public life with the means of comfort" after years of financial struggle. In less than four years of heading the Post Office, Kendall wrote, "its revenue ha[d] increased upwards of 40 percent . . . and but for the commercial convulsion of 1837," the revenue increase "would have been more surprising." Recalling his travels to the West during his youth, Kendall noted, "not a stage[coach] turned its wheel beyond Pittsburgh," but by 1839, "the Country [was now] intersected with stage lines south from [Pittsburgh] to New Orleans about 1500 miles . . . and west about an equal distance, standing 200 to 300 miles up the Missouri River." The progress of westward expansion and transportation improvements, to which the Post Office was inextricably linked, made him proud: "There is scarcely a settlement of half a dozen families in the distant wilderness which has not a mail carrier to it on horseback."[5] Not mentioned in Kendall's letter was the crucial role of the American state in facilitating this expansion—in subsidizing the spread of newspapers through the Post Office, in purchasing the bonds that financed transportation projects, in helping to carry out Indian Removal, and in subscribing to much of the shares of stock that capitalized financial institutions whose credit fueled a U.S. economy that was becoming more nationally and globally integrated by the day.

Kendall's achievements owed a great deal to his own inner talents, hard work, and firmly held principles, his close relationship with the president, and importantly, preexisting political institutions. From obtaining the public printing as a young man in the Kentucky state legislature, to establishing the *Globe* in Washington and becoming postmaster general, governmental institutions helped elevate Kendall's social standing. The four slaves that Kendall acquired through marriage were protected by federal courts and marshals, a complicated system of property rights, and several clauses in the original U.S. Constitution. In the 1840s inventor Samuel F. B. Morse hired Kendall to manage the patent rights associated with the construction of the nation's first telegraph line. Morse had obtained a patent for the project in 1840 and a $30,000 grant from Congress in 1843. The two men sought at least partial federal ownership of the telegraph, including an unsuccessful plan to sell the patent to Congress, in order to minimize investment risks and prevent monopolistic price gouging by railroad companies. Throughout all of these projects, Kendall maintained an arduous work schedule, which took its toll on what he characterized as his "precarious" health and "feeble constitution." But a strong inner spirit kept him going.[6]

The funding structure that Kendall had long been accustomed to, going back to the days of editing the *Argus of Western America* in Frankfort, would undergo significant changes by the mid-nineteenth century. More efficient technology dropped production costs, allowing newspapers to be printed on a mass scale. Greater literacy, urbanization, immigration, and a more integrated national market created a larger and more diverse audience of readers. To meet these demands, newspaper enterprises required more employees, a managerial hierarchy, reporters, delivery men, and more expensive start-up costs. Gone were the days when a single person was editor, proprietor, and printer. Newspapers also had to offer more in terms of content—no longer could they print stories exclusively within the realm of elite politics and commerce. Readers clamored for more stories that were local in nature, and ones based on crime, sex, and violence.[7] Hence the rise of the "penny press," in which the newspaper business compensated for low profit margins with a higher volume of sales. Benjamin Day's subscription list of nearly 20,000 for his *New York Sun* in 1835 eclipsed that of most partisan presses at the time. True, the partisan press never went away, as the careers of Thurlow Weed and Horace Greeley attest. But with advertisers supplanting political parties as the chief sources of revenue for most newspapers, editors increasingly wrote to avoid alienating customers, not to secure printing contracts.[8]

By examining the careers of Kendall and his contemporaries, *The Bank War and the Partisan Press* has added important dimensions to how we narrate the Bank War. Through its focus on newspaper editors, financiers, and public officials, it has demonstrated how the BUS used its network of branch offices to defend itself while the Jacksonians sought political advantage by appropriating the levers of power contained in the Post Office and other bureaucratic agencies. Both sides disseminated their messages through communications networks funded by public and private money. In the process, this book has contextualized and broadened our understanding of this watershed moment in American political history with insights on political institutions, the development of the American state, the business model of partisan newspapers, and the unpredictable ways in which the Bank War could play out on the ground level. Editors fanned the flames of violent rhetoric that sometimes culminated in the physical violence of riots and duels, all the while passing through a revolving door of financial institutions and the Post Office—a government agency whose influence over the politics and daily lives of antebellum Americans was considerable. Kendall's career illuminated the two-sided nature of political patronage as practiced by the Jacksonian Democrats: it could and did provide social advancement for white men who were not born into wealth, but it often prioritized loyalty over merit and from time to time evinced glaring examples of corruption.

If the key events of the Bank War took place within a larger political economy characterized by public-private businesses partially regulated by government agencies whose reach was national in scope, it was clear by the mid- to late 1830s that this dynamic was shifting. The aftershocks of the Bank War, especially the destruction of the BUS, Jackson's Specie Circular, and the Deposit and Distribution Act of 1836, contributed to the onset of a major financial panic that began in early 1837. Economists in the last two decades have zeroed in on the American origins of this global phenomenon, particularly in relation to the bursting of an inflationary bubble in the old

Southwest that grew out of the mutually reinforcing sales of land, cotton, and slavery—all of which was fueled by exuberant bank lending. This is not to deny, of course, the importance of international factors. Any comprehensive telling of the panic must include the trade and investment relationships with Great Britain and the global movements of gold and silver that linked Mexico, China, and the United States through complex networks of credit and debt.[9]

Somewhat surprisingly, vigorous public spending on transportation projects at the state level continued unabated during this depressed economy, which contributed to budget deficits. Businesses declared bankruptcy, and transportation projects were abandoned midstream. Many states defaulted on their debts, which opened up opportunities for those who favored private investment of infrastructure. State leaders who wished to resume bond payments abandoned their support for publicly financed internal improvements and banks, imposed borrowing limits, privatized postal carriers, increased property taxes, and adopted other constitutional restrictions. Those who advocated exclusively private means of funding transportation projects carved out an important niche. Data suggest that in the remaining years before the Civil War, most large-scale transportation improvements, as measured by dollars invested, were controlled by private for-profit companies rather than governments. In contrast to canals, most funds for railroads were private. More policymakers and businessmen began to believe that private companies were better at estimating costs and sticking within their allotted budgets. The incentive of returning profits to shareholders and bondholders, according to this thinking, worked better than the inflated contracts and waste of taxpayer dollars that often resulted from public management.[10]

Legislatures in New York, Ohio, and several other states rejected special charters for banks, transportation companies, and telegraphs in favor of general incorporation statutes, which institutionalized the principle of antimonopolism. The older arrangement for state-sanctioned corporate charters, prevalent in the early republic and harkening back to English common law, granted certain legal privileges and immunities—among them, monopoly status, fictitious legal personhood, and limited liability—in exchange for providing a clear public good. Included in this arrangement were strict limits imposed by the legislature or central authority. It was clear from the numerous congressional reports and the amount of BUS-related correspondence and financial statements that Biddle submitted to Congress—sometimes willingly, sometimes begrudgingly, and sometimes not at all—that the bank was under almost constant regulatory scrutiny. Even the deposit banks that supplanted the Second Bank's fiscal duties had regulations. These were consistent with the older model. But by the 1840s, corporations were assuming broader powers, winning legal immunities in court, and increasingly prioritizing the interests of private stockholders above their public duties. Especially in the North, laissez-faire gained wider currency as a viable theory of political economy.[11]

The magnitude and rapidity of these changes have been hotly debated by historians, and it is important to remind ourselves that the United States was not entering some libertarian paradise with an absolutist commitment to limited government. Kendall helped to reform the bureaucracy based on his impulses toward efficiency and fiscal accountability, but we would not characterize these impulses as unabashedly antiregulatory predicated on a visceral hostility to government. Kendall's reforms included regulations.[12] Economic historians have known for many decades that railroads did not immediately replace canals and stagecoaches overnight. In the same vein, public investment in transportation at the state and local levels remained strong in the southern states.[13] Some corners of the economics and legal professions, Social Darwinists, and, especially, the wealthiest titans of industry found in laissez-faire a convenient and self-serving justification for economic inequality; but regulation, expectations for ethical behavior, duties, morality, civic virtue, self-sacrifice, and providing for the general welfare— ideas and values traditionally associated with classical republicanism—did not vanish by the Civil War era and Gilded Age. A distinguished lineage of historians have reminded us that laissez-faire undergirded general incorporation, but laissez-faire in this context meant antiprivilege and antimonopoly; not antistatist, or antiregulation.[14] Applying this general principle to the Bank War, and taking the Jacksonian view charitably, this meant that the Jacksonians were not killing the Second Bank to deliberately weaken the state; rather, the point was to make sure that the state was upholding equal opportunity for white men by not granting privileges and monopolies to the favored few.

As two of the chief combatants in a Bank War phenomenon that was nominally nonviolent, Kendall and Biddle stood for two fundamentally different visions of the federal government's relationship with monopolies. Kendall's vision of antimonopolism stressed equal opportunity. Captured most pointedly in the destruction of the Second Bank, this vision was ascendant when the Jacksonian Democrats dominated national-level politics in the three decades prior to 1860.[15] But with the Civil War and Gilded Age bringing the newly formed Republican Party to power, the federal government returned to a cozier relationship with big business that resembled the political economy envisioned by Biddle. The specific contexts had changed— by the 1870s the United States was further along in its path to becoming a leading industrial superpower, including a more centralized banking system, greenback notes, a new bond market, and ever more byzantine forms of corporate organization—but as the historian Richard White pointed out in one article, "The [transcontinental] railroads took up a kind of politics that the Jacksonians had associated with the Second Bank of the United States."[16] Some enduring patterns persisted. Like the BUS, railroads were government-sponsored monopolies that aroused popular outcry because of the corruption implicit in appropriating public money for private gain. In issuing complex credit instruments and commercial paper whose value depended heavily on confidence and reputation, railroads had much in common with banks. Railroads were financial entities just as much as they were transportation companies. Moreover, railroad companies in the 1870s and 1880s planted stories, loaned to journalists, and recruited them as agents and lobbyists. Railroad magnate Collis P. Huntington, like Biddle, commissioned articles and wrote many of them anonymously.[17] Echoing broad similarities to Clayton's report, an 1872 congressional investigation of Credit Mobilier, a finance and construction trust administered by a small group of directors of the Union Pacific railroad, brought to light a level of scandal and corruption operating on multiple levels, including bribery of members of Congress. If there was an antebellum-era analog to the more ubiquitous Gilded Age railroad lobby, Biddle's campaign to recharter the BUS would make a strong candidate.[18]

In the remaining years of his life, Biddle continued to solicit votes and favorable media coverage through small bribes. The 1820s had been much kinder to the bank president than the 1830s. He closed the latter decade with a series of poor business decisions that revealed questionable financial prudence at best and chicanery at worst. Even historians who have generally been sympathetic to Biddle have noted these lapses in judgment.[19] The Philadelphia financier, once hailed as a proud, precocious, and talented prodigy from a distinguished family, died in 1844 with a semitarnished reputation that future generations of historians would continually reassess. Kendall, who defended slave owners as postmaster general against the onslaught of abolitionist mailings in 1835 and who played a major role in creating a mass political party that would eventually come to speak primarily for slave interests, lived to see the conclusion of the Civil War that destroyed these very same slave interests. He died in 1869. The 190-year period that has transpired since the Bank War renders tenuous any direct and exact parallels to the present. But broadly speaking, the questions of monopoly, executive overreach, regulation, favoritism, corporate lobbying, social advancement, monetary policy, equal opportunity, and economic inequality continue to elicit lively debates today.

APPENDIX ONE

⟡

How the Bank Worked

Understanding the precise manner in which the BUS contributed to—and was located within—the domestic and international economies has presented many challenges for students of early American history. Even to a highly informed reader, grappling with this topic can be quite daunting. There are numerous reasons for this confusion, not the least of which being that the nature of the topic itself can be abstract, esoteric, and even counterintuitive at times. There are few modern parallels to the financial system of the antebellum era, with its hundreds of different state-chartered banks, all circulating their own currencies of differing values backed by gold and silver. In addition, when financiers corresponded with one another, they often wrote in ways that appear to modern readers as dense, technical, and borderline unintelligible.[1] Too many historians and economists, unfortunately, have not done a very good job explaining the credit system to a lay audience in clear and straightforward language, opting to recapitulate much of the convoluted prose of antebellum Americans.

Related to this, the standard practices of banking were still developing in the 1820s and 1830s. Balance sheets and bank-related commentary from financiers and politicians did not evince a uniform terminology. The terms "promissory note," "bill," "draft," "check," "note," and "loan," for example, might be used interchangeably to describe the same type of financial transaction. A financial statement might say "bills discounted on personal security" in one congressional report and "notes discounted" in another when both were the same.[2] It is entirely possible that a great many antebellum Americans, even those from educated backgrounds, conceived of the financial system in different ways and expressed views about topics they did not entirely comprehend. Historians who wish to understand the fundamental principles of the antebellum-era credit system have expressed some frustration over the lack of clear explanations, and it is at least partially in this spirit that I have written the following paragraphs.[3] If my own explanations have proved inaccurate or inadequate, it is only because of the humble realization that I also have found these concepts too difficult to grasp.

How Do Banks Work?

At the most basic level, a bank brings together lenders and borrowers to promote trade and economic growth. Lenders (also known as depositors or savers) tend to value security, liquidity, and the greatest possible return on their investments through high interest rates. Borrowers (also known as investors) have the opposite goal: they want to use money in the long term with low interest rates. Banks intermediate—or reconcile the differences between—these two goals, and hence, banks are known as *financial intermediaries*. In linking the interests of lenders and borrowers, banks provide a service that entails some risk. To compensate for this risk, they charge fees and interest, which can be defined as the price of obtaining money. The greater the risk, the higher interest rate lenders will demand in exchange for parting with their money.[4]

Pooling peoples' savings together in one location in the form of bank deposits contains a number of important economic advantages. For example, banks can take some of these savings and lend them out to companies that need money to start transportation projects. By accumulating deposits, by selling shares of stock, and by keeping some gold and silver on hand at any particular time, banks can offer better terms to prospective borrowers in comparison to individual lenders. Lending $500 could be a risky proposition for a merchant in the antebellum era, but a bank could offer the same amount with less risk. Spreading risk was, and is, fundamental to the concept of credit. It is worth noting that insurance companies, another type of financial intermediary, spread risk in ways that are similar to banks. The advantages of making credit available at lower interest rates were so essential that many historians have argued that the development of a robust banking system, especially within the agricultural sector and in bond markets, was a necessary precondition for the Industrial Revolution.[5] As the financial crises of 1931 and 2008 demonstrated, the banking system is the lifeblood of the economy. If a recession originates in the financial sector, recovery can be a painfully slow process.

How the Second Bank of the United States Worked

Like most other commercial banks, the BUS loaned to borrowers and collected profits from interest. Part of these profits could be returned as dividends to private stockholders, who subscribed to 80 percent of the Second Bank's capital. A merchant seeking a loan, for example, could come to a BUS branch office with some form of commercial paper such as a bill of exchange.[6] The bank would take possession of the merchant's bill, deduct interest, and offer in return BUS notes, a circulating medium that passed from hand to hand as cash. Effectively the bank was purchasing an earning asset—another term for issuing a loan—because the bill of exchange had value and earned interest over time. In northeastern cities, the bank would often loan to merchants who needed cash to pay for imports. The money used to pay for customs duties (tariffs) would, through several intermediate steps, be deposited in the U.S. Treasury as public money. From that point the Treasury could decide what to do with the public money, whether it was to pay off overseas bondholders who had purchased U.S. Treasury bonds (public debt) or fund government expenditures.[7]

In its capacity as the Treasury Department's chief fiscal agent, the Second Bank serviced the nation's public debt and provided convenient facilities for the collection and distribution of federal revenue. The bulk of the Treasury's receipts came from customs duties and land sales and, secondarily, from dividends on subscribing to 20 percent of the bank's stock. Added to this were small amounts of revenue drawn from internal taxes such as excise taxes and fees, and from direct taxes such as land taxes, slave taxes, and poll taxes. In terms of government outlays (spending), the bank helped to pay for veterans' pensions, interest on the public debt, and the salaries of military officers and public officials, including judges, foreign diplomats, and members of Congress and the federal bureaucracy.[8]

The secretary of the Treasury maintained a special account with the BUS, providing instructions to the bank president on how best to carry out the administration's fiscal priorities.[9] This involved a complex process since the areas in which the government received and spent money were geographically separate. About 90 percent of the federal government's revenue was derived from customs duties on the East Coast. More than half of this amount came from New York City alone. And yet, federal expenditures were required in every part of the union. The BUS was responsible for carrying out this interregional transfer free of charge. With its vast network of branches and commercial agencies, the bank had a built-in institutional framework that proved essential for mobilizing revenue from the North and redistributing it for employment in the South and West.[10]

Bank Notes and Bills of Exchange

Paper money in the antebellum era consisted of a dizzying array of credit instruments that functioned as promises to pay specie on demand. Banks extended credit by creating paper money, but they were not the only actors and institutions who possessed this power. Merchants, storeowners, exchange brokers, factors, mercantile houses, private firms, insurance companies, and large slave-trading firms performed a lot of the same functions as banks in this period.[11] While many antebellum Americans were skeptical of paper money, there were others who recognized its superiority compared to barter and relying exclusively on gold and silver for trade. Precious metals gradually deteriorated and were expensive to transport and insure. The benefits of gold mining diminished over time until there were new discoveries or the development of new extractive technologies, both of which were difficult to predict with any consistency. Gold strikes, moreover, had a destabilizing effect on the nation's money supply. But paper money reduced the cost of transactions and freed up resources for more productive ends. Though there is some risk of inflation, more money in circulation tends to lower interest rates, which spurs borrowing and economic growth. It is now a standard lesson among mainstream economists and economic historians that fiat currencies managed by central banks are better at stabilizing wild swings in prices and employment compared to monetary regimes where paper money is convertible to gold and/or silver.[12]

In the strictest legal and constitutional sense, coins were the only currency with *legal tender* status in the antebellum era, which meant that individuals were obligated to accept them in payment for debts. But in day-to-day practice, BUS notes were the next closest thing.[13] They were payable for all public duties, which is to say that Americans could use BUS notes to pay for customs duties, land sales, and local taxes. This helped give BUS notes legitimacy and a relatively uniform value in any part of the nation. Without the

APPENDIX ONE

confidence and stability that the bank's bills and notes conferred, antebellum Americans would have needed to rely much more on specie for daily transactions, which would stifle economic growth and material advancement.

Unlike BUS notes, most notes from state-chartered financial institutions were confined to a local or regional circulation. State bank notes tended to decrease in value the farther one traveled from the issuing bank. To take a hypothetical example, let's say a merchant from Lexington, Kentucky, traveled to Albany, New York. In his possession were notes from a state bank in Lexington. After arriving in Albany, the merchant discovered that he needed to pay off some debts quickly and so he took the Kentucky bank notes to a nearby bank in Albany to exchange them for specie. The Albany bank would accept the notes, but only offered in return an amount of specie far less than the face value of the Kentucky bank notes. In other words, the Albany bank *discounted* the notes. It did this because it had to send these notes back to Lexington to be redeemed in specie, and then the specie would have to be sent back to New York.[14] This would have implied significant amounts of time in the form of several weeks of travel over hundreds of miles of distance, and risk in the event that the specie was lost or stolen. There was also a possibility that the bank in Lexington did not have a solid reputation, perhaps because it issued too many notes or because there were lots of counterfeits in circulation. The discount rate on any given credit instrument depended on supply and demand, the distance between the buyer and seller, the bank's reputation, and other miscellaneous factors.

One of the most important credit instruments in domestic and international trade was the *bill of exchange*. This was a short-term (sixty to ninety days), liquid, interest-bearing order that represented the value of agricultural exports and commercial imports.[15] Bills of exchange dated back to the sixteenth century and bear some resemblance to a personal check one might use to pay rent today. They passed from hand to hand, but unlike bank notes, they required endorsements, or signatures, for each transaction (see Figures 1 and 2 in Chapter 5). Virtually every actor in a market economy relied to some degree on credit, mostly because there was a delay between the time a product was produced and when it was consumed. Bills of exchange were one way of providing this credit.[16] If a borrower signed the back of a bill to obtain credit, s/he was pledging her/his own reputation that the loan would be repaid. In the event of default, anyone who signed the back of a credit instrument could be sued to recover funds and damages. Such legal proceedings illustrated the extent to which one's own personal reputation was crucial to the credit system in antebellum America.[17]

When he became president of the Second Bank in 1823, Nicholas Biddle started directing the BUS branch offices toward buying and selling millions of dollars of bills of exchange.[18] This was a way of making the bank's lending practices more liquid in comparison to loans secured by stocks, whose prices could decline during a recession, or real estate, an illiquid asset. Soon the BUS became the nation's largest dealer in domestic and foreign bills. Factors, planters, merchants, and other actors who engaged in long-distance trade used bills of exchange to avoid the time, risk, and hassle of transporting specie over long distances to pay for goods.[19] Let's say a Mississippi planter wished to buy manufactured goods for his plantation. After the fall harvest, the planter gave his cotton crop, worth approximately $1,000, to a factor for shipment to New Orleans. The factor then drew up a bill of exchange for $1,000, payable in ninety days, drawn on the BUS branch in New Orleans, and gave it to the planter.[20] With bill in hand, the planter then walked into the Second Bank's branch office in Natchez. As part of the discounting process, the bank would take possession of the bill, deduct interest up front, and give the planter $985 in bank notes. The bank was lending to the planter at 6 percent interest, which was the price the planter paid for the risk that he would be unable to pay back the loan. At the end of the ninety days, when the bill came to maturity, or fell due, the factor paid back the full $1,000 to the bank. By issuing its own notes, the BUS was providing planters and other actors with cash that they could use to buy crops, slaves, tools, land, and other commodities. It was greasing the wheels of commerce. The bank's credit was crucial in this instance because without it, the planter would have had to wait several months before his cotton reached its ultimate destination in Great Britain.

The BUS was most impactful in the old Southwest, where the mutually reinforcing booms in land, cotton, and slavery required abundant credit facilities. Out of all the bank's branches, the ones located in the Ohio and Mississippi River Valleys were the most profitable.[21] They also purchased the most bills of exchange (see Appendix 2). Conversely, the BUS was least important in New England, a well-capitalized region with plenty of state banks.[22] Any look at the balance sheets of the BUS branch offices in Nashville and New Orleans demonstrates the institution's dominance in the South and West, which was related to the seasonal trade in bills of exchange founded on cotton exports. The United States was still overwhelmingly agricultural at this time, especially in this region, so it was the purpose of banks, including the BUS, to loan to farmers and planters in order to keep them afloat between the spring planting and the fall harvest. This explains why the duration of many loans lasted as long as six months. The number of bills purchased on the books of the branch office in Nashville peaked in April, when some of the last crops had been shipped by river toward New Orleans.[23] It took several weeks for the crops to arrive in New Orleans, and, unsurprisingly, the time of year in which the New Orleans branch purchased the most bills was in July (see Figure 3 in Chapter 5). At the Nashville branch, the number of bills in its possession declined steadily throughout the year as the bills matured. By December the fall harvest was complete, and merchants and factors would start drawing up bills again.

Because of its network of branch offices, the BUS provided convenient credit facilities for actors engaged in long-distance trade. During the winter and spring months, when cotton was moving to market for export, the BUS branches in the South purchased foreign bills of exchange drawn on (or payable in) London. The BUS would then ship these bills up to its northeastern branches, which sold them to American import merchants. By the summer and fall, the northeastern merchants would use these bills to pay for manufactured goods produced in England. Meanwhile, the bank's southern branches had issued notes to planters as part of the discount process. Planters could then pay their debts to southern merchants, who reimbursed northeastern creditors, who in turn, sent remittances to merchant banking houses. Over the course of the year, bills of exchange and bank notes flowed in a northeasterly direction.[24]

The BUS repeated this process over and over on a nationwide scale involving millions of dollars, and in doing so it provided financial services that linked the needs of southern planters and northeastern merchants at very low cost to both. By purchasing bills of exchange in some locations (the South in late spring) and then selling them in others (the North in the fall) for only a small profit, the bank equalized and rationalized interregional exchange rates. It smoothed out seasonal fluctuations in trade and provided cheap credit where it was needed. Without these services, the availability of bills of exchange during certain months of the year would have run dry, leading to higher exchange rates. Merchants would have needed to ship specie to pay for goods, which was not cheap. According to one estimate, in 1830 the cost of moving specie between the coast and the interior was about 4 percent of the value of the specie. Biddle's supporters argued that the bank's facilities served a salutary public interest by preventing private exchange brokers and middlemen from charging usurious interest rates on commercial paper. At least one economic historian has pointed out that by reducing the cost of interregional and international trade, the BUS contributed to the nation's economic growth.[25]

Many of these principles were also applicable to the Second Bank's role in facilitating trade between the United States and Great Britain. Under a presumably automatic and self-regulating balance-of-payments system, countries engaged in trade were supposed to sort out surpluses and deficits through the flow of gold and silver (or bills of exchange in certain circumstances). If countries pegged their currencies to gold at a fixed rate and kept government intervention minimal, the thinking went, then prices, production, and employment would work themselves out naturally over time. Wild swings in prices and employment were sometimes necessary, it was believed, to bring budgets and exchange rates back into line. This was the prevailing view of Enlightenment-era free trade theorists like Adam Smith, David Hume, and David Ricardo.[26] While this was an idealized theory that did not always materialize in practice, one can see many of the broad patterns at play in the antebellum era. Exporting commodities to Great Britain created bills of exchange in the United States whereas importing manufactured goods sent bills to Great Britain, taking them out of circulation. If the value of American imports exceeded the value of exports to Great Britain—in other words, if there was a trade deficit—this meant that the supply of bills of exchange was higher in Great Britain and scarcer in the United States. Scarcity of bills of exchange, according to supply and demand, would have meant that it was more expensive to obtain them. If bills were *really* scarce, it would have actually become cheaper to send specie abroad to pay for goods. Lower specie reserves in the United States would impel banks to contract credit, thereby lessening merchants' ability to continue importing. Theoretically the balance of trade would eventually stabilize.[27]

There was an added layer of complexity to this arrangement in that the flow of metals between the two countries depended not just on trade but on foreign investment, too. For most of the 1820s and 1830s, Great Britain maintained a trade surplus with the United States, principally because the value of manufactured goods produced in Great Britain was greater than the value of American crop exports. But Britain was also investing heavily in the United States at this time. After the celebrated completion of the Erie Canal in 1825, American securities—the stocks and bonds that capitalized banks, internal improvements, and state and municipal governments—began to appear more frequently in London money markets. When taking into account both investments and trade, the net balance in many years favored the United States. In this situation, gold in Great Britain flowed to the United States.[28]

The Bank in a Global Context

In recent years historians have come to emphasize the Second Bank's global dimensions with respect to the flow of precious metals, credit instruments, and workers (slave, free, and everything in between) that characterized the rise of industrial capitalism in the early nineteenth century. In the 1820s the British started funneling investment capital into the United States, in part because Biddle had cultivated a positive reputation among the financial community for making consistent payments on the national debt, maintaining liquid domestic and foreign exchange markets, implementing effective monetary policies during the 1825–1826 financial crisis, and for propagating a stable and uniform currency. Under Biddle's management, the BUS established a formal partnership with Baring Brothers, a major merchant banking house whose commercial reach spanned several continents. The BUS-Barings partnership facilitated Anglo-American trade and the brokering of U.S. sovereign debt. In exchange for American cotton exports, Barings and the Bank of England granted generous lines of "open credits" to American import merchants, allowing them to satisfy Americans' consumptive tastes and borrow without security on a continual basis.[29]

American brokerage firms like Thomas Biddle & Company and Prime, Ward & King purchased U.S. Treasury bonds from the BUS and marketed them to Barings for sale in London money markets. Treasury bonds came in several varieties based on duration and yield. All of them comprised the nation's public debt, which British investors played a major role in financing. Through Barings's credit and the Second Bank's commercial facilities, rural planters in the American South were wedded to British manufacturers, including all of the importers, factors, commission agents, exchange dealers, exporters, and insurance agents in between.[30] Access to British capital thus depended mainly on American-grown cotton, the crucial ingredient upon which the textile mills of the early Industrial Revolution relied. It was through cotton sales that American merchants settled foreign debts with Great Britain. American bank notes could not be used to pay these debts, but foreign bills of exchange in pounds sterling, whose value was based upon the price of cotton, helped Americans secure British credit, buy British manufactured goods, and make payments to the British bondholders who owned American securities. The BUS always kept large specie reserves on hand, in part to satisfy its fiscal and regulatory responsibilities and in part to pay British merchant banking houses in the event that they refused to honor bills of exchange.[31]

Jacksonians often claimed that the BUS unfairly siphoned specie away from the South and West, but in fact, as Biddle explained in congressional testimony, the BUS leveraged its position as a major player in both national and global trade to keep specie in the country.[32] Since the late eighteenth century, American merchants had been part of a global network of trade connecting China, the United States, Mexico, and Great Britain. American merchants sent produce and manufactured goods to Mexico and South America in exchange for Spanish silver dollars, which entered American ports at New York, Philadelphia, Baltimore, and, especially, New Orleans. The United States was nominally on a bimetallic standard, but in practice, a silver standard. In 1830 silver comprised 85 percent of the Second Bank's specie reserves. Much of this silver was rerouted to China to pay for silk, tea, nankeens, and chinaware.[33] Biddle found these payments to China inconvenient for American commerce, and in 1827, using Barings's open line of credit, he created a six-month foreign bill of exchange, drawn on London, that would substitute specie shipments. The use of these credit instruments successfully kept specie on the order of $5 million to $7 million per year in the United States. This was possible only because of the imperial presence of Barings and the British East India Company, which exploited the Chinese addiction to opium. The Chinese used these foreign bills of exchange to purchase opium produced on plantations in British-held India. Silver that had previously stayed in China was now exported to Great Britain, and Mexican silver that had previously gone to China now stayed in the United States. All of these forces set up the preconditions for a bubble in land, cotton, and slaves from 1834 to 1836 that burst in 1837.[34]

There is compelling evidence to suggest that the BUS played a role in the expansion of slavery in the old Southwest, which in turn fueled the rise of global capitalism. Deliberately or not, the bank seems to have evolved in a way so that one of its chief functions was to channel foreign and northern capital for productive use in the South's economy. The bank's preexisting institutional framework in the form of branch offices promoted this southwesterly flow of investment capital. Most of the bank's shares of capital stock were set aside for branch offices located in free states.[35] Yet the bank's notes and bills of exchange circulated mostly in the slaves states. From January 1, 1832, to January 1, 1833, all of the bank's branches purchased approximately $67.5 million in bills of exchange. Of this sum, $46.3 million, or 68.6 percent, were purchased at branch offices located in slave states. In February 1832, more than two out of every three BUS notes (67.9 percent) were issued by branches located in slave states (see Appendix 3). With such a large portion of its commercial paper circulating in the southern states, it is hard to imagine how this could not have aided the expansion of slavery in some form or another, particularly since slavery was so dominant in the South. The bank need not have directly bought and sold human beings to still bear some responsibility for the expansion of slavery—its notes and bills were undoubtedly used by planters, merchants, and factors to buy the cotton and tools on plantations where slaves worked. Slave traders often preferred using commercial paper drawn on northern financial institutions and firms like the BUS because southern notes, bills, and checks tended to depreciate more in value. The liquidity of the Second Bank's notes and bills was an advantage because slave traders often had to make quick sales to pay for their debts. When the BUS purchased a domestic bill of exchange and lent out its own notes in return as cash, slave traders could then use these notes to buy slaves.[36]

To be clear, the BUS was only one of numerous financial institutions and economic actors to finance the domestic slave trade. Bills of exchange on the order of several thousands of dollars, drawn on northern firms like the Phenix Bank of New York; Mackie, Lockhart & Company; Foster & Giraud; and Philadelphia's Samuel Moss & Son, appear in the surviving business records of Franklin & Armfield, the nation's largest slave-trading firm. This firm eventually grew so large that it took on its own lending capabilities.[37] Nonetheless, there is both an interpretative and empirical basis to the claim that the BUS financed and profited from the domestic slave trade in direct and indirect ways. Previous generations of historians have noted that the bank financed cotton exports and land sales in the old Southwest, but it is only recently that they have linked these trends to slavery. As planters and slaves pushed the boundaries of settlement further west, a cyclical pattern emerged: planters bought slaves to pick cotton on new lands they had just purchased, sold the cotton, and used the profits from cotton and land sales to buy more land and more slaves.[38] If one financed cotton and land sales in the South, one was implicitly financing the expansion of slavery, too. In addition, the practice of collateralizing and bundling slave mortgages into complex securities, which dated back to the colonial period, lubricated the South's credit system, raised cash, and, according to at least one historian, allowed for economic growth to accelerate faster than it would have otherwise.[39]

We now know that planters, merchants, factors, and slave-trading firms like Franklin & Armfield used the Second Bank's currency and benefited from the institution's ability to extend low-interest loans, stimulate interregional trade, and keep crop, land, and slave prices stable.[40] Historian Edward Baptist found that Franklin drew up to $40,000 at a time from the BUS to buy more slaves in the Upper South and estimated that about 5 percent of all the commercial credit handled by the BUS in 1831–1832 passed at some point through the hands of Franklin & Armfield. When the bank wound up its affairs in the late 1830s and early 1840s as a private institution, it became one of the largest owners of plantations, slaves, and slave-grown products in Mississippi.[41] Recent works by historians of slavery and capitalism have come at the Bank War from a new angle, giving us an opportunity to rethink how we teach and narrate a long-studied topic. These lines of inquiry should continue.

APPENDIX TWO

Average Percentage of Domestic Bills of Exchange Purchased at Each Branch Office According to Region, 1832

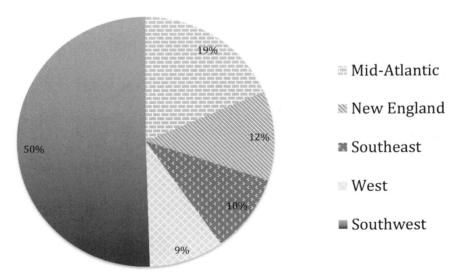

Methodology: Because the number of bills purchased at the various BUS branch offices tended to vary widely according to season, it made sense to calculate an average percentage based on several data points throughout a single year. According to financial statements presented in congressional reports, some of which included the bank's quarterly reports, 1832 contains the most complete financial information, including the number of bills purchased at each branch office. By combining data from three different congressional reports, one can compile seven different data points. Averaging these data points is thus intended to smooth out seasonal variations. The data points are January 1, 1832; February/March 1832; April 1, 1832; July 1, 1832; October 1, 1832; November 1, 1832; and January 1, 1833. Calculations performed by author.

Definition of Regions: For the purposes of this pie chart, the BUS branch offices were divided into the following regions: (1) Mid-Atlantic: Philadelphia, New York, Baltimore, Washington, and Utica; (2) New England: Portland, Portsmouth, Boston, Providence, Hartford, and Burlington; (3) Southeast: Richmond, Norfolk, Fayetteville, Charleston, and Savannah; (4) West: St. Louis, Cincinnati, Pittsburgh, and Buffalo; and (5) Southwest: Nashville, Louisville, Lexington, Mobile, Natchez, and New Orleans.

Sources: H. R. Rept. No. 460, 22nd Congress, 1st Session, Serial Volume 227, 267; S. Doc. No. 17, 23rd Congress, 2nd Session, Serial Volume 267, 126–140; House Document 8, 22nd Congress, 2nd Session, Serial Volume 233, 4.

BUS Note Circulation, Divided by Branch Offices in Slave States and Free States, February 1832

Branch Office (Free States)	Note Circulation (Free States)	Branch Office (Slave States)	Note Circulation (Slave States)
Philadelphia	$4,407,264.63	Baltimore	$1,116,477.50
Portland	$218,670.00	Washington	$938,777.50
Portsmouth	$281,295.00	Richmond	$1,186,010.00
Boston	$972,365.00	Norfolk	$1,218,505.00
Providence	$421,690.00	Fayetteville	$1,293,920.00
Hartford	$361,887.50	Charleston	$1,476,000.00
New York	$1,720,027.50	Savannah	$2,369,355.00
Cincinnati	$1,539,525.00	Mobile	$1,716,730.00
Pittsburgh	$1,249,232.50	New Orleans	$8,004,525.00
Buffalo	$1,070,385.00	Natchez	$1,455,565.00
Utica	$751,605.00	St. Louis	$844,555.00
Burlington	$518,885.00	Nashville	$3,532,425.00
Agency, Cincinnati	$1,830.00	Louisville	$1,452,175.00
Agency, Chillicothe	$225.00	Lexington	$1,998,535.00
Total in Free States	$13,514,887.13	Total in Slave States	$28,603,555.00

Source: H. R. Rept. No. 460, 22nd Congress, 1st Session, Serial Volume 227, 269. Percentage calculations performed by author.

Note: Total note circulation (free + slave states): $42,118,442.13. Percentage of notes issued by BUS branches in slave states: 67.9 percent. The BUS established two commercial agencies in Cincinnati, Ohio, and Chillicothe, Ohio. Commercial agencies were similar to BUS branch offices, but unlike branch offices, agencies did not maintain accounts with other banks.

Notes

Abbreviations

AKMP   *Amos Kendall Miscellaneous Papers*, Filson Historical Society

CNB   *The Correspondence of Nicholas Biddle: Dealing with National Affairs, 1807–1844*, ed. Reginald Charles McGrane (Boston: Houghton Mifflin, 1919)

FHS   Filson Historical Society, Louisville

FLPU   Firestone Library, Princeton University

H. R. Rept.   House of Representatives Report

HSP   Historical Society of Pennsylvania, Philadelphia

INHP   Independence National Historical Park, Philadelphia

JWWP   *James Watson Webb Papers*, Yale University Sterling Library

LOC   Library of Congress, Washington, DC

MHS   Missouri Historical Society, St. Louis

NARA II   National Archives and Records Administration, College Park, Maryland

PAJ   *The Papers of Andrew Jackson*, ed. Sam B. Smith et al., 10 vols. to date (Knoxville: University of Tennessee Press, 1980–)

PHC   *The Papers of Henry Clay*, ed. James F. Hopkins et al., 10 vols. (Lexington: University of Kentucky Press, 1959–1992)

RD   *Register of Debates*

S. Doc.   Senate Document

SHC   Southern Historical Collection, University of North Carolina, Chapel Hill

WHMC   Western Historical Manuscript Collection, Columbia, Missouri

Introduction

1. William Stickney, *Autobiography of Amos Kendall* (Boston: Lee and Shepard, 1872), 91–162; Donald B. Cole, *A Jackson Man: Amos Kendall and the Rise of American Democracy* (Baton Rouge: Louisiana State University Press, 2004), 36–51; Culver Smith, *The Press, Politics, and Patronage: The American Government's Use of Newspapers, 1789–1875* (Athens: University of Georgia Press, 1977), 88–89.

2. *United States Telegraph*, July 19, 1828; Robert V. Remini, *The Election of Andrew Jackson* (Philadelphia: J. B. Lippincott, 1962), 82. One historian, Donald J. Ratcliffe, has recently published compelling evidence that challenges the standard interpretation that Jackson was the most popular candidate in the 1824 election. While Jackson won a plurality of the popular vote in eighteen states, there were six states, including vote-rich New York, that did not keep official records of the popular vote because they determined votes in the Electoral College based on the preferences of the state legislature. By looking at voting records from state elections and the preferences of state lawmakers, Ratcliffe estimates that John Quincy Adams garnered the support of about 40 percent of the New York state legislature, which would have given him 77,000 additional votes in the national popular vote. Judged by this metric, Adams may have won the overall popular vote in 1824 by a margin of about 34,000 votes. Ratcliffe, "Popular Preferences in the Presidential Election of 1824," *Journal of the Early Republic* 34, no. 1 (Spring 2014), especially 68–73; and *The One-Party Presidential Contest: Adams, Jackson, and 1824's Five-Horse Race* (Lawrence: University Press of Kansas, 2015), 3, 234–237, 255.

3. Thomas Patrick Moore et al. to Andrew Jackson, May 23, 1829, in *The Papers of Andrew Jackson*, ed. Sam B. Smith et al. (Knoxville: University of Tennessee Press, 1980–) (hereafter cited as *PAJ*) 7, 25–26.

4. Most of Kendall's personal papers were destroyed in a fire. Scattered letters are spread across numerous manuscript collections located in several states. Amos Kendall to unknown, April 4, 1839, *Amos Kendall Miscellaneous Papers* (hereafter cited as *AKMP*); Stephen Campbell, "The Spoils of Victory: Amos Kendall, the Antebellum State, and the Growth of the American Presidency in the Bank War, 1828–1834," *Ohio Valley History* 11, no. 2 (Summer 2011): 3–25.

5. Kendall to Martin Van Buren, November 10, 1827, *Martin Van Buren Papers*, Library of Congress (hereafter cited as LOC); Kendall to Joseph Desha, April 9, 1831, *Joseph Desha Papers*, LOC; John J. Crittenden to Kendall, September 1, 1830, *John Crittenden Collection*, Filson Historical Society (hereafter, FHS). Cole, *A Jackson Man*, 36–51; James A. Padgett, "Correspondence between Governor Joseph Desha and Amos Kendall, 1831–1835," *Register of the Kentucky Historical Society* 38 (January 1940), 5–24.

6. See Appendix 1 for a deeper explanation of paper money in the antebellum era.

7. During this era, a bank's cashier was effectively its treasurer. The cashiers

of each BUS branch office corresponded often with Biddle on important financial matters. The BUS's functions are enumerated in the original 1816 charter, which can be found in *Annals of Congress*, House, 14th Congress, 1st Session, Appendix, 1812–1825. See also *RD*, 21st Congress, 1st Session, House, Appendix, 128–142. The number of directors is listed in Davis R. Dewey, *The Second United States Bank* (Washington, DC: Government Printing Office, National Monetary Commission, 1910), 290. H. R. Rept. No. 121, 22nd Congress, 2nd Session, Serial Volume 236, 84–86; S. Doc. No. 17, 23rd Congress, 2nd Session, Serial Volume 267, 311–312.

8. When characterizing Biddle as a central banker, it is important to keep several things in mind. Many of the regulatory practices that Biddle implemented were not spelled out explicitly in the bank's charter but evolved gradually as BUS officers realized the value of their large specie holdings. When the notes of state banks accumulated in BUS branches, Biddle instructed his cashiers to promptly redeem them in specie. Lower specie reserves would force state banks to contract their note circulation, thus minimizing the risk of inflation and excessive lending. Biddle could make minor adjustments in the nation's overall money supply by selling government bonds, for example, but these measures were not on the same scale as the more impactful open market operations conducted by today's Federal Reserve System, which is tasked with the dual mandate of providing price and employment stability. Although Biddle did rescue a handful of state banks from collapse, in general, the BUS prioritized its own safety, its profits, its political reputation, and its specie reserves above the prevention of financial panic. Biddle to Robert Lenox, April 22, 1828, *Biddle Letterbooks*, LOC; Biddle to Thomas Cadwalader, December 29, 1831, *Nicholas Biddle Papers*, LOC; *Frankfort Commonwealth*, April 29, 1834; Eric Lomazoff, "Turning (Into) 'The Great Regulating Wheel': The Conversion of the Bank of the United States, 1791–1811," *Studies in American Political Development* 26 (April 2012), 1–23; Jane Knodell, *The Second Bank of the United States: "Central" Banker in an Era of Nation-building, 1816–1836* (London: Routledge, 2017), 117–123. My understanding of central banking in the antebellum era is drawn principally from Michiel Hendrik De Kock, *Central Banking* (London: Crosby Lockwood Staples, 1939); J. Van Fenstermaker, *The Development of American Commercial Banking: 1782–1837* (Kent, OH: Kent State University Press, 1965); Peter Temin, *The Jacksonian Economy* (New York: W. W. Norton, 1969); George D. Green, *Finance and Economic Development in the Old South: Louisiana Banking, 1804–1861* (Palo Alto, CA: Stanford University Press, 1972); Richard Timberlake, *The Origins of Central Banking in the United States* (Cambridge, MA: Harvard University Press, 1978). Helpful treatises that elucidate some of the discourses of financial theory in the antebellum era include Nathan Appleton, *An Examination of the Banking System of Massachusetts in Reference to the Renewal of Bank Charters* (Boston: Stimpson and Clapp, 1831); and Condy Raguet, *A Treatise on Currency and Banking* (Philadelphia: Crigg and Elliot, 1840). Biddle's management skills during the prosperity of

the mid-1820s had won the BUS praise and temporarily allayed the concerns of some of its most vocal critics. For contemporaneous criticisms of Biddle's actions, see Peter Austin, *Baring Brothers and the Birth of Modern Finance* (London: Pickering and Chatto, 2007), 23–24.

9. Yet another source of bitterness was that the bank had taken possession of several tracts of land worth tens of thousands of dollars in western locales like Kentucky and Ohio, mostly because of loan defaults and foreclosures left over from the Panic of 1819. For Jackson's objections to the BUS, see Jackson to Hamilton, January 4, 1830, in *PAJ 8*, 12–16. For the bank's property holdings in the West, see Cope to Biddle, July 26, 1832, *United States Bank Papers*, HSP. Henry Clay described the BUS as the largest proprietor of real estate in Lexington and Frankfort in 1829. Clay to Biddle, November 28, 1829, in *The Papers of Henry Clay*, ed. James F. Hopkins et al. (Lexington: University of Kentucky Press, 1959–1992) *8*, 129 (hereafter cited as *PHC*).

10. The view that Jackson hated banks and paper money is well known among historians and is supported by the enactment of the Specie Circular in 1836. However, this view should not be overstated. Jackson participated actively in the Atlantic economy by working with financial agents and merchants in Nashville, New Orleans, and Philadelphia, who used BUS checks to facilitate the sales of Jackson's cotton in Liverpool and the purchase of chinaware. The fact that even the BUS's most vociferous critics still used its credit facilities would seem to lend credence to the interpretation that the Bank War was more about power and patronage than raw economic concerns. And despite Jackson's emotionally charged opposition to banks, his letters show that he understood the banking system well enough to make edits on financial matters in the drafting stages of his 1832 BUS veto message and several annual messages to Congress. In addition, while serving as military governor of the Florida territory, Jackson recommended the establishment of a BUS branch in the city of Pensacola. Jackson to Andrew Jackson Jr., May 31 and June 27, 1832; Maunsel White to Jackson, June 9, 1832; Henry Toland to Jackson, July 16, 1832; Jackson to Maunsel White, December 22, 1832, in *PAJ 10, 1832*, 295, 332–333, 421–422, 745–746; S. Doc. No. 17, 249–251.

11. For two contrasting perspectives on the Bank War, see Sean Wilentz, *The Rise of American Democracy: From Jefferson to Lincoln* (New York: W. W. Norton, 2005), 359–481; and Daniel Walker Howe, *What Hath God Wrought: The Transformation of America, 1815–1848* (New York: Oxford University Press, 2007), 328–395.

12. For a recent historiographical article, see Stephen Mihm, "The Fog of War: Jackson, Biddle, and the Destruction of the Bank of the United States," in *The Companion to the Era of Andrew Jackson*, ed. Sean Patrick Adams (Malden, MA: Wiley-Blackwell, 2013), 348–375.

13. For the relationship between the BUS and the Panic of 1837, see Temin, *The Jacksonian Economy*. For liberal entrepreneurialism, see Bray Hammond, *Banks and Politics in America from the Revolution to the Civil War* (Princeton,

NJ: Princeton University Press, 1957). For classical republicanism, see Major Wilson, "The 'Country' Versus the 'Court': A Republican Consensus and Party Debate in the Bank War," *Journal of the Early Republic* 15 (Winter 1995): 619–647.

14. Robert Remini, *Andrew Jackson and the Bank War* (New York: W. W. Norton, 1967), 10. The emphasis on Jackson's strong personality, both as a driver of policy and as a significant factor in his electoral success and general popularity, can be traced to James Parton, *Life of Andrew Jackson in Three Volumes* (New York: Mason Brothers, 1860).

15. For the market revolution paradigm, see Harry Watson, *Liberty and Power: The Politics of Jacksonian America* (New York: Hill and Wang, 1990); and Charles Sellers, *The Market Revolution: Jacksonian America, 1815–1846* (New York: Oxford University Press, 1991). Critics argued that this paradigm exaggerated average Americans' antipathy to capitalism, overlooked the importance of slavery and governmental institutions, and downplayed the examples in which Americans welcomed the era's educational opportunities, greater living standards, and consumer choices. See Winifred Barr Rothenberg, *From Market-Places to a Market Economy: The Transformation of Rural Massachusetts* (Chicago: University of Chicago Press, 1992); Howe, *What Hath God Wrought*. For the Second Bank's relationship to the Atlantic economy, see Jessica M. Lepler, *The Many Panics of 1837: People, Politics, and the Creation of a Transatlantic Financial Crisis* (Cambridge: Cambridge University Press, 2013); and Edward E. Baptist, *The Half Has Never Been Told: Slavery and the Making of Capitalism* (New York: Basic Books, 2014), 215–259.

16. For examples of monographs written between 1950 and 1970, see Walter Buckingham Smith, *Economic Aspects of the Second Bank of the United States* (Cambridge, MA: Harvard University Press, 1953); Remini, *Andrew Jackson and the Bank War*; and Jean Alexander Wilburn, *Biddle's Bank: The Crucial Years* (New York: Columbia University Press, 1967). One of the last monographs on the Bank War to be published is John M. McFaul, *The Politics of Jacksonian Finance* (Ithaca, NY: Cornell University Press, 1972). Two more recent works that are often cited in historiographical articles are Edward L. Kaplan, *The Bank of the United States and the American Economy* (Westwood, CT: Greenwood Press, 1999); and Richard H. Kilbourne Jr., *Slave Agriculture and Financial Markets in Antebellum America: The Bank of the United States, 1831–1852* (London: Pickering and Chatto, 2006). Both differ with my own work in significant ways. Kaplan's is a synthetic, derivative work with little evidence of archival research. Kilbourne's uncovers some of the bank's little-known investments in the Mississippi Valley based on an examination of Biddle papers and plantation and legal records. However, there is much less focus on party politics, political institutions, and newspaper editors.

17. APD scholars emerged in the 1980s. They were concerned initially with the development of the modern American state in the late nineteenth and early twentieth centuries, though researchers since then have applied their thinking

to the early republic and antebellum eras. For some of the earliest iterations of APD, see Stephen Skowronek, *Building a New American State: The Expansion of National Administrative Capacities, 1877–1920* (Cambridge: Cambridge University Press, 1982); and Theda Skocpol, "Bringing the State Back In: Strategies of Analysis in Current Research," in *Bringing the State Back In*, ed. Peter Evans, Dietrich Rueschemeyer, and Theda Skocpol (New York: Cambridge University Press, 1985), 28. Those who have applied an institutional analysis to earlier decades in American history include Max Edling, *A Revolution in Favor of Government: Origins of the U.S. Constitution and the Making of the American State* (New York: Oxford University Press, 2003), 18–24; and Richard R. John, *Spreading the News: The American Postal System from Franklin to Morse* (Cambridge, MA: Harvard University Press, 1995). For a helpful historiographical article, see Richard R. John, "Governmental Institutions as Agents of Change: Rethinking American Political Development in the Early Republic, 1787–1835," *Studies in American Political Development* 11 (Fall 1997): 347–380.

18. William Novak, *The People's Welfare: Law and Regulation in Nineteenth Century America* (Chapel Hill: University of North Carolina Press, 1996), 86–107; John Lauritz Larson, *Internal Improvement: National Public Works and the Promise of Popular Government* (Chapel Hill: University of North Carolina Press, 2001), 193–233; Howard Bodenhorn, *State Banking in Early America: A New Economic History* (New York: Oxford University Press, 2003), 5, 11–16; Richard Ellis, *Aggressive Nationalism: McColluch v. Maryland and the Foundation of Federal Authority in the Young Republic* (New York: Oxford University Press, 2007); Richard John, *Network Nation: Inventing American Telecommunications* (Cambridge, MA: Harvard University Press, 2010), 90.

19. Smith, *The Press, Politics, and Patronage*; Richard Kielbowicz, *News in the Mail: the Press, Post Office, and Public Information, 1700–1860s* (New York: Greenwood Press, 1989); Gerald Baldasty, *The Commercialization of News in the Nineteenth Century* (Madison: University of Wisconsin Press, 1992); John, *Spreading the News*; Jeffrey Pasley, *"The Tyranny of Printers": Newspaper Politics in the Early American Republic* (Charlottesville: University of Virginia Press, 2001); Robert W. McChesney and John Nichols, *The Death and Life of American Journalism: The Media Revolution That Will Begin the World Again* (New York: Nation Books, 2010); Paul Starr, *The Creation of the Media: Political Origins of Modern Communications* (New York: Basic Books, 2004), 83–150; Leonard D. White, *The Jacksonians: A Study in Administrative History 1829–1861* (New York: MacMillan, 1954); Richard John, "Affairs of Office: The Executive Departments, the Election of 1828, and the Making of the Democratic Party," in *The Democratic Experiment: New Directions in Political History,* Meg Jacobs et al. (Princeton, NJ: Princeton University Press, 2003), 51–54.

20. The historian Brian Balogh wrote that it is ironic that Americans, in their collective memory, often associate the West with rugged individualism because the region relied so heavily on state support. Acquiring, exploring, surveying,

and selling western lands all required governmental sponsorship at both the national and state levels, to say nothing of enforcing property rights (including slave property), conducting foreign policy, protecting borders, and maintaining the postal system. One explanation for this disconnect may be that these institutions operated at the margins of society and were not always perceptible to ordinary Americans. Brian Balogh, *A Government Out of Sight: The Mystery of National Authority in Nineteenth-Century America* (Cambridge: Cambridge University Press, 2009).

21. A state can be considered weak for some segments of the population (i.e., white males) but oppressive for others (i.e., African Americans and Native Americans) at the same time. Additionally, there is disagreement as to whether certain policies—among them, tariffs, slavery, Gag Rule, and Indian Removal— were representative of a strong or weak state. And to note that the American state was decentralized is not the same as claiming that it exercised only limited influence over Americans' lives. The notion of a "weak" American state dates back to Tocqueville and Weber with added reinforcement from the American historian Louis Hartz. Tocqueville saw the American state as fundamentally distinct from civil society and the public sphere. In showing how governmental institutions funded by public money helped capitalize newspapers, which in turn influenced civil society, my work contests this assumption. Those who see the early United States as weak and decentralized typically point to the protection of individual rights, checks and balances, and the shared authority between states and national governments outlined in the Constitution. The presumed absence of a professional police force, centralized bureaucracy, large federal budget, and long-standing wars of imperial expansion (a main driver of state development) seemed to add to this claim. To varying degrees, scholars have challenged these assumptions in recent decades. For the view that slavery expanded the powers of the state, see Don E. Fehrenbacher, *The Slaveholding Republic: An Account of the United States Government's Relation to Slavery* (New York: Oxford University Press, 2001); and David F. Ericson, *Slavery in the American Republic: Developing the Federal Government, 1791–1861* (Lawrence: University Press of Kansas, 2011). For the more commonly held view that slavery weakened the American state, see Robin Einhorn, *American Taxation, American Slavery* (Chicago: University of Chicago Press, 2006). For key works that have influenced my thinking on "the state," see James G. March and Johan P. Olsen, "The New Institutionalism: Organizational Factors in Political Life," *American Political Science Review* 78, no. 3 (September 1984): 734–749; Ira Katznelson, "Flexible Capacity: The Military and Early American Statebuilding," and Robert O. Keohane, "International Commitments and American Political Institutions in the Nineteenth Century," in *Shaped by War and Trade*, ed. Ira Katznelson and Martin Shefter (Princeton, NJ: Princeton University Press, 2002), 60, 86; Novak, *The People's Welfare*, ix, 3–36 and "The Myth of the 'Weak' American State," *AHR* 113, no. 3 (June 2008): 752–772; and John, "Governmental Institutions as Agents of Change," 357–358.

22. For the arbitrary division between the state and market common in nine-teenth-century liberalism, see Gautham Rao, *National Duties: Custom Houses and the Making of the American State* (Chicago: University of Chicago Press, 2016), 10–11. For early New York corporations, see Brian Phillips Murphy, *Building the Empire State: Political Economy in the Early Republic* (Philadelphia: University of Pennsylvania Press, 2015).

23. For recent studies that emphasize the American origins of the panic, see Peter Rousseau, "Jacksonian Monetary Policy, Specie Flows, and the Panic of 1837," *Journal of Economic History* 62, no. 2 (June 2002): 457–488; Namsuk Kim and John Joseph Wallis, "The Market for American State Government Bonds in Britain and the United States, 1830–43," *Economic History Review* 58, no. 4 (November 2005): 736–764; Knodell, *The Second Bank of the United States*; and Knodell, "Rethinking the Jacksonian Economy: The Impact of the 1832 Bank Veto on Commercial Banking," *Journal of Economic History* 66, no. 3 (September 2006): 541–574.

Chapter 1. Public Printers, Private Struggles: The Party Press and the Early American State

1. Andrew Jackson to John Randolph, November 11, 1831, in *PAJ* 9, 684.

2. William Barry to Susan Barry, June 11, 1829, *William Barry Letters*, FHS.

3. Jackson's interpretation of the law was not shared by many of his contemporaries, including his predecessor, John Quincy Adams. Richard J. Ellis, *The Development of the American Presidency* (London: Routledge, 2012), 425–426.

4. Within one year of taking office, Jackson dismissed 423 postmasters. The regional dimension of these appointments signaled a clear attempt at party-building. Most of the federal officeholders he dismissed were from New England, the Middle Atlantic states, and the old Northwest—regions where the Jacksonian Party was weakest. Jackson fired only 2 percent of the postmasters in the South. Richard John, *Spreading the News: The American Postal System from Franklin to Morse* (Cambridge, MA: Harvard University Press, 1995), 221–236; Daniel Walker Howe, *What Hath God Wrought: The Transformation of America, 1815–1848* (New York: Oxford University Press, 2007), 226, 281, 333; Spencer Darwin Pettis to Jackson, March 27, 1830, in *PAJ* 8, 162.

5. Henry Clay, "Fowler's Garden Speech," May 16, 1829, in *PHC* 8, 41–54. Jackson to John Overton, May 13, 1830, in *PAJ* 8, 260–262. For Jacksonian opposition to the removals, see Van Buren to Jackson, March 31, 1829, in *PAJ* 7, 129–134, and Randolph to Jackson, November 8, 1831, in *PAJ* 9, 674–676.

6. For the financial travails of editors, see William H. Lyon, *The Pioneer Editor in Missouri 1808–1860* (Columbia: University of Missouri Press, 1965); Thomas C. Leonard, *The Power of the Press: The Birth of American Political Reporting* (New York: Oxford University Press, 1986), 55; and Charles G. Steffen, "Newspapers for Free: The Economies of Newspaper Circulation in the Early Republic," *Journal of the Early Republic* 23, no. 3 (Autumn 2003): 381–419.

7. Edward J. Balleisen, *Navigating Failure: Bankruptcy and Commercial Society in Antebellum America* (Chapel Hill: University of North Carolina Press, 2001), 2.

8. For some smaller newspaper establishments, one or two persons might serve as printer, editor, proprietor, news-gathering correspondent, clerk, and subscription agent at once. In larger establishments such as the *New York Courier and Enquirer*, greater demand and readership required a stricter division of labor. Lyon, *The Pioneer Editor in Missouri 1808–1860*, 105.

9. Paul Starr, *The Creation of the Media: Political Origins of Modern Communications* (New York: Basic Books, 2004), 83–150.

10. Robert V. Remini, *The Election of Andrew Jackson* (Philadelphia: J. B. Lippincott, 1963), 76.

11. For the public sphere, see Jurgen Habermas, *The Structural Transformation of the Public Sphere: An Inquiry into a Category of Bourgeois Society*, translated by Thomas Burger with the assistance of Frederick Lawrence (Cambridge, MA: MIT Press, 1989); Steffen, "Newspapers for Free," 381–419; and Donald J. Ratcliffe, *The One-Party Presidential Contest: Adams, Jackson, and 1824's Five-Horse Race* (Lawrence: University Press of Kansas, 2015), 264–265.

12. Jackson to Blair et al., January 1, 1829, in *PAJ 7*, 3–4; Shadrach Penn Jr. to Jackson, March 20, 1831, in *PAJ 9*, 140–141; William Brent to Clay, October 2, 1829; Claiborne Jr. to Clay, November 28, 1829; Prentiss to Clay, July 1, 1831, all in *PHC 8*, 106, 130, 369–370.

13. J. Mills Thornton III, *Politics and Power in a Slave Society* (Baton Rouge: Louisiana State University Press, 1978), 129–142.

14. Jeffrey L. Pasley, *"The Tyranny of Printers:" Newspaper Politics in the Early American Republic* (Charlottesville: University of Virginia Press, 2001), 20; "Minnows, Spies, and Aristocrats: The Social Crisis of Congress in the Age of Martin Van Buren," *Journal of the Early Republic* 27, no. 4 (Winter 2007): 599–653; *Printers, Editors, and Publishers in the U.S. Congress, 1789–1861*, 2001–2007, available at http://pasleybrothers.com/newspols/congress.htm, accessed June 30, 2012.

15. William A. Ames, *A History of the National Intelligencer* (Chapel Hill: University of North Carolina Press, 1972), 60–61.

16. Clay to Fendall, September 18, 1830, in *PHC 8*, 261–262.

17. Jackson did not appoint Stambaugh marshal but later gave him an interim appointment as Indian agent. The Senate rejected his nomination for a more permanent appointment in March 1831. Cameron to Jackson, February 24, 1830, in *PAJ 8*, 92.

18. Steffen, "Newspapers for Free," 382–383.

19. *Saturday Evening Post*, quoted in the *Missouri Free Press*, September 19, 1833.

20. Ames, *A History of the National Intelligencer*, 226–227; Gerald Baldasty, *The Commercialization of News in the Nineteenth Century* (Madison: University of Wisconsin Press, 1992), 19.

21. *Fayetteville Observer*, November 19, 1833.

22. *National Intelligencer*, November 10, 1831.

23. John C. Rives to Francis P. Blair, June 15, 1833, *Blair-Lee Papers*, Firestone Library, Princeton University (hereafter cited as FLPU); Steffen, "Newspapers for Free," 385–389.

24. According to the U.S. federal census of 1840, there were 1,390 newspapers and 224 periodicals in the nation. *University of Virginia Library, Historical Census Browser* 2004, available at http://mapserver.lib.virginia.edu/php/start .php?year=V1840, accessed July 2, 2012.

25. Kendall to Jackson, December 3, 1831, in *PAJ* 9, 721–722.

26. Prentiss to Clay, February 22, 1831; F. H. Pettis to Clay, December 16, 1830, in *PHC 8*, 326, 313.

27. *Frankfort Commonwealth*, April 9, 1833.

28. For example, see William Whiteley et al. to Jackson, February 26, 1829, in *PAJ 7*, 65–66.

29. For some of the specific names and offices involved in Jackson's removals of civil servants and appointment of party loyalists, including newspaper editors and printers, see Caleb Atwater to Jackson, February 16 and 28, 1829, and Ingalls to Jackson, August 9, 1829, in *PAJ 7*, 27, 43–47, 67–68, 357–363; Cameron to Jackson, February 24, 1830, in *PAJ 8*, 92.

30. Jackson to Thomas Hart Benton, February 16, 1830; Spencer Darwin Pettis to Jackson, March 15 and 27, 1830; Jackson to Samuel Delucenna Ingham, March 16, 1830, in *PAJ 8*, 76, 130–131, 162.

31. Despite his later rift with the president, Green seems to have gotten his wish. Jackson appointed Meehan to the position of librarian of Congress on May 28, 1829. Green to Jackson, April 23, 1829, in *PAJ 7*, 171–172.

32. Atwater to Jackson, February 28, 1829, in ibid., 68; One useful study of the patronage system, particularly in terms of printing contracts, is Culver Smith, *The Press, Politics, and Patronage: The American Government's Use of Newspapers, 1789–1875* (Athens: University of Georgia Press, 1977).

33. There were notable exceptions, of course, including *Niles' Weekly Register*, which eschewed the overt partisanship of organs like the *Globe*. Editors of commercial presses, moreover, risked losing readership and advertising if they became too partisan. For example, see Niles to Clay, October 28, 1830, in *PHC 8*, 281.

34. Punshon to Jackson, February 6, 1829, in *PAJ 7*, 32; Clay to Langdon, December 20, 1830, and Clay, "Fowler's Garden Speech," May 16, 1829, in *PHC 8*, 41–54 and 314–315; Atwater to Jackson, February 16, 1829; Parsons to Jackson, May 25, 1829, in *PAJ 7*, 43–47.

35. Jacksonians had charged in 1828 that *Boston Statesman* editor Nathaniel Greene (1797–1877) was denied the annual printing contract for the city of Boston for political reasons despite submitting the lowest bid. Ingalls to Jackson, August 9, 1829, in *PAJ 7*, 357–363.

36. Publishing rates for projects like those pursued by Force and Clarke depended on the quality of paper and the number of letters that printers opted to fit into one page. These rates usually set the standard for printing contracts for

the various executive departments, unless another law or resolution prevailed. H. R. Rept. No. 849, 24th Congress, 1st Session, Serial Volume 295, 3–12; Clay to Peter B. Porter, November 22, 1829, and "Remark in the Senate," June 21, 1834, in *PHC 8*, 128–129, 733–734; Jackson to Edward Livingston, July 21, 1832, in *PAJ 10*, 436; William B. Lewis to Biddle, November 15, 1829, in Reginald Charles McGrane, ed., *The Correspondence of Nicholas Biddle: Dealing with National Affairs, 1807–1844* (Boston: Houghton Mifflin, 1919) (hereafter cited as *CNB*), 85–87.

37. Ames, *History of the National Intelligencer*, 62.

38. Ibid., 225–226; *National Intelligencer*, January 29, 1828; *Register of Debates* (hereafter, *RD*), 24th Congress, 1st Session, Senate, Document 11. Those who recorded debates in Congress for print practiced a form of shorthand known as stenography. In fact, reporters in the House of Representatives at this time were sometimes known as stenographers.

39. Baldasty, *Commercialization of the News*, 20; *Niles' Weekly Register*, May 30, 1834.

40. Ames, *A History of the National Intelligencer*, 225–231.

41. S. Doc. No. 17, 23rd Congress, 2nd Session, Serial Volume 267, 318. As a further illustration of the hybrid public-private nature of party presses, it is important to point out that when editors accepted printing contracts, they did not automatically become federal or state employees. According to judicial precedent, a publisher of the laws was not a commissioned officer. Therefore, the editors who acquired patronage through printing contracts, but were not appointed to federal office, might be likened to private contractors today who work for the government. Clay, "Fowler's Garden Speech," May 16, 1829, in *PHC 8*, 41–54.

42. S. Doc. No. 17, 317.

43. Samuel Harrison Smith should not be confused with Samuel Smith, a military general and U.S. senator from Maryland. Ames, *History of the Intelligencer*, 62–63.

44. Over the course of their financial relationship with BUS, Gales and Seaton signed several deeds of trust, including ones in December 1820 and June 1826. S. Doc. No. 17, 317–319.

45. Ames, *History of the Intelligencer*, vii, 84.

46. *Globe*, September 11, 1832; *Frankfort Argus*, March 13, 1833; Fletcher M. Green, "Duff Green, Militant Journalist of the Old School," *American Historical Review* 52, no. 2 (January 1947): 257; Robert Washington Kerr, *History of the Government Printing Office (at Washington D.C.)* (Lancaster, PA: Inquirer Printing and Publishing, 1881), 20; Ames, *History of the National Intelligencer*, 237.

47. Amos Kendall to unknown, April 4, 1839, *AKMP*.

48. Green, "Duff Green, Militant Journalist of the Old School," 247; William Stephen Belko, *The Invincible Duff Green: Whig of the West* (Columbia: University of Missouri Press, 2006), 3–4, 270–280.

49. Parsons to Jackson, May 25, 1829, in *PAJ* 7, 241–242.

50. Similarly, Clay advised Covington, Kentucky, editor Richard Langdon that his new business should be "actually commenced and in circulation" before he submitted an application for patronage from the Kentucky state legislature. Clay to Langdon, December 20, 1830; Prentiss to Clay, February 22, 1831, in *PHC* 8, 314–315, 326–327.

51. Parsons to Jackson, May 25, 1829, in *PAJ* 7, 241–242.

52. *Scioto Gazette*, February 17, 1830.

53. Donald J. Ratcliffe, *The Politics of Long Division: The Birth of the Second Party System in Ohio, 1818–1828* (Columbus: Ohio State University Press, 2000), 87, 188.

54. Lyon, *Pioneer Editor in Missouri*, 54, 72.

55. *Missouri Intelligencer*, May 23, 1835, quoted in Lyon, *Pioneer Editor in Missouri*, 55.

56. Ewing to Jackson, September 26, 1833, *Blair-Lee Papers*, FLPU.

57. Ewing helped collect subscription money in Missouri for Blair's *Globe*.

58. Alexander to Blair, April 11, 1833, *Blair-Rives Papers*, LOC.

59. *Globe*, August 6 and October 31, 1833.

60. For an example of an editor getting excited about the garnering of printing contracts, see Samuel Harrison Smith's experience in Ames, *A History of the Intelligencer*, 30.

61. Ames, *History of the Intelligencer*, 154.

62. John Steele to Daniel Dunklin, February 25, 1832, *Daniel Dunklin Collection*, Western Historical Manuscript Collection, Columbia, Missouri (hereafter, WHMC). Benton largely shared Dunklin's views on currency issues and finance. Perry McCandless, "Thomas Hart Benton, His Source of Political Strength in Missouri, 1815–1838." (PhD diss., University of Missouri, Columbia, 1953); Robert E. Shalhope, "Thomas Hart Benton and Missouri State Politics: A Re-Examination," *Missouri Bulletin* 25, no. 3 (April 1969): 171–191.

63. Benton to Ewing, November 12, 1831, *Thomas Hart Benton Papers*, Missouri Historical Society, St. Louis (hereafter, MHS); Miller to Dunklin, March 8 and September 16, 1832, *Dunklin Collection*, WHMC. For more on the development of the Jacksonian Party in Missouri, see James E. Moss, "William Henry Ashley: A Jackson Man with Feet of Clay," *Missouri Historical Review* 61, no. 1 (January 1966): 1–20; and Stephen Campbell, "Hickory Wind: The Role of Personality and the Press in Andrew Jackson's Bank War in Missouri, 1831–1837," *Missouri Historical Review* 101, no. 3 (April 2007): 146–167.

64. Miller to Dunklin, March 8, 1832, *Dunklin Collection*, WHMC.

65. Steele to Dunklin, April 16, 1832, *Dunklin Collection*.

66. Dunklin to Miller, March 31, 1832; Steele to Dunklin, April 24, 1832, *Dunklin Collection*.

67. Steele to Dunklin, April 24, 1832, *Dunklin Collection*.

68. Manning to Dunklin, September 13, 1834, *Dunklin Collection*.

69. Miller to Dunklin, March 8, 1832; Steele to Dunklin, March 16, 1832,

in *Dunklin Collection. Missouri Free Press,* June 6, 1833; Rudolph Eugene Forderhase, "Jacksonianism in Missouri, From Predilection to Party, 182c–1836"
(PhD diss., University of Missouri, 1968), 395.

70. Richard M. Clokey, *William H. Ashley: Enterprise and Politics in the
Trans-Mississippi West* (Norman: University of Oklahoma Press, 1980), 270.

71. *Missouri Argus,* January 22, 1836, quoted in Clokey, *William H. Ashley,*
268. For editors, writing under pseudonyms served multiple purposes. An editor could use a pseudonym if he wished to make a strong statement without
retaliation, either physically or in print (although duels did arise out of insult
trading in newspapers from time to time). Alternatively, he may have wanted
to create the impression that there was widespread popular support for the
position he advocated. In this way, partisan editors may have wished to manufacture—rather than reflect—public opinion. But there was also a less deceitful
purpose. As debates over the ratification of the U.S. Constitution and the *Feder-
alist Papers* demonstrated, authors wrote pseudonymously to avoid ad hominem
attacks. That is, they wanted ratification to be decided based on their collective
notions of reason, rationality, and the merits of certain arguments, rather than
the types of character attacks that often characterized political debates. Max
Edling, *A Revolution in Favor of Government: Origins of the U.S. Constitution
and the Making of the American State* (New York: Oxford University Press,
2003), 18–24.

72. *Missouri Argus,* July 22, 1836, and January 22, 1836, quoted in Clokey,
William H. Ashley, 268.

73. Clokey, *William H. Ashley,* 268–270; Moss, "William Henry Ashley,"
1–20; Campbell, "Hickory Wind," 146–167.

74. For free labor ideology, see Eric Foner, *Free Soil, Free Labor, and Free
Men: The Ideology of the Republican Party before the Civil War* (New York:
Oxford University Press, 1970).

*Chapter 2. "A Very Able State Paper": Amos Kendall and
the Rise of the* Globe

1. Leonard D. White, *The Jacksonians: A Study in Administrative History
1829–1861* (New York: Macmillan, 1954), 252; Richard Kielbowicz, *News in
the Mail: The Press, Post Office, and Public Information, 1700–1860s* (New
York: Greenwood Press, 1989), 2. For a useful historiographical article on the
importance of political institutions and "the American state," see Richard John,
"Governmental Institutions as Agents of Change: Rethinking American Political Development in the Early Republic, 1787–1835," *Studies in American Political Development* 11 (Fall 1997): 347–380.

2. For examples of this view, see Harry Watson, *Liberty and Power: The
Politics of Jacksonian America* (New York: Hill and Wang, 1990); John Lau-
ritz Larson, *Internal Improvement: National Public Works and the Promise of
Popular Government in the Early Republic* (Chapel Hill: University of North
Carolina Press, 2001); and Richard Ellis, *Aggressive Nationalism:* McColluch v.

Maryland *and the Foundation of Federal Authority in the Young Republic* (New York: Oxford University Press, 2007).

3. Economists, who are often trained to consider counterfactuals, may ponder whether the Second Party System could have developed without public subsidies. While this is potentially a fruitful avenue of inquiry, for the purposes of this study, it is beside the point. What matters here is the actual historical record of how the Second Party System developed, and this record included public subsidies.

4. Don E. Fehrenbacher, *The Slaveholding Republic: An Account of the United States Government's Relation to Slavery* (New York: Oxford University Press, 2001); David F. Ericson, *Slavery in the American Republic: Developing the Federal Government, 1791–1861* (Lawrence: University Press of Kansas, 2011); Matthew Karp, *This Vast Southern Empire: Slaveholders at the Helm of American Foreign Policy* (Cambridge, MA: Harvard University Press, 2016).

5. Robert V. Remini, *The Election of Andrew Jackson* (Philadelphia: J. B. Lippincott, 1963), 76.

6. Lynn Hudson Parsons, *The Birth of Modern Politics: Andrew Jackson, John Quincy Adams, and the Election of 1828* (New York: Oxford University Press, 2009), 139.

7. *PAJ 8, 1830*, 168. Kendall's circular and exchanges with newspaper editors appeared in *Niles' Weekly Register*, April 18, 1829, 125–126.

8. For one example showing Jackson's appreciation for Kendall, see Andrew Jackson to William Berkeley Lewis, August 10, 1830, in *PAJ 8*, 470.

9. Jackson to John Berrien, June 11, 1829, in *PAJ 7, 1829*, 275–276. Jackson nominated Kendall as a recess appointment on March 21, 1829.

10. Amos Kendall to Jackson, January 5, 1830, in *PAJ 8*, 17–18. See also Jackson to John Boyle, March 25, 1831, in *PAJ 9, 1831*, 149.

11. Jackson to Kendall, May 10, 1830, in *PAJ 8*, 251–252.

12. For one example of Green's behavior, see Samuel B. Barrell to James Watson Webb, February 6, 1832, *James Watson Webb Papers*, Yale University Sterling Library (hereafter cited as *JWWP*).

13. Donald B. Cole, *A Jackson Man: Amos Kendall and the Rise of American Democracy* (Baton Rouge: Louisiana State University Press, 2004), 117–147; Fletcher M. Green, "Duff Green, Militant Journalist of the Old School," *American Historical Review* 52, no. 2 (January 1947): 247. For Duff Green's views on the BUS, see William Stephen Belko, *The Invincible Duff Green: Whig of the West* (Columbia: University of Missouri Press, 2006), 3–4, 270–280; Kendall to Blair, November 20, 1830, *Blair Family Papers*, LOC; Kendall to Isaac Hill, July 13, 1830, *AKMP*; Kendall to Blair, October 2, 1830, *Blair-Lee Papers*, FLPU.

14. James A. Hamilton to Jackson, July 29, 1830, in *PAJ 8*, 456.

15. Kendall to Blair, July 10 and November 20, 1830, *Blair Family Papers*, LOC. Kendall to Blair, March 1 and October 2, 1830, *Blair-Lee Papers*, FLPU; Culver Smith, *The Press, Politics, and Patronage: The American Government's Use of Newspapers* (Athens: University of Georgia Press, 1977), 124; William

Stickney, *Autobiography of Amos Kendall* (Boston: Lee and Shepard, 1872), 371–374. Stickney used Kendall's notes to publish the autobiography three years after Kendall's death.

16. Jackson to Lewis, June 26, 1830; Hamilton to Jackson, July 29, 1830, in *PAJ* 8, 396–397, 456.

17. Kendall to Jackson, December 3, 1831, in *PAJ* 9, 720–723.

18. Smith, *Press, Politics, and Patronage*, 122–130.

19. Kendall to Blair, October 2, 1830; Richard M. Johnson to Blair, n.d., circa 1831, *Blair-Lee Papers*, FLPU; William Barry to Joseph Desha, February 2, 1831, *Joseph Desha Papers*, LOC.

20. Kendall to Blair, July 10 and November 20, 1830, *Blair Family Papers*, LOC; Kendall to Blair, March 1 and October 2, 1830, *Blair-Lee Papers*, FLPU; Stickney, *Autobiography of Amos Kendall*, 371–374.

21. These features included the mobilization of mass political parties, relatively open and democratic voting requirements for white men, greater attention to popular vote totals rather than following the wishes of political elites exclusively, and high voter turnout rates between 60–80 percent, at least in state elections in northern states where party competition was fierce. By 1792 state-imposed property tests on the right to vote had either been removed or made meaningless by inflation, and tax-paying qualifications meant little when a county road tax paid by labor on the roads could satisfy the requirement. Constitutional reforms that eliminated the property requirement for voting in northern states between 1815 and 1821, thus, formalized what had already become common practice. Donald J. Ratcliffe, *The Politics of Long Division: The Birth of the Second Party System in Ohio, 1818–1828* (Columbus: Ohio State University Press, 2000), xii; Ratcliffe, *The One-Party Presidential Contest: Adams, Jackson, and 1824's Five-Horse Race* (Lawrence: University Press of Kansas, 2015), 4–10.

22. Parsons, *The Birth of Modern Politics*, 134–135.

23. Kendall to Blair, October 2, 1830, *Blair-Lee Papers*, FLPU; Kendall to Blair, November 20, 1830, *Blair Family Papers*, LOC; Kendall and Blair to John C. Rives, November 14, 1833, *AKMP*.

24. As one historian has written, gossip, innuendo, and surreptitious dealmaking among the wives of cabinet members revealed the extent to which women shaped Washington politics. Catherine Allgor, *Parlor Politics: In Which the Ladies of Washington Build a City and a Government* (Charlottesville: University of Virginia Press, 2000); *National Intelligencer*, February 19, 1831.

25. For details of the cabinet breakup, see Robert V. Remini, *Andrew Jackson and the Course of American Freedom, 1822–1832* (New York: Harper and Row, 1981), 306–315.

26. *House Journal*, 21st Congress, 2nd Session, 8–33.

27. Hays to Jackson, January 3, 1831; Campbell to Jackson, January 14, 1831; Jackson to White, April 29, 1831, in *PAJ* 9, 6–7, 20–23, 220–221.

28. Jackson to Kendall, December 6, 1830; Jackson to Coffee, December 6,

1830; Jackson to Hays, December 7, 1830, in *PAJ 8*, 680–682; Jackson to John Overton, January 16, 1831, in *PAJ 9*, 27–28.

29. William Prentiss to Henry Clay, February 22, 1831, in *PHC 8*, 327; Samuel Jackson Hays to Jackson, January 3, 1831 in *PAJ 9*, 7.

30. George W. Campbell to Jackson, January 14, 1831, in *PAJ 9*, 20–23.

31. Kendall to Blair, October 2, 1830, *Blair-Lee Papers*, FLPU.

32. Kendall to Blair, April 25, 1830; November 20, 1830, in *Blair Family Papers*, LOC.

33. Kendall to Blair, March 1, 1830, *Blair-Lee Papers*, FLPU.

34. Kendall to Blair, April 25, 1830, *Blair Family Papers*, LOC.

35. Clay to Johnston, July 18, 1829, in *PHC 8*, 77.

36. Stickney, *Autobiography of Amos Kendall*, 375.

37. Hicks to Blair, July 13, 1831; *Blair-Rives Papers*, LOC. Daniel Walker Howe, *What Hath God Wrought: The Transformation of America, 1815–1848* (New York: Oxford University Press, 2007), 282.

38. Kendall to Blair, November 20, 1830, *Blair Family Papers*, LOC. Alexander Kyle had been a papermaker from Kentucky and was the father of Kendall's second wife, Jane. Cole, *A Jackson Man*, 147.

39. "Kendall and Blair agree," n.d. circa late 1830; Kendall to Blair, October 2, 1830, *Blair-Lee Papers*, FLPU; Kendall to Blair, November 20, 1830, *Blair Family Papers*, LOC.

40. Kendall to Jackson, December 3, 1831, in *PAJ 9*, 720–723.

41. Ibid:

42. Kendall to unknown, April 4, 1839, *AKMP*.

43. Cole, *A Jackson Man*, 62; 129; 146. For his part, Blair had a different recollection of the events Kendall described. He felt that he did not owe Kendall any compensation. Kendall to Jackson, December 3, 1831, in *PAJ 9*, 722.

44. Kendall to Blair, November 20, 1830, *Blair Family Papers*, LOC. Charles G. Steffen, "Newspapers for Free: The Economies of Newspaper Circulation in the Early Republic," *Journal of the Early Republic* 23, no. 3 (Autumn 2003): 385–389.

45. Pettis to Jackson, March 15, 1830; and Jackson to Ingham, March 16, 1830, in *PAJ 8*, 130–131; Thomas Hart Benton to Finis Ewing, November 12 and 21, 1831, *Thomas Hart Benton Papers*, MHS; Ewing to Blair, April 16, 1832, *Blair-Rives Papers*, LOC.

46. Robert W. Lewes to Blair, August 7, 1832, *Blair-Rives Papers*, LOC.

47. Richard Hauton to Blair, March 31, 1831; Ammon Hicks to Blair, July 13, 1831; Tandy Collins to Blair, July 17, 1831, all in *Blair-Rives Papers*, LOC.

48. John Wells to Blair, May 29, 1832; John C. Rives to George Adams, June 27, 1833 (the person requesting delivery of the *Globe* planned to be in Dubuque but had to pick up the *Globe* at the post office in Galena, Illinois); John P. Sheldon to Blair, August 16, 1833, all in *Blair-Rives Papers*, LOC; John Donelson to Jackson, October 31, 1831, in *PAJ 9*, 650–651.

49. Brian Balogh, *A Government out of Sight: The Mystery of National*

Authority in Nineteenth-Century America (Cambridge: Cambridge University Press, 2009). One can make a compelling case that slaves and Indians were more likely than ordinary white males to experience the heavy hand of the state.

50. For state subsidies of banks and internal improvements, see Harry N. Scheiber, *Ohio Canal Era: A Case Study of Government and the Economy, 1820–1861* (Columbus: Ohio University Press, 1969); and Howard Bodenhorn, *State Banking in Early America: A New Economic History* (New York: Oxford University Press, 2003).

51. Jackson to Edward Livingston, July 21, 1832, in *PAJ 10*, 436.

52. Pierce Van Voorhis to Blair, November 29, 1833, *Blair-Rives Papers*, LOC. Blair would have to wait a few more years before obtaining congressional printing.

53. Cole, *A Jackson Man*, 194; Steffen, "Newspapers for Free," 381–419.

54. William L. D. Ewing to Jackson, September 24, 1831, in *PAJ 9*, 590.

55. James Gordon Bennett to Webb, March 15, 1833, *JWWP*; Rives to Blair, April 17, 1833; June 15, 1833; June 19, 1833; and June 27, 1833, all in *Blair-Lee Papers*, FLPU.

56. William E. Huntzicker, "The Popular Press, 1833–1865," in James D. Startt and William David Sloan, *The History of American Journalism, Number 3* (Westport, CT: Greenwood Press, 1999), 36; Smith, *The Press, Politics, and Patronage*, 153–155.

57. Kielbowicz, *News in the Mail*, 70–71; White, *Jacksonians*, 284–289.

58. Richard John, "Affairs of Office: The Executive Departments, the Election of 1828, and the Making of the Democratic Party," in Meg Jacobs et al., *The Democratic Experiment: New Directions in Political History* (Princeton, NJ: Princeton University Press, 2003), 66–74; White, *Jacksonians*, 38–39.

Chapter 3. The Monster Strikes Back: Nicholas Biddle and the Public Relations Campaign to Recharter the Second Bank, 1828–1832

1. Biddle to Webster, December 2, 1828; Biddle to Potter, January 9, 1830, in *CNB*, 58–59, 95–96. Parts of this chapter have been published as Stephen Campbell, "Funding the Bank War: Nicholas Biddle and the Public Relations Campaign to Re-Charter the Second Bank of the United States, 1828–1832," *American Nineteenth Century History* 17, no. 3 (Fall 2016): 273–299.

2. For Biddle's desire for political neutrality, see Biddle to Harper, January 9, 1829; Biddle to McLean, January 10 and 11, 1829, in *CNB*, 67–71. McGrane incorrectly identified the name of the cashier at the Lexington branch BUS as "John" Harper. The correct first name was "James."

3. Biddle to Gales, March 2, 1831, in *CNB*, 125–126; William Ames, *A History of the National Intelligencer* (Chapel Hill: University of North Carolina Press, 1972), 172–225.

4. For a similar argument regarding the national reach of the branch offices of the First Bank of the United States, see Eric Lomazoff, "Turning (Into) 'The

Great Regulating Wheel,': The Conversion of the Bank of the United States, 1791–1811," *Studies in American Political Development* 26 (April 2012): 1–23.

5. Grundy to Jackson, May 22, 1829, in *PAJ* 7, 236.

6. For conflicts at the BUS branch offices, see Appleton to Biddle, February 10, 1829, *Appleton Family Papers*, Massachusetts Historical Society, Boston, Massachusetts. McLean to Biddle, January 5, 1829; Biddle to McLean, January 11, 1829; Dun to Biddle, August 14, 1829; Biddle to Dickins, September 16, 1829, all in *CNB*, 63–75; Jackson to Overton, June 8, 1829; Memorandum on Nicholas Biddle's letter, circa late-September 1829, in *PAJ* 7, 270–272, 459; Pope to Jackson, June 19 and August 6, 1831, in *PAJ* 9, 316–319, 467–471.

7. Memorandum, Between October 1829 and January 1830, in *CNB*, 93–94.

8. Ingham to Jackson, November 24 and 27, 1829; Berrien to Jackson, November 27, 1829; Jackson to Hamilton, December 19, 1829, in *PAJ* 7, 568–569, 578, 580, 642.

9. For the drafting and revision process of Jackson's first annual message, see *PAJ* 7, 587–629, especially "Draft by John Henry Eaton on the Bank of the United States," November 1829, 587–589. For the finalized version delivered to Congress, see *House Journal*, 21st Congress, 1st Session, 11–28.

10. S. Doc. No. 104, 21st Congress, 1st Session, Serial 193, 1–8. Evidence for Biddle's authorship of the report is presented in Thomas Payne Govan, *Nicholas Biddle, Nationalist and Public Banker, 1786–1844* (Chicago: University of Chicago Press, 1959), 125–127.

11. Biddle to Samuel Smith, April 22, 1830, *Biddle Letterbooks*, LOC.

12. *RD*, 21st Congress, 1st Session, House, Appendix, 104–133.

13. Ibid., 120; Jane Ellen Knodell, *The Second Bank of the United States: "Central" Banker in an Era of Nation-building, 1816–1836* (London: Routledge, 2017), 4.

14. For the year 1831, the bank paid $11,153.25 for printing orders, almost double the amount from the previous year, corresponding to an escalation in the Bank War. S. Doc. No. 17, 23rd Congress, 2nd Session, Serial Volume 267, 322–325.

15. "Report of a Committee of Directors of the Bank of the United States," December 3, 1833, *Manuscripts and Political Papers*, 39, Independence National Historical Park, Philadelphia (hereafter cited as INHP).

16. S. Doc. No. 17, 23rd Congress, 2nd Session, Serial Volume 267, 322–325; H. R. Rept. No. 460, 22nd Congress, 1st Session, Serial Volume 227, 292–293.

17. Hamilton to Jackson, January 4, 1830; Jackson to Hamilton, May 3 and June 3, 1830; Jackson to Lewis, June 28, 1830, all in *PAJ* 8, 12–16, 221, 342–344, 403.

18. Ingalls to Jackson, August 9, 1829, in *PAJ* 7, 357–363; David Henshaw, *Remarks upon the Bank of the United States: Being an Examination of the Report of the Committee of Ways and Means, Made to Congress, April, 1830. By a Merchant.* (Boston: True and Greene, 1831).

19. Tucker to Biddle, January 26 and April 8, 1831, *Biddle Papers*; S. Doc. No. 17, 23rd Congress, 2nd Session, Serial Volume 267, 324–325.

20. Gallatin to Biddle, February 17, 1831; Robinson to Biddle, February 19, 1831, *Biddle Papers*.

21. Burrows to Biddle, February 13 and 17, 1831, *Biddle Papers*; Swartwout to Jackson, April 19, 1831, in *PAJ* 9, 196–197. Although Burrows was working with Biddle to support the Bank's recharter effort in early 1831, Burrows reversed course several months later. He attempted to blackmail Biddle and began negotiating with President Jackson, to no avail. In early 1832 Burrows resumed his financial dealings with Biddle. James A. Morrison, "This Means (Bank) War! Corruption and Credible Commitments in the Collapse of the Second Bank of the United States," *Journal of the History of Economic Thought* 37, no. 2 (2015): 232–234.

22. Ingersoll to Biddle, February 17, 1831, *Biddle Papers*.

23. Norvell to Biddle, March 11, 1831, *Biddle Papers*.

24. Norvell's exchange with Biddle did not appear in Morrison's article or in Ralph C. H. Catterall's exhaustively researched *The Second Bank of the United States* (Chicago: University of Chicago Press, 1903), which is often cited by today's historians. Govan mentioned Norvell briefly but did not link him to the Jacksonian charges of bribery and corruption. Govan, *Nicholas Biddle*, 147–154. Biographical information on Ingersoll and Norvell can be obtained in *Biographical Directory of the United States Congress, 1774–present*, available at http://bioguide.congress.gov/biosearch/biosearch.asp, accessed July 27, 2015.

25. Unknown to Biddle, March 17, 1831, *Biddle Papers*. The unknown correspondent may have been James Robertson, the cashier at the BUS branch office in Richmond.

26. Ibid.

27. For an example of this viewpoint, see Biddle to James Hunter, May 4, 1831, in *CNB*, 126–127.

28. "Report of Directors of BUS," 39–41.

29. For the connection of psychological factors and financial panics, see Douglas W. Diamond and Philip H. Dybvig, "Bank Runs, Deposit Insurance, and Liquidity," *JPE* 91 (June 1983): 401–419; Jessica M. Lepler, *The Many Panics of 1837: People, Politics, and the Creation of a Transatlantic Financial Crisis* (Cambridge: Cambridge University Press, 2013), 94–122.

30. Norvell to Biddle, June 21, 1831, *Biddle Papers*; Jeffrey L. Pasley, "Minnows, Spies, and Aristocrats: The Social Crisis of Congress in the Age of Martin Van Buren," *Journal of the Early Republic* 33, no. 1 (Winter 2007): 599–653.

31. In 1828, there were 7,651 post offices. In April 1839, Kendall estimated that there were about 13,000 post offices. For canals, see George Rogers Taylor, *The Transportation Revolution 1815–1860* (New York: Reinhart & Company, 1951), 34, 79, and 133. For Post Office statistics, see *American State Papers*, 20th Congress, 2nd Session, No. 72, "Condition of the Post Office Department"; and Amos Kendall to unknown, April 4, 1839, *AKMP*. Paul Starr, *The*

Creation of the Media: Political Origins of Modern Communications (New York: Basic Books, 2004), 112–127.

32. Knodell, *The Second Bank of the United States*, 74.

33. Richard John, *Spreading the News: The American Postal System from Franklin to Morse* (Cambridge, MA: Harvard University Press, 1995) and *Network Nation: Inventing American Telecommunications* (Cambridge, MA: Harvard University Press, 2010).

34. Gary B. Nash, *The Unknown American Revolution: The Unruly Birth of Democracy and the Struggle to Create America* (New York: Penguin Books, 2005), 140–144.

35. Lynn Hudson Parsons, *The Birth of Modern Politics: Andrew Jackson, John Quincy Adams, and the Election of 1828* (New York: Oxford University Press, 2009), 185; Donald J. Ratcliffe, *The One-Party Presidential Contest: Adams, Jackson, and 1824's Five-Horse Race* (Lawrence: University Press of Kansas, 2015), 6.

36. Daniel Peart, "Looking beyond Parties and Elections: The Making of United States Tariff Policy during the Early 1820s," *Journal of the Early Republic* 33 no. 1 (Spring 2013): 87–108.

37. Decennial federal census records indicate that the U.S. population in 1790 was 3.9 million. In 1830 it was 12.8 million.

38. *RD*, House, Appendix, 22nd Congress, 1st Session, 33–46. The editor of the *Philadelphia Inquirer* was Jesper Harding, who would later receive numerous printing orders and loans from the BUS totaling nearly $40,000, most of which occurred after the bank veto. S. Doc. No. 17, 23rd Congress, 2nd Session, Serial Volume 267, 313; *CNB*, Appendix, 358.

39. Benton's nickname was "Old Bullion" because of his strong belief that only gold and silver constituted a respectable and safe currency for a republic founded on liberty and equality. Because the branch drafts could only be redeemed for specie in Philadelphia, Benton believed that they gave an advantage to merchants and speculators over laborers and farmers in the West. The bank's board, however, had concluded as early as 1820 that issuing the branch drafts saved valuable time for it would have been impracticable for the president and cashier of the Philadelphia branch to spend the entirety of their days signing every branch draft. The board also wanted to facilitate the collection of public revenue in the South and West, and to provide the regions with a sound currency. The BUS had also applied to Congress on numerous occasions throughout the 1820s for approval in issuing the drafts only to see congressmen who shared Benton's views stymie passage. Furthermore, the Treasury Department, attorney general, and several courts in the 1820s had examined the legality of the branch drafts and concluded that they did not violate the bank's charter. H. R. Rept. No. 460, 55–57; Thomas Hart Benton, *Thirty Years' View Vol. 1* (New York: D. Appleton, 1856), 187–193, 221; S. Doc. No. 17, 6, 53, 65–72.

40. For example, see the *St. Louis Beacon*, October 20, 1831.

41. Gales to Richard Smith, February 12, 1831; Gales to Biddle, Febru-

ary 13, 1831; M. Robinson to Biddle, February 19, 1831, in *Biddle Papers*; Biddle to Gales, March 29, 1831, *Biddle Letterbooks*; Ames, *A History of the National Intelligencer*, 172–225.

42. Jeffrey L. Pasley, *"The Tyranny of Printers": Newspaper Politics in the Early American Republic* (Charlottesville: University of Virginia Press, 2001), 19–20.

43. *Niles' Weekly Register*, January 4, 1834; John C. Rives to Blair, June 19, 1833, *Blair-Lee Papers*, FLPU; Ames, *History of the National Intelligencer*, 152, 219–235.

44. There are few surviving letters and records from Gales and Seaton. Much of what historians know about them comes from the letters they wrote to Biddle, their newspaper columns, and what their contemporaries wrote about them. For the two editors' debts, including those owed to the BUS, see Gales to Biddle, August 8, 1832, *Simon Gratz Collection*, Case 8, Box 10, Gales Folder, Historical Society of Pennsylvania, Philadelphia (hereafter, HSP); Ames, *History of the National Intelligencer*, 152–153, 214, 219–235.

45. S. Doc. No. 17, 319; Ames, *History of the National Intelligencer*, 153.

46. *Frankfort Argus*, March 3, 1830.

47. William H. Lyon, *The Pioneer Editor in Missouri 1808–1860* (Columbia: University of Missouri Press, 1965), 110–111; Ames stated several times in his book that Gales and Seaton were poor businessmen. Ames, *History of the National Intelligencer*, 152, 219–235. Calculations performed by author.

48. For examples of Gales and Seaton printing political documents, letters, and speeches free of cost, see Gales and Seaton to Clay, October 12, 1832, in *PHC 8*, 582; William J. Graves to Gales and Seaton, May 25, 1838, *William J. Graves Papers*, FHS; Ames, *History of the National Intelligencer*, 153.

49. Nicholas's brother Thomas, of Missouri, was not the same person as Nicholas's cousin of the same name. The latter was a Philadelphian who founded the brokerage firm Thomas Biddle & Company.

50. Because Thomas Biddle was nearsighted, he insisted on firing pistols at a distance of five feet, ignoring the admonitions of friends who urged a lengthier distance. *St. Louis Beacon*, September 1 and 22, 1831; *Hartford Times*, April 19, 1877; John Fletcher Darby, *Personal Recollections of many prominent people whom I have known, and of events—especially those relating to the history of St. Louis—during the first half of the present century* (St. Louis: G. I. Jones, 1880), 194; *Journal of the House of Representatives of the State of Missouri at the First Session of the Sixth General Assembly* (Bowling-Green, MO: Office of the Salt River Journal, 1831); John Mullanphy to Nicholas Biddle, August 29, 1831, *Biddle Family Papers, Autograph Letters*, LOC.

51. *St. Louis Times*, reprinted in the *St. Louis Beacon*, September 8, 1831; Nicholas B. Wainwright, "The Life and Death of Major Thomas Biddle," *Pennsylvania Magazine of History and Biography* 104, no. 3 (July 1980): 326–344; Walter Barlow Stevens, *St. Louis: The Fourth City 1764–1911 Volume I* (St. Louis: S. J. Clarke Publishing, 1909), 222–228; Edward Dobyns letter, circa 1866, *Duels Collection*, MHS.

52. Dobyns letter, *Duels Collection*, MHS.

53. C. R. Barns, *The Commonwealth of Missouri* (St. Louis, 1877), 489, quoted in Wainwright, "Life and Death of Major Biddle," 337; *The Memoirs of David Meriwether*, FHS; *Hartford Times*, April 19, 1877.

54. Wainwright, "Life and Death of Major Biddle," 338; Darby, *Personal Recollections*, 189–194.

55. Dobyns letter, *Duels Collection*, MHS; Darby, *Personal Recollections*, 189–194; Wainwright, "Life and Death of Major Biddle," 340.

56. Linn to Dunklin, September 13, 1831, *Daniel Dunklin Collection*, WHMC; *St. Louis Beacon*, September 1, 1831; *St. Louis Times*, reprinted in the *St. Louis Beacon*, September 8, 1831; Stevens, *St. Louis, The Fourth City*, 222–228. For southern honor, see Bertram Wyatt-Brown, *Southern Honor: Ethics and Behavior in the Old South* (New York: Oxford University Press, 1982); and Kenneth Greenberg, *Honor and Slavery: Lies; Duels; Baseball; Gambling Etc. in the Old South* (Princeton, NJ: Princeton University Press, 1996).

57. For the connection between violent rhetoric and violent action, see Robert E. Shalhope, *The Baltimore Bank Riot: Political Upheaval in Antebellum Maryland* (Champaign: University of Illinois Press, 2009), 2, 83.

58. Specialists of antebellum Missouri, dueling, and southern honor are familiar with the Biddle-Pettis duel but have made only a passing reference to the Bank War. Similarly, most accounts of the Bank War do not mention the duel at all, and the few ones that do have not offered any sustained analysis. James Earl Moss, "William Henry Ashley: A Jackson Man with Feet of Clay," *Missouri Historical Review* 61, no. 1 (January 1966): 1–20; Elihu H. Shephard, *The Early History of St. Louis and Missouri: From Its First Exploration by White Men in 1673 to 1843* (St. Louis: Southwestern Book and Publishing Company, 1870), 98–101; Wainwright's 1980 article might be an exception to this characterization, but the author focused more on Thomas Biddle's personal life rather than the larger bank question.

59. Mullanphy to Biddle, August 29, 1831, *Biddle Family Papers, Autograph Letters*, LOC.

60. Dobyns letter, *Duels Collection*, MHS. Though historians can note that Dobyns may have been correct in characterizing what many Missourians believed at the time, internal correspondence among the bank's officers suggests that far from wanting to control the politics of Missouri, bank officers were reluctant to establish a branch in St. Louis for fear that it would not be profitable. Moreover, the branch only operated for roughly three years. Unknown to Thomas Cadwalader, March 17, 1827, *Thomas Cadwalader Papers*, Box 98, HSP.

61. *Niles' Weekly Register*, September 10 and October 8, 1831.

62. Ibid.; *Annals of Congress*, House, 14th Congress, 1st Session, Appendix, 1812–1825; *House Journal*, 21st Congress, 1st Session, 11–28.

63. *House Journal*, 22nd Congress, 1st Session, 9–21; *RD*, 22nd Congress, 1st Session, Appendix, 25–33.

64. Jackson to John Randolph, December 22, 1831, in *PAJ* 9, 782–783.

65. The evidence presented here challenges the interpretations of Perkins and Morrison, who contended that compromise between Biddle and Jackson was possible at several points during the Bank War, especially in 1831. For Jackson's consistent opposition to the BUS, see Jackson to Van Buren, December 6, 1831; Jackson to Hamilton, December 12, 1831; Randolph to Jackson, December 19, 1831, in *PAJ* 9, 731–733, 768–769, 780–782; Cadwalader to Biddle, December 26, 1831, in *CNB*, 160–161.

66. Shippen to Biddle, December 6, 1831; Mercer to Biddle, December 12, 1831; Smith to Biddle, December 17, 1831; Webster to Biddle, December 18, 1831; McLane to Biddle, January 5, 1832, in *CNB*, 88–91, 136–138, 140–146, 154–161, 165–168; Clay to Biddle, September 11, 1830, and December 15, 1831; and Biddle to Clay, December 22, 1831, in *PHC* 8, 263–264, 432–433, 435. Clay's letter to Biddle on December 15 marked a reversal from his previous recommendation to Biddle on September 11, 1830, where he predicted that an early application would play into the hands of the Jackson Party.

67. To make the claim that Cadwalader and the bank's stockholders were more important in Biddle's thinking than Clay and Webster, I had to consult a large number of letters, paying close attention to chronology. In December 1830 John Norvell wrote to Biddle, in reference to an early push for recharter, "In any event, it appears to me to be the interest of the stockholders and officers to bring the matter at once to issue." McGrane misspelled Norvell's last name as "Norvall." Norv[e]ll to Biddle, December 16, 1830; Cadwalader to Biddle, December 20, 21, 22, 23, and 25, 1831; Biddle to Cadwalader, December 24, 1831; Biddle to Smith, January 4, 1832, in *CNB*, 120, 146–158, 161–165; Biddle to Cadwalader, December 29, 1831, in *Biddle Papers*.

68. Historians who have emphasized Clay's role in Biddle's decision to apply for an early recharter include Robert Remini, *Henry Clay: Statesman for the Union* (New York: W. W. Norton, 1991), 379; Sean Wilentz, *The Rise of American Democracy: From Jefferson to Lincoln* (New York: W. W. Norton, 2005), 367–368; and Edward E. Baptist, *The Other Half Has Never Been Told: Slavery and the Making of American Capitalism* (New York: Basic Books, 2014), 250. For the view that Jackson and Biddle could have compromised, see Remini, *Andrew Jackson and the Bank War*, 43; Edwin J. Perkins, "Lost Opportunities for Compromise in the Bank War: A Reassessment of Jackson's Veto Message," *Business History Review* 61, no. 4 (Winter 1987): 531–551; Morrison, "This Means (Bank) War!" 221–245.

69. Anthony Imbert, "Set to between Old Hickory and Bully Nick," *lithograph* (New York: 1834), Library of Congress, American cartoon print filing series, available at: https://www.loc.gov/item/2008661767/ accessed June 12, 2017. According to one legislative record, 3,552 white males over the age of twenty lived in St. Louis County at the time. If we assume the low estimate of 1,000 people attending was accurate, this was a fairly high turnout. *Journal of the House of Representatives of the State of Missouri.*

Chapter 4. Monster News! Veto and Reelection

1. The BUS issued a total of 350,000 shares at about $100 per share. The U.S. Treasury owned 70,000 shares and foreign stockholders owned 83,045 shares, leaving almost 200,000 shares for domestic ownership. On January 23, 1832, McLane, with Biddle's cooperation, gave to the Senate a list of all of the bank's foreign stockholders and the number of shares that each of them had purchased from the Philadelphia and New York branch offices. The largest foreign owner, Baring Brothers, owned 7,915 shares, or almost 10 percent of all shares owned by foreigners. S. Doc. No. 31, 22nd Congress, 1st Session, Serial Volume 212, 3–13. Calculations performed by author.

2. S. Doc. No. 37, 22nd Congress, 1st Session, Serial Volume 212, 1–4.

3. Dallas to Gilpin, January 25 and February 10, 1832, *George M. Dallas Papers*, HSP.

4. "Memorial of the President and Directors of the Bank of the United States on Behalf of the Stockholders Praying for a Renewal of the Charter," January 5, 1832, *Manuscripts and Political Papers*, CAT #1755, INHP; *RD*, Senate, 22nd Congress, 1st Session, 53–55.

5. H. R. Rept. No. 460, 22nd Congress, 1st Session, Serial Volume 227, 315; Ingham to Biddle, December 4, 1829, *Letters to Banks*, NARA II.

6. H. R. Rept. No. 460, 513–525; H. R. Rept. No. 121, 22nd Congress, 2nd session, Serial Volume 236, 2.

7. For an example, see Isaac Lawrence's reply to Biddle on January 30. In addition, George Poe Jr., an agent of the Mobile branch BUS, urged John L. Tindall, president of the Bank of the State of Alabama, to help pass pro-BUS resolutions intended for Congress. Tindall responded to Poe twelve days later by getting the Bank of the State of Alabama to pass the requested resolutions. Lawrence to Biddle, January 30, 1832; Poe to Tindall, February 11, 1832; Tindall to Poe, February 23, 1832, *Biddle Papers*, LOC.

8. Kentucky Memorial, to the Congress of the United States, January 28, 1832, *Biddle Papers*; Jean Alexander Wilburn, *Biddle's Bank: The Crucial Years* (New York: Columbia University Press 1967), 55.

9. For examples of memorials presented to the Senate, see *Senate Journal*, 22nd Congress, 1st Session, 91. Typically a senator or representative from a given state would present a memorial (or petition) in Congress. Many memorials did not list the specific names of those who signed them but indicated that they came from a certain state bank or perhaps a group of citizens from a given city or county. All memorials sent to Congress concerning the recharter of the BUS occurred after the bank's board meetings on December 16, 1831, and January 5, 1832. *A Century of Lawmaking for a New Nation*, available at http://memory.loc.gov/ammem/hlawquery.html, accessed July 23, 2015; Wilburn, *Biddle's Bank*, 31–55; Robert Remini, *Andrew Jackson and the Bank War* (New York: W. W. Norton, 1967), 41.

10. Unknown to Blair, February 4, 1832, *Blair-Lee Papers*, FLPU. Educated nineteenth-century Americans would have likely been familiar with the charac-

ters of Shylock and Molock from Shakespeare's *The Merchant of Venice*. On that note, there is a strong possibility that this antibanking editorial contained anti-Semitic themes.

11. For the perspective that Benton and Clayton were intentionally trying to delay the passage of the bank bills to exact a political benefit, see O'Fallon to Biddle, March 3, 1832, *Biddle Papers*.

12. *RD*, House, 22nd Congress, 1st Session, 2092–2163.

13. H. R. Rept. No. 460, 109, 553–557.

14. The bank's stockholders elected the board of directors. There were 4,553 votes allocated to the bank's stockholders for electing board members, and Biddle controlled 1,684, or over 30 percent, of them. The board, in turn, appointed members of the institution's various committees, including the exchange committee that typically handled loan applications. Ibid., 284.

15. Ibid., 190.

16. Cadwalader to Biddle, March 14, 1832, *Cadwalader Family Papers*, Box 98, HSP. By March 1833 Gales and Seaton owed $80,338 to the BUS from notes discounted on personal security, split between the Philadelphia and Washington branches. By September 1834 their debts had been reduced to $57,107. S. Doc. No. 17, 23rd Congress, 2nd Session, Serial Volume 267, 317.

17. H. R. Rept. No. 460, 369–410.

18. Ibid., 379.

19. A financial statement included in Clayton's report showed that the bank divided its deposits into three columns: "Deposites on account of Treasurer U.S."; "Deposites of account of public officers"; and "Individuals." The total amount in the second of these three columns is highest at the Washington branch BUS, which would make sense if one considers that this branch was facilitating part of the bank's fiscal responsibilities by paying public officials, including members of Congress. S. Doc. No. 17, 320–321; James A. Morrison, "This Means (Bank) War! Corruption and Credible Commitments in the Collapse of the Second Bank of the United States," *Journal of the History of Economic Thought* 37, no. 2 (2015): 238–239; H. R. Rept. No. 460, 270, 379, 424, 532, 568–571.

20. H. R. Rept. No. 460, 297–327, 369–410.

21. James L. Crouthamel, *James Watson Webb: A Biography* (Middletown, CT: Wesleyan University Press, 1969), 31; *New York Courier and Enquirer*, August 23, 1832, quoted in *Niles' Weekly Register*, September 1, 1832; Hoskin to Webb, July 1, 1832; Lispenard Stewart, "In the Matter of Proving the Last Will and Testament of the Late Robert Stewart, Esq.," January 24, 1844, 12–13, in *JWWP*.

22. Lispenard Stewart, "Last Will and Testament of Robert Stewart," in *JWWP*; Samuel B. Barrell to Webb, February 6, 1832; Hoskin to Webb, July 1, 1832; "Indenture," James Watson Webb to Daniel E. Tylee and Stephen Webb, December 8, 1832, in *JWWP*; Crouthamel, *James Watson Webb*, 31, 69, 80–81; *National Intelligencer*, May 10, 1832; *New York Courier and Enquirer*, June

6, 1832, and August 23, 1832, quoted in *Niles' Weekly Register*, September 1, 1832. From August 9, 1831, to February 10, 1832, Webb and Noah had several notes discounted at the BUS for a total of $71,575. S. Doc. No. 17, 40.

23. *Congressional Globe*, 25th Congress, 2nd Session, House, "Report of the Dueling Committee," 326–333; and Jeffrey L. Pasley, "Minnows, Spies, and Aristocrats: The Social Crisis of Congress in the Age of Martin Van Buren," *Journal of the Early Republic* 27, no. 4 (Winter 2007): 599–653.

24. *Congressional Globe*, "Report of the Dueling Committee," 326–333.

25. Ibid., 330.

26. Ibid.; Steven M. Stowe, *Intimacy and Power in the Old South: Ritual in the Lives of the Planters* (Baltimore: Johns Hopkins University Press, 2007), 45; Pasley, "Minnows, Spies, and Aristocrats," 644.

27. Pasley, "Minnows, Spies, and Aristocrats," 649; Stowe, *Intimacy and Power in the Old South*, 264.

28. Stowe, *Intimacy and Power in the Old South*, 39.

29. For the view that newspapers could transform violent words into violent actions, see Robert Shalhope in *The Baltimore Bank Riot: Political Upheaval in Antebellum Maryland* (Champaign: University of Illinois Press, 2009), 33.

30. H. R. Rept. No. 460, 314.

31. Ibid., 1–29.

32. Jackson to Coffee, February 19, 1832, in *PAJ 10*, 96–98.

33. Ibid., 297–327; *CNB*, 357–359. For the impact of Clayton's report on Jackson's thinking, see Hamilton to Jackson, May 7, 1832, in *PAJ 10*, 266–267.

34. Jackson to Allan Ditchfield Campbell, May 13, 1832, in *PAJ 10*, 270. For similar themes and sentiments, see Jackson to Hamilton, March 28, 1832, in ibid., 193–194.

35. Richard M. Clokey, *William H. Ashley: Enterprise and Politics in the Trans-Mississippi West* (Norman: University of Oklahoma Press, 1980), 217; Rudolph Eugene Forderhase, "Jacksonianism in Missouri, From Predilection to Party, 1820–1836" (PhD diss., University of Missouri, 1968), 365; James Gowen to Jackson, August 13, 1830, in *PAJ 8*, 478; Watmough to Sergeant, May 1, 1832, *Biddle Papers*; James L. Crouthamel, "Three Philadelphians in the Bank War: A Neglected Chapter in American Lobbying," *Pennsylvania History: A Journal of Mid-Atlantic Studies* 27, no. 4 (October 1960): 361–378.

36. *House Journal*, 22nd Congress, 1st Session, 1066–1075; *Senate Journal*, 22nd Congress, 1st Session, 345–346.

37. William Barry to Susan Barry, July 4, 1832, in William T. Barry, "Letters of William T. Barry," *William and Mary Quarterly* 14, no. 4 (April 1906): 233.

38. *Senate Journal*, 22nd Congress, 1st Session, 451–453.

39. Ibid., 433–446. Evidence for Kendall's influence on Jackson's veto message can be found in *PAJ 10*, 379–409.

40. Leonard White, *The Jacksonians: A Study in Administrative History 1829–1861* (New York: Macmillan, 1954), 22–23; Robert Remini, *Andrew*

Jackson and the Course of American Freedom, 1822–1832, Volume II (New York: Harper and Row, 1981), 369–370.

41. Dallas to Gilpin, July 10, 1832, *George M. Dallas Papers*, HSP.

42. This viewpoint is evident in Charles Sellers, "Who Were the Southern Whigs?" *American Historical Review* 59, no. 2 (January 1954): 335–346; J. Mills Thornton III, *Politics and Power in a Slave Society: Alabama, 1800–1860* (Baton Rouge: Louisiana State University Press, 1978), 31–58, 137; and William J. Cooper Jr., *Liberty and Slavery: Southern Politics to 1860* (Columbia: University of South Carolina Press, 1983), 171.

43. Jane Knodell, "Rethinking the Jacksonian Economy: The Impact of the 1832 Bank Veto on Commercial Banking," *Journal of Economic History* 66, no. 3 (September 2006): 541–574.

44. For this view, see Arthur M. Schlesinger Jr., *The Age of Jackson* (Boston: Little, Brown, 1945), 78; Bray Hammond, *Banks and Politics in America from the Revolution to the Civil War* (Princeton, NJ: Princeton University Press, 1957), 359–361; Remini, *Andrew Jackson and the Bank War*, 39; and Edward E. Baptist, *The Half Has Never Been Told: Slavery and the Making of American Capitalism* (New York: Basic Books, 2014), 249. For an opposing view, see Wilburn, *Biddle's Bank*, 31–45.

45. *Frankfort Commonwealth*, April 29, 1834; Biddle to Lenox, April 22, 1828, *Biddle Letterbooks*, LOC; Biddle to Cadwalader, December 29, 1831; Cadwalader to Isaac Lawrence, June 29, 1832, *Biddle Papers*; H. R. Rept. No. 121, 85–86.

46. John Snead, John O'Fallon, and C. W. Lawrence were just a few of many examples of individuals who worked for both BUS branches and state banks at different stages in their careers. H. R. Rept. No. 121, 85–86; S. Doc. No. 104, 21st Congress, 1st Session, Serial Volume 193, 6.

47. The 1834 Senate report showed that in 1826, the BUS issued loans totaling $237,436 to members of Congress. In 1834 the figure was $238,586. In 1832 the bank loaned $478,069, which would seem to indicate a major increase. Perhaps because this figure would look suspicious in the year of Jackson's veto, the bank offered an explanation marked by asterisks next to the Philadelphia and Washington branches, which stated: "In this sum is included a stock loan of one hundred thousand dollars" and "a large portion of this debt, as in other offices, is created by the discount of domestic bills of exchange. At this and several of the branches every renewal of a note discounted is included—including $50,000 for P.O. acceptances." The Senate report did not list the dates or terms of the loans. S. Doc. No. 17, 320–321. It is worth stressing that adding up the dollar amounts of various bank loans over time may not give us the best indicator of the bank's influence. This is because loans were either repaid, renewed, or went into default. Thus, bank *loans* are a different type of transaction than bank *expenditures*.

48. S. Doc. No. 17, 38–39.

49. Ibid., 44–45.

50. Ibid.

51. Ibid., 46–47.

52. My estimate for the bank's expenditures on printing orders is based primarily on two sources: "Report of Directors of BUS," 40, stated that between December 1829 and December 1833 the bank spent $58,000 to defend itself. This sum included printing and circulating reports to Congress, speeches in Congress, and other miscellaneous publications. Most of this period occurred before the veto. The sums listed in this source are roughly in line with the figures presented in a Senate report published in December 1834, which gave a figure of $94,708.25 spent on printing orders from January 1829 to September 1834. If we subtract the period from the July 1832 veto to September 1834, we arrive at similar figures. S. Doc. No. 17, 320. The estimate for the bank's loans to newspaper editors and members of Congress is based on figures published in several sources: H. R. Rept. No. 460, 108–110 lists loans of several thousand dollars to Thomas Ritchie and Gales and Seaton. The two tables presented on pages 320–321 of S. Doc. No. 17 do not indicate if the loans issued to members of Congress were intended to influence voting on the BUS. There is also Biddle's own estimate, which appears in CNB, 357–359. Readers might be curious about the terms of the loans that Biddle extended to editors and congressmen, including principal, interest, duration, security, renewal, etc. While one can gather bits and pieces of this information after extensive research, the available documentary evidence, unfortunately, makes it difficult, if not impossible, to answer all of these questions. We may know the principal of a loan issued to Duff Green, for example, but may not know the interest rate, duration, security provided, or whether the loan was renewed, fell due, or defaulted.

53. Robert V. Remini stated, "Although it can not be determined precisely the exact amount of money the Bank contributed to the campaign, it is likely that something approximating $100,000 was spent by the institution to defeat Andrew Jackson." Remini's estimate only concerned the election of 1832 and not the months between January 1830 and July 1832, the key months of Biddle's lobby. Thomas Payne Govan wrote, "During 1831 and 1832 the Bank had spent a total of eighty thousand dollars for the preparation, printing, and circulation of documents, of which twenty thousand dollars had been paid on the orders of Biddle 'without any account of the manner in which, or the persons to whom, they were disbursed.'" While it is possible that Govan's research, presented elsewhere in his book, led him to this figure, the only citation he presented for this particular quote was Henry Dilworth Gilpin's diary. Govan's estimates for BUS expenditures on printing and circulation are roughly in line with my own slightly higher figure. However, Govan, unabashedly sympathetic to Biddle, did not estimate the loans the loans to members of Congress and editors. Ralph C. H. Catterall noted that Biddle "published floods of articles at the bank's expense," that the unusual loans to congressmen left the bank "open to censure," and that Biddle's spending of $30,000 for unspecified purposes was

"totally indefensible." Yet Catterall did not consider these actions to be full-proof evidence of corruption, nor did he not offer a systematic estimate of Biddle's loans and expenditures. Remini, *Andrew Jackson and the Bank War*, 99; Govan, *Nicholas Biddle, Nationalist and Public Banker, 1786–1844* (Chicago: University of Chicago Press, 1959), 241; Catterall, *The Second Bank of the United States* (Chicago: University of Chicago Press, 1903), 205, 243, 254–265.

54. A useful website for converting dollar amounts in the past to their equivalent in today's dollars is Louis Johnston and Samuel H. Williamson, "Seven Ways to Compute the Relative Value of a U.S. Dollar Amount—1774 to Present," *MeasuringWorth*, 2013, available at http://www.measuringworth.com/us compare/, accessed December 19, 2014. One can also use this website to obtain GDP numbers for past years (hence, the figure of $1 billion).

55. The U.S. Treasury Department's estimate for the 1832 federal budget of $34,611,466.03 appeared in House Doc. No. 3, 22nd Congress, 2nd Session, Serial Volume 233, 1–4. The bank's specie holdings varied based on multiple factors, including the country's balance of payments, payments on the national debt, and the time of year. To account for seasonal variability, it makes sense to obtain balance sheets from the same month over several years. Balance sheets, which capture a financial institution's assets and liabilities at any given moment, are rare for the BUS. But thankfully, there are at least three available for the date of August 1, published in the *Aurora and Pennsylvania Gazette*, September 3, 1828; *Niles' Weekly Register*, September 10, 1831; and the *New York Spectator*, March 24, 1834. To arrive at the average of $9 million in specie and $16 million in deposits over this six-year period, I simply added up all of the totals and divided by three.

56. Jackson to Robert Johnston Chester, July 20, 1832, in *PAJ 10*, 434.

57. Jackson to Kendall, July 23, 1832; Henry Leavitt Ellsworth to Jackson, July 21, 1832, in *PAJ 10, 437, 439.*

58. Henry Toland to Jackson, July 16, 1832, in *PAJ 10*, 421–422.

59. *Missouri Republican*, July 24 and 31, 1832; *St. Louis Beacon*, August 2, 1832; *Missouri Intelligencer*, August 4, 1832; *Globe*, August 9, 1832.

60. The Cincinnati Commercial Agency was distinct from the BUS branch in the same city. Herman Cope to Biddle, July 26, 1832, *United States Bank Papers*, HSP.

61. In 1834 the bank reported that it owned an estimated $102,988.93 in "other real estate" in Louisville. This sum did not include the property it needed to build branch offices. S. Doc. No. 17, 188. See also Clay to Biddle, November 28, 1829, in *PHC 8*, 129.

62. A House report published in March 1833 reprinted numerous letters between the cashiers, directors, and presidents of the Philadelphia and Lexington branches from the fall of 1832. These letters identified the key actors, editors, and newspapers involved in the attempted bank run. H. R. Rept. No. 121, 127–129.

63. Ibid., 134.

64. Ibid., 130–131, 140.

65. Ibid., 135–139.

66. For conflicts at the BUS branch offices in the lead-up to the 1828 election, see Chapter 3.

67. H. R. Rept. No. 121, 131–132.

68. S. Doc. No. 17, 321–322.

69. Remini, *Andrew Jackson and the Course of American Freedom*, 374.

70. *Globe*, September 17, 1832.

71. *Christian Register*, October 1, 1831.

72. *National Intelligencer*, August 29, 1832.

73. The U.S. Constitution's Three-Fifths Clause, which inflated the number of House members allotted to the slave-owning states and therefore boosted the electoral votes given to the candidate who could win the most southern states, redounded to Jackson's benefit. This imbalance was reflected in the fact that Jackson won 76.6 percent of the votes in the Electoral College but 54.2 percent of the popular vote. Third-party candidates William Wirt and John Floyd garnered a combined 6.3 percent of the electoral vote and 7.8 percent of the popular vote. Some states continued the older practice of determining Electoral College votes through the state legislature rather than the popular will.

74. *Annals of Congress*, House, 14th Congress, 1st Session, Appendix, 1818.

75. Foreigners owned 62 percent of stock in the First Bank of the United States in 1803, 40 percent of which came from Great Britain. By 1832 foreigners owned about one-quarter of the Second Bank's stock. See Edwin J. Perkins, *Financing Anglo-American Trade: The House of Brown, 1800–1880* (Cambridge, MA: Harvard University Press, 1975), 88–113.

76. Unlike today in the United States, where federal, state, and local elections occur on the same ballot and the same today in November, in the antebellum era, federal, state, and local elections could all be held on different days of the year. Even Jackson's reelection in 1832 was not so much one national election but more like two dozen separate state elections, only some of which occurred on the same day.

77. Crabb to Jackson, November 6, 1832, in *PAJ 10*, 554–557.

78. Matthew A. Crenson, *The Federal Machine: Beginnings of Bureaucracy in Jacksonian America* (Baltimore: Johns Hopkins University Press, 1975), 23, 50–51; Donald J. Ratcliffe, *The One-Party Presidential Contest: Adams, Jackson, and 1824's Five-Horse Race* (Lawrence: University Press of Kansas, 2015), 273.

79. Ratcliffe has argued that the election of 1824 created a major electoral realignment and party divisions that lasted well into the 1830s and 1840s. See his *The Politics of Long Division: The Birth of the Second Party System in Ohio, 1818–1828* (Columbus: Ohio State University Press, 2000), 14, 174, 314–318; and *The One-Party Presidential Contest*, 6, 124–125, 133. See also "1832 Presidential Election," Gerhard Peters and John T. Woolley, *The American Presidency Project*, 1999–2016, available at http://www.presidency.ucsb

.edu/showelection.php?year=1832, accessed August 8, 2016. Percentage calculations performed by author. Some experts have warned us not to equate support for Jackson with opposition to the bank. Indeed, a group of politicians in the Border South, identified pejoratively by their opponents as "counterfeit Jacksonians" for their pro-BUS stances, suggests that one could run successfully for office under the "Jacksonian" banner while still supporting a federal program of internal improvements, moderately high tariffs, and a national bank. Throughout the 1830s the presence of pro-BUS Jacksonians gradually disappeared as the party firmed up its political ideology. John Miller to Daniel Dunklin, March 8, 1832, and September 16, 1832, *Daniel Dunklin Collection*, WHMC; Clokey, *William H. Ashley*, 181–279.

80. Ratcliffe, *The Politics of Long Division*, 11, and *The One-Party Presidential Contest*, 123, 260–261.

81. Lynn Hudson Parsons, *The Birth of Modern Politics: Andrew Jackson, John Quincy Adams, and the Election of 1828* (New York: Oxford University Press, 2009), x, 133–139, 185.

82. The view that emphasizes Jacksonians' superior organizational skills is presented in Remini, *Andrew Jackson and the Course of American Freedom*, 374–384. This view is complicated and challenged in Ratcliffe, *The Politics of Long Division*, 169–200; and "Antimasonry and Partisanship in Greater New England, 1826–1836," *Journal of the Early Republic* 15, no. 2 (Summer 1995): 236. For the view that Gales and Seaton were a bit more dispassionate in their editorial style compared to their opponents, see *Niles' Weekly Register*, January 4, 1834; Parsons, *The Birth of Modern Politics*, 137; and William Ames, *A History of the National Intelligencer* (Chapel Hill: University of North Carolina Press, 1972), 187.

83. Remini, *Andrew Jackson and the Bank War*, 106.

84. Ratcliffe, *The Politics of Long Division*, 313–317, and *The One-Party Presidential Contest*, 265.

Chapter 5. Two Sides of the Same Coin: The Panic of 1833–1834 and the Loss of Public Support

1. Draft by Amos Kendall on the Bank of the United States, December 1832; Draft by Andrew Jackson on the Bank of the United States, December 1832, in *PAJ 10*, 649–652.

2. Jackson to Polk, December 16, 1832, in *PAJ 10*, 729.

3. House Document No. 8, 22nd Congress, 2nd Session, Serial Volume 233, 3; H. R. Rept. No. 121, 22nd Congress, 2nd Session, Serial Volume 236, 3–5; Toland to Jackson, July 16, 1832; and Jackson to Polk, December 16, 1832, in *PAJ 10*, 421–422, 730.

4. H. R. Rept. No. 460, 22nd Congress, 1st Session, Serial Volume 227, 273; S. Doc. No. 17, 23rd Congress, 2nd Session, Serial Volume 267, 129.

5. Jessica Lepler, *The Many Panics of 1837: People, Politics, and the Creation of a Transatlantic Financial Crisis* (Cambridge: Cambridge University Press,

2013), 23; Howard Bodenhorn, *State Banking in Early America: A New Economic History* (New York: Oxford University Press, 2003), 291.

6. H. R. Rept. No. 121, 54–55, 71.

7. S. Doc. No. 17, 8–10, 23–24, 54; Peter Austin, *Baring Brothers and the Birth of Modern Finance* (London: Pickering and Chatto, 2007), 18, 45–47.

8. Biddle to Charles A. Wickliffe, December 6, 1832, *Biddle Papers*, LOC.

9. Jane Knodell, *The Second Bank of the United States: "Central" Banker in an Era of Nation-building, 1816–1836* (London: Routledge, 2017), 106–109.

10. H. R. Rept. No. 121, 12; S. Doc. No. 17, 97–98.

11. H. R. Rept. No. 121, 37–42.

12. Anti-BUS Jacksonians like Taney argued that by placing so much power in the exchange committee, the bank's board was exceeding the power granted to it by the bank's 1816 charter. The bank's private directors responded that all of the bank's transactions in foreign and domestic exchange were recorded in an account book that was placed on a desk that was available to all of the bank's directors, including the public directors. S. Doc. No. 17, 2–6, 52.

13. H. R. Rept. No. 121, 17–31; 50–65; 91; S. Doc. No. 17, 11.

14. H. R. Rept. No. 121, 64, 91.

15. *Niles' Weekly Register*, September 28, 1833.

16. "Report of a Committee of Directors of the Bank of the United States," December 3, 1833, *Manuscripts and Political Papers*, 34–35, INHP.

17. S. Doc. No. 17, 18; Jackson to Van Buren, November 25, 1832, in *PAJ* 10, 613–614; Sean Wilentz, *The Rise of American Democracy: From Jefferson to Lincoln* (New York: W. W. Norton, 2005), 395; Davis R. Dewey, *The Second United States Bank* (Washington, DC: Government Printing Office, National Monetary Commission, 1910), 282. Jackson appointed Taney while Congress was out of session. The Senate never confirmed Taney's appointment, voting him down 28 to 18. *Globe*, June 28, 1834. See Chapter 6 for a discussion of the political orientation of the deposit banks.

18. H. R. Rept. No. 121, 29.

19. S. Doc. No. 17, 17–18.

20. Biddle to Rathbone, November 21, 1832; Biddle to Perkins, November 26, 1832, Biddle to Lenox, October 1, 1833, in *Biddle Papers*, LOC; *Globe*, November 30, 1833; Biddle to William Appleton, July 4, 1834, in *CNB*, 237–241.

21. S. Doc. No. 17, 73.

22. Ibid., 73, 96.

23. Ibid., 79.

24. Ibid., 79–85.

25. H. R. Rept. No. 121, 154–159; House Document 8, 29.

26. House Document 8, 30.

27. Ibid., 29–33.

28. Ibid., 31.

29. Ibid., 32.

30. S. Doc. No. 17, 94.

31. H. R. Rept. No. 121, 31.

32. Charles Sellers, *The Market Revolution: Jacksonian America, 1815–1846* (New York: Oxford University Press, 1991), 337; Jacob P. Meerman, "The Climax of the Bank War: Biddle's Contraction, 1833–34," *Journal of Political Economy* 71, no. 4 (August 1963): 378–388.

33. Richard H. Kilbourne Jr., *Slave Agriculture and Financial Markets in Antebellum America: The Bank of the United States, 1831–1852* (London: Pickering and Chatto, 2006), 48. To calculate the fall in commodity prices, I consulted Arthur Harrison Cole, *Wholesale Commodity Prices in the United States 1700–1861* (Cambridge, MA: Harvard University Press, 1938), 242–287.

34. Francis Granger to Thurlow Weed, January 13, 1834, *Thurlow Weed Papers*, Rush Rhees Library, University of Rochester, Rochester, New York; unknown to Webb, February 21, 1834, *JWWP*; *Niles' Weekly Register*, January 4, 1834; Robert E. Shalhope, *The Baltimore Bank Riot: Political Upheaval in Antebellum Maryland* (Champaign: University of Illinois Press, 2009), 13–44; Douglas W. Diamond and Philip H. Dybvig, "Bank Runs, Deposit Insurance, and Liquidity," *Journal of Political Economy* 91 (June 1983): 401–419.

35. J. Mordecai to Thomas Biddle, March 5, 1834, *Thomas Biddle Correspondence*, HSP; *National Intelligencer*, December 17, 1833; Isaac Franklin to Rice Ballard, March 10, 1834, *Rice Ballard Papers*, Southern Historical Collection, University of North Carolina, Chapel Hill (hereafter cited as SHC); *Richmond Enquirer*, quoted in *Niles' Weekly Register*, January 25, 1834; Calvin Schermerhorn, *The Business of Slavery and the Rise of American Capitalism, 1815–1860* (New Haven, CT: Yale University Press, 2015), 158–160.

36. Meerman, "Climax of the Bank War," 378–388; Douglass North, *The Economic Growth of the United States* (New York: W. W. Norton, 1961), 183 and 201; *RD*, 23rd Congress, 1st Session, Senate, 518; Cole, *Wholesale Commodity Prices*, 242–287. Calculations performed by author. Peter Temin, *The Jacksonian Economy* (New York: W. W. Norton, 1969), 113–147; *Niles' Weekly Register*, January 4 and May 3, 1834; *Globe*, February 18 and July 17, 1834.

37. Editors, in their descriptions of the panic, frequently cited a "pressure in the money market," a "scarcity of money," the "derangement of the currency," or a "want of confidence." The U.S. economy was still predominantly agricultural in the 1830s, meaning that most Americans' jobs were seasonal, volatile, and dependent on local conditions. The idea of having a fixed job or occupation of employment was by no means universal then, so calculating unemployment in some ways would be anachronistic. During Biddle's Panic, the unemployment rate may have reached 25 percent in some locales, but it was probably not close to this number nationwide. *New York Spectator*, March 24, 1834; Philip Kearney to H. D. Smith, January 19, 1834, *Philip Kearny Papers*, FHS. Also helpful are the works of financial theorists at the time, including Nathan Appleton, *An Examination of the Banking System of Massachusetts in Reference to the Renewal of Bank Charters* (Boston: Stimpson and Clapp, 1831), 8 and 17; and

Condy Raguet, *A Treatise on Currency and Banking* (Philadelphia: Crigg and Elliot, 1840), 105–116. For the role of confidence and psychology during the Panic of 1837, see Lepler, *The Many Panics of 1837*.

38. Michael F. Holt, *The Rise and Fall of the American Whig Party: Jacksonian Politics and the Onset of the Civil War* (New York: Oxford University Press, 1999), xiii; "Fac Simile of the Expunged Resolution of the U.S. Senate, as It Appears in the Record of the Senate, of March 28th, 1834," January 16, 1837, *Thomas Hart Benton Papers*, MHS.

39. Donald J. Ratcliffe, "The Crisis of Commercialization: National Political Alignments and the Market Revolution," in Melvin Stokes and Stephen Conway, eds., *The Market Revolution in America: Social, Political, and Religious Expressions, 1800–1880* (Charlottesville: University of Virginia Press, 1996), 185.

40. Ibid., 177–201; Donald J. Ratcliffe, "Antimasonry and Partisanship in Greater New England, 1826–1836," *Journal of the Early Republic* 15, no. 2 (Summer 1995): 199–239.

41. Biddle to William Appleton, January 27, 1834; Biddle to Watmough, February 8, 1834, in *CNB*, 219–221; *Globe*, November 30, 1833.

42. Biddle to Hamilton, February 1, 1834, in *Biddle Papers*, LOC; Biddle to Charles Hammond, March 11, 1834, in *CNB*, 225–226; S. Doc. No. 17, 100.

43. *Niles' Weekly Register*, July 26, 1834.

44. William Stickney, *Autobiography of Amos Kendall* (Boston: Lee and Shepard, 1872), 418; *Kentucky Gazette*, April 26, 1834. A Senate committee report issued in December 1834 was much more favorable to the bank; *RD*, 23rd Congress, 2nd Session, Senate, Appendix, 185–208.

45. Biddle to Chauncey, February 10, 1834, in *Manuscripts and Political Papers*, INHP.

46. For Biddle to have learned of Webster's tepid support was significant because the Massachusetts senator had spent years defending the BUS in Congress and even received a paid legal retainer for representing the bank in court. Webster to Biddle, December 21, 1833; Binney to Biddle, February 4, 1834, in *CNB*, 218–220.

47. George Edward Reed and W. W. Griest, eds., *Pennsylvania Archives Fourth Series: Volume VI, Papers of the Governors 1832–1845* (Harrisburg: State of Pennsylvania, 1901), 53–54.

48. *Globe*, March 3, 1834.

49. S. Doc. No. 17, 83–84.

50. R. Fisher to Biddle, July 7, 1834, in *CNB*, 241–242.

51. *New York American*, July 14, 1834, quoted in the *National Intelligencer*, July 17, 1832.

52. Ibid; Biddle to Rathbone, July 11, 1834, *Biddle Papers*; *Niles' Weekly Register*, July 26, 1834.

53. Webb to Biddle, March 18, 1834, in *CNB*, 227.

54. Tracy to Weed, July 26, 1834, *Weed Papers*.

55. Lay to Weed, July 16, 1834, *Weed Papers.*

56. *Globe*, September 11, 1834.

57. See the *Globe*, February 13, 14, 17, 18, 19, 20, 21, 22, 25, and March 3, 4, 1834. For examples of bank-related public meetings in Kentucky, see *Kentucky Gazette*, April 12 and 26, 1834; *Frankfort Commonwealth*, June 10 and 24, 1834.

58. *Globe*, February 14, 1834; *United States Telegraph*, February 15, 1834; *Cincinnati Gazette*, in the *Missouri Republican*, March 6, 1834.

59. Anonymous to Jackson, February 17, 1834, *Manuscripts and Political Papers*, CAT #7289, INHP.

60. Donald B. Cole, *The Presidency of Andrew Jackson* (Lawrence: University Press of Kansas, 1993), 221; H. W. Brands, *Andrew Jackson: His Life and Times* (New York: Doubleday, 2005), 504.

61. Jon Meacham, *American Lion: Andrew Jackson in the White House* (New York: Random House, 2008), 298–301; Richard C. Rohrs, "Partisan Politics and the Attempted Assassination of Andrew Jackson," *Journal of the Early Republic* 1, no. 2 (Summer 1981): 149–163.

62. *Workingman's Advocate*, May 3, 1834; *New Hampshire Statesman*, May 3, 1834.

63. Carl E. Prince, "The Great 'Riot Year': Jacksonian Democracy and Patterns of Violence in 1834," *Journal of the Early Republic* 5, no. 1 (Spring 1985): 1–19.

64. This type of election would be similar to primary elections in today's politics.

65. For the Moyamensing election riot, see the *Globe*, October 4, 8, and 20, 1834; *National Gazette and Literary Register*, October 6, 1834; *New York Spectator*, October 16, 1834; and *Niles' Weekly Register*, October 18, 1834. Many of these outlets republished reports from Philadelphia newspapers, which included the *Philadelphia Sentinel*, the *United States Gazette*, the *Philadelphia Gazette*, and the *Pennsylvanian*.

66. *Philadelphia Gazette*, in *Niles' Weekly Register*, October 18, 1834.

67. *Philadelphia Sentinel*, in *Niles' Weekly Register*, October 18, 1834; *American Sentinel*, in the *National Gazette and Literary Register*, October 6, 1834; Reed and Griest, *Pennsylvania Archives Fourth Series: Volume VI*, 185–186.

68. The *Globe*, October 4, 8, and 20, 1834; *National Gazette and Literary Register*, October 6, 1834; *New York Spectator*, October 16, 1834; *Niles' Weekly Register*, October 18, 1834; *Missouri Republican*, October 31, 1834; *Indiana Journal*, November 7, 1834; *Jeffersonian Republican*, November 8, 1834.

69. Brian Balogh, *A Government Out of Sight: The Mystery of National Authority in Nineteenth-Century America* (Cambridge: Cambridge University Press, 2009).

70. For a discussion of how the Gold Coinage Act of 1834 and the policies pursued by Mexican president Antonio Lopez de Santa Anna contributed to

the flow of gold and silver into the United States, see Austin, *Baring Brothers*, 147–182. The money supply in the United States grew at an average annual rate of 30 percent between 1834 and 1836, a marked increase from the 2.7 percent growth during the previous three-year period. Jane Knodell, "Rethinking the Jacksonian Economy: The Impact of the 1832 Bank Veto on Commercial Banking," *Journal of Economic History* 66, no. 3 (September 2006): 542–548.

71. There would be several more attempts to pass a recharter of Biddle's institution. Congressional Whigs sent a bill for a new national bank to President John Tyler's desk in 1841. A states' rights man, Tyler vetoed the bill. Not until 1862, with southern states kicked out of Congress, would the federal government charter another corporation, the Union Pacific Railroad. Richard White, *Railroaded: The Transcontinentals and the Making of Modern America* (New York: W. W. Norton, 2011), 19.

Chapter 6. An Unholy Trinity: Banks, Newspapers, and Postmasters during the Post Office Scandal, 1834–1835

1. *National Intelligencer*, March 29, 1834; *RD*, 23rd Congress, 1st Session, Senate, 1138–1205.

2. Ibid. Leigh's estimate of $2 million may have been conservative. In 1839 Amos Kendall, as postmaster general, estimated that the Post Office collected $4.5 million per year in revenue. Much of this revenue paid for the salaries of department clerks and private contractors who carried the mail. Kendall to unknown, April 4, 1839, *AKMP*.

3. For the Post Office, see Richard John, *Spreading the News: The American Postal System from Franklin to Morse* (Cambridge, MA: Harvard University Press, 1995), 48; and *RD*, "Newspaper Postage," Index to the Appendix, 22nd Congress, 1st Session, Senate, 148. For the deposit removal controversy, see Frank Otto Gatell, "Spoils of the Bank War: Political Bias in the Selection of Pet Banks," *American Historical Review* 70, no. 1 (October 1964): 35–58; and Sean Wilentz, *The Rise of American Democracy: From Jefferson to Lincoln* (W. W. Norton, 2005), 391–455.

4. John, *Spreading the News*, 245–248; Donald B. Cole, *A Jackson Man: Amos Kendall and the Rise of American Democracy* (Baton Rouge: Louisiana State University Press, 2004), 193–213.

5. Matthew A. Crenson, *The Federal Machine: Beginnings of Bureaucracy in Jacksonian America* (Baltimore: Johns Hopkins University Press, 1975), xi.

6. Cole, *A Jackson Man*, 124; *American State Papers: Post Office Department*, 1829, 184, and *American State Papers*, 20th Congress, 2nd Session, No. 72, "Condition of the Post Office Department"; John, *Spreading the News*, 3; Kendall to unknown, April 4, 1839, *AKMP*.

7. John, *Spreading the News*, 48; *RD*, "Newspaper Postage," 148; "Report to the Committee on the Post Office and Post Roads," 23rd Congress, 1st Session, Senate, Document 422, 4 and 55; "Postage on Newspapers and Periodicals," 22nd Congress, 1st Session, House, 1.

8. Lynn Hudson Parsons, *The Birth of Modern Politics: Andrew Jackson, John Quincy Adams, and the Election of 1828* (New York: Oxford University Press, 2009), 134.

9. Henry Clay to Philip Fendall, August 17, 1830, in *PHC 8*, 253–254; *Annals of Congress*, 2nd Congress, 1st Session, House, 289–290; Robert McChesney and John Nichols, *The Death and Life of American Journalism: The Media Revolution That Will Begin the World Again* (New York: Nation Books, 2010), especially chapter 3.

10. *RD*, "Postage on Newspapers and Periodicals"; Richard Kielbowicz, *News in the Mail: The Press, Post Office, and Public Information, 1700–1860s* (New York: Greenwood Press, 1989); John, *Spreading the News*, 39.

11. Legislative records indicate that in 1828 the Post Office paid $3,167.87 to editors of the *National Intelligencer* and $3,127.50 to the editors of the *National Journal* for advertising space. Ibid; *RD*, "Memorial of Francis P. Blair," Document 462, 23rd Congress, 1st Session, Senate, 1–8; *American State Papers: Advances for Printing, & C*, 1830, 251.

12. For advertising rates, see the *Pensacola Gazette and Florida Advertiser*, May 8, 1830; *Globe*, April 10, 1832; and *Frankfort Argus*, April 30, 1834.

13. Daniel Bradford to Charles Kitchel Gardner, September 27, 1835, *Daniel Bradford Collection*, FHS; Stephen Campbell, "The Spoils of Victory: Amos Kendall, the Antebellum State, and the Growth of the American Presidency in the Bank War, 1828–1834," *Ohio Valley History* 11, no. 2 (Summer 2011): 11.

14. *Kentucky Gazette*, June 14, 1834; *Extra Telegraph*, quoted in the *National Intelligencer*, September 5, 1832.

15. *RD*, Document No. 261, "Clerks—General Post Office," 23rd Congress, 1st session, House, 1–3.

16. Joseph Coe to Blair, December 19, 1831; Severu E. Parker to Blair, September 7, 1832; Lewis Gassard to Blair, May 27, 1834, *Blair-Rives Papers*.

17. *National Journal*, September 13, 1831; *National Union*, quoted in the *National Intelligencer*, September 5, 1832.

18. Clay to Webster, June 7, 1830, in *PHC 8*, 220.

19. Parsons, *The Birth of Modern Politics*, 135.

20. *Cincinnati Daily Gazette*, quoted in the *National Intelligencer*, August 29, 1832.

21. *New York Courier and Enquirer*, quoted in the *National Intelligencer*, September 18, 1832.

22. *Niles' Weekly Register*, September 15, 1832.

23. *New York Courier and Enquirer*, quoted in the *National Intelligencer*, September 18, 1832.

24. J. P. Morris to Blair, April 25, 1832, *Blair-Rives Papers*, LOC.

25. Robert M. Gibbes to Biddle, December 11, 1831, in *CNB*, 139; Cole, *A Jackson Man*, 157–176.

26. William Duane to Hugh Hamilton, August 10, 1833, *Manuscripts and Political Papers*, INHP; Adams and Gregory to Kendall, September 25, 1833; George

W. Meriwether to Taney, October 3, 1833, *Letters from Banks*, NARA II. Michael F. Holt, *The Rise and Fall of the American Whig Party: Jacksonian Politics and the Onset of the Civil War* (New York: Oxford University Press, 1999), 23; William Stickney, *Autobiography of Amos Kendall* (Boston: Lee and Shepard, 1872), 375.

27. *National Intelligencer*, August 13, 1833.

28. These measures aligned with other financial regulations implemented under Jackson's two terms as president, including prohibitions on the issuance of notes of small denominations, a new gold-to-silver ratio, usury laws, and the establishment of dozens of banks in the South and West capitalized by public stock ownership. Alfred Thruston to Roger Taney, November 5, 1833, *Letters from Banks*, NARA II; Richard M. Johnson to John Tilford, February 26, 1836, *Richard M. Johnson Miscellaneous Papers*, FHS; Larry Schweikart, *Banking in the American South from the Age of Jackson to Reconstruction* (Baton Rouge: Louisiana State University Press, 1987), 15–17. For other examples of regulation in the Jacksonian economy, see John McFaul, *The Politics of Jacksonian Finance* (Ithaca, NY: Cornell University Press, 1972); and Howard Bodenhorn, *State Banking in Early America: A New Economic History* (New York: Oxford University Press, 2003), 11–13.

29. Martin Gordon to Kendall, October 15, 1833, *Letters from Banks*, NARA II; *Niles' Weekly Register*, April 19 and May 3, 1834.

30. Cole, *A Jackson Man*, 182–190; Gatell, "Spoils of the Bank War" and "Secretary Taney and the Baltimore Pets: A Study in Banking and Politics," *Business History Review* 39, no. 2 (Summer 1965): 205–227; Bray Hammond, *Banks and Politics in America from the Revolution to the Civil War* (Princeton, NJ: Princeton University Press, 1957), 329.

31. Gatell, "Spoils of the Bank War," 38; Cole, *A Jackson Man*, 196.

32. Stickney, *Autobiography*, 388.

33. Ibid., 390. David Grimsted, "Robbing the Poor to Aid the Rich: Roger B. Taney and the Bank of Maryland Swindle," *Supreme Court Historical Society Yearbook* (1987): 53–123.

34. John, *Spreading the News*, 243.

35. *RD*, "Report to the Committee on the Post Office and Post Roads," 35.

36. Robert E. Shalhope, *The Baltimore Bank Riot: Political Upheaval in Antebellum Maryland* (Champaign: University of Illinois Press, 2009), 33.

37. Jacob P. Meerman, "Climax of the Bank War; Biddle's Contraction, 1833–34," *Journal of Political Economy* 71 (August 1963): 380.

38. Shalhope, *The Baltimore Bank Riot*, 1–12; Grimsted, "Robbing the Poor to Aid the Rich," 53–123; Stickney, *Autobiography*, 390; Jason Schott to Taney, October 5, 1833; Thomas Ellicott to Taney, October 8, 1833, in *Letters from Banks*, NARA II; Adam Malka, "'The Open Violence of Desperate Men': Rethinking Property and Power in the 1835 Baltimore Bank Riot" *Journal of the Early Republic* 37, no. 2 (Summer 2017): 193–223.

39. *RD*, 22nd Congress, 1st Session, House of Representatives, February 9, 1832, 140–142.

40. Richard D. Davis to Thurlow Weed, March 3, 1834, *Thurlow Weed Papers*, Rush Rhees Library, University of Rochester, Rochester, New York.

41. Richard Johnson to Blair, n.d., circa 1835, *Blair-Lee Papers*, FLPU; Gatell, "Spoils of the Bank War," 57; Stickney, *Autobiography*, 381; Hammond, *Banks and Politics*, 329.

42. Jackson to Arthur Lee Campbell, April 10, 1826; Arthur Lee Campbell to William Barry, March 4, 1833, *Arthur Lee Campbell Papers*, FHS.

43. Gatell, "Spoils of the Bank War," 55; Arthur Lee Campbell to Matthew Monroe Campbell, February 6, 1836, *Matthew Monroe Miscellaneous Papers*, FHS; Jackson to Arthur Lee Campbell, April 10, 1826; Campbell to Kendall, October 22, 1836, in *Arthur Lee Campbell Miscellaneous Papers*, FHS.

44. In the early republic and antebellum eras, before general incorporation statutes, Americans could only establish banks through a special corporate charter granted by the state legislature. This process was often susceptible to corruption. Politically powerful members of state legislatures were often friends with the merchants and investors who lobbied them for this charter. State lawmakers often received a bonus payment or an inside deal on the bank's initial stock offering as a favor for granting the charter. Brian Phillips Murphy, *Building the Empire State: Political Economy in the Early Republic* (Philadelphia: University of Pennsylvania Press, 2015), 27–55; Richard Ellis, *Aggressive Nationalism:* McColluch v. Maryland *and the Foundation of Federal Authority in the Young Republic* (New York: Oxford University Press, 2007).

45. *New Hampshire Statesman*, quoted in the *New York Spectator*, February 19, 1834.

46. Gatell, "Spoils of the Bank War," 52. William C. Mallalieu and Sabri M. Akural, "Kentucky Banks in the Crisis Decade: 1834–1844," *Register of the Kentucky Historical Society* 65, no. 4 (1967): 296; John, *Spreading the News*, 209; Fletcher M. Green, "Duff Green, Militant Journalist of the Old School," *American Historical Review* 52, no. 2 (January 1947): 247.

47. When Jackson selected Barry to serve as postmaster general in 1829, he included the position in the president's official cabinet. *American State Papers*, "Receipts and Expenditures to April 1, 1829," 21st Congress, 2nd Session, Senate, Document 106. Jackson to John Christmas McLemore, September 28, 1829, in *PAJ* 7, 456. In addition to advertising routes in the *Telegraph*, the Post Office Department would advertise routes for bidding in two newspapers for each state or territory through which the proposed routes ran. *National Intelligencer*, October 17, 1829.

48. Edwin Porter was an associate of James Reeside, a leading mail contractor from Philadelphia and friend of Andrew Jackson with whom he traded horses. Jackson to Reeside, circa March 1830, in *PAJ* 8, 115.

49. One complaint of the petitioners was that Porter, Reeside, and their friends and associates would disguise their de facto monopoly by submitting bids for different mail routes using only small variations of the names Porter,

Reeside & Co. The firms may have had different names, but the petitioners argued that the contracts and profits were essentially going to the same group of people. Before petitioning Jackson the petitioners had addressed their concerns to Barry, who gave a perfunctory reply. After receiving a second letter from the petitioners, Barry gave a second reply and then cut off correspondence. Addison Powell and William Rosser Hinton to Andrew Jackson, circa October 1830, in *PAJ 8*, 570–573.

50. Brown and Reeside denied the petitioner's accusations in their own affidavits. Barry denied all charges of wrongdoing through written letters. Jackson to Barry, October 23, 1830 (two letters); Jackson to Powell, November 13, 1830, in *PAJ 8*, 573–575, 625; Lewis to Jackson, June 27, 1831; Jackson to John Wilson Campbell, November 1, 1831, in *PAJ 9*, 347–349, 654–655.

51. RD, "Report to the Committee on the Post Office and Post Roads," Document 422.

52. RD, "Report from the Postmaster General," 23rd Congress, 1st Session, Senate, Document 75.

53. For the Jacksonian defense of Barry, see *Kentucky Gazette*, March 8, 1834, and April 12, 1834.

54. RD, "Report from the Secretary of the Treasury," 23rd Congress, 1st Session, Senate, Document 441, 1–2.

55. RD, "Memorial of Francis P. Blair," Document 462, 1–8.

56. RD, "Report to the Committee on the Post Office and Post Roads," Document 422, 3–32.

57. Ibid., 15–21.

58. Ibid., 14.

59. Ibid., 15.

60. Ibid., 19–20.

61. Ibid., 25.

62. Ibid., 27.

63. Ibid., 28–29.

64. Ibid.; Donald B. Cole, *The Presidency of Andrew Jackson* (Lawrence: University Press of Kansas, 1993), 239.

Conclusion: 1835 and Beyond

1. Matthew A. Crenson, *The Federal Machine: Beginnings of Bureaucracy in Jacksonian America* (Baltimore: Johns Hopkins University Press, 1975), 166; Donald B. Cole, *The Presidency of Andrew Jackson* (Lawrence: University Press of Kansas, 1993), 239.

2. *Niles' Weekly Register*, July 18, 1835.

3. Crenson, *The Federal Machine*, 4, 47–54, 74, 102, 108–111, 132–136, 152. Kendall was not solely responsible for the improvement in the Post Office's budget. A commercial boom starting in 1835 increased the amount of revenue the department collected through postage. Many of Kendall's ideas for reform became part of the Post Office Act of 1836. Kendall to Henry Johnson, July 5,

1836, *Amos Kendall Miscellaneous Papers*, LOC; Donald B. Cole, *A Jackson Man: Amos Kendall and the Rise of American Democracy* (Baton Rouge: Louisiana State University Press, 2004), 193–213. Crenson, based on somewhat tenuous evidence, argued that the transition to a more professionalized bureaucracy occurred because of a breakdown of social values and a sense of moral decline. A more recent assessment by Richard John critiqued Crenson for relying too heavily on Kendall's *Autobiography*, a document many contemporaries avoided for its unreliability and one that showcased Kendall's tendency to exaggerate his own role in the events in which he participated. Some of Kendall's reforms had been proposed by his predecessors, John McLean and William Barry. Richard John, "Affairs of Office: The Executive Departments, the Election of 1828, and the Making of the Democratic Party," in Meg Jacobs et al., eds., *The Democratic Experiment: New Directions in Political History* (Princeton, NJ: Princeton University Press, 2003), 50–84.

4. Barry had approved a contract of $122,600 with the stagecoach firm Stockton & Stokes. Kendall terminated this contract as part of his reforms, but William B. Stokes of Stockton & Stokes appealed to Congress, claiming an illegal breach of contract. In two separate Supreme Court decisions handed down in 1838 and 1845, the High Court affirmed an earlier decision by the solicitor of the Treasury ordering Kendall to pay the $122,600 to Stockton & Stokes, but it rejected the additional $40,000 fee that Stockton & Stokes had demanded of Kendall in a private suit. *RD*, "Memorial of Amos Kendall," 29th Congress, 1st Session, House, Document 37, December 15, 1845; Leonard White, *The Jacksonians: A Study in Administrative History* (New York: Macmillan, 1954), 38–39 and 278–279; Richard John, *Spreading the News: The American Postal System from Franklin to Morse* (Cambridge, MA: Harvard University Press, 1995), 245–248; Cole, *A Jackson Man*, 193–213.

5. Kendall to unknown, April 4, 1839, *AKMP*.

6. Ibid; Cole, *A Jackson Man*, 193–200; Richard John, *Network Nation: Inventing American Telecommunications* (Cambridge, MA: Harvard University Press, 2010), 24–25, 66; Kendall to Jackson, December 3, 1831, in *PAJ* 9, 720–723.

7. Patricia Cline Cohen, *The Murder of Helen Jewett* (New York: Vintage, 1999).

8. The party organ lasted until the Civil War, when after repeated scandals both parties created a more cost-effective Government Printing Office (GPO) that included an independent printing plant and independent employees. Paul Starr, *The Creation of the Media: Political Origins of Modern Communications* (New York: Basic Books, 2004), 83–150. For more on the policy, technological, political, and economic factors that spearheaded the transformation to more commercialized media, see Gerald Baldasty, *The Commercialization of News in the Nineteenth Century* (Madison: University of Wisconsin Press, 1992).

9. Though there were earlier signs of distress, May 1837 is usually cited as the onset of the panic. The standard orthodoxy for many years that empha-

sized the international origins of the panic was Peter Temin, *The Jacksonian Economy* (New York: W. W. Norton, 1969). For challenges to Temin's thesis that have returned to the panic's American origins, see Peter Rousseau, "Jacksonian Monetary Policy, Specie Flows, and the Panic of 1837," *Journal of Economic History* 62, no. 2 (June 2002): 457–488; Namsuk Kim and John Joseph Wallis, "The Market for American State Government Bonds in Britain and the United States, 1830–43," *Economic History Review* 58, no. 4 (November 2005): 736–764; and Jane Knodell, "Rethinking the Jacksonian Economy: The Impact of the 1832 Bank Veto on Commercial Banking," *Journal of Economic History* 66, no. 3 (September 2006): 541–574. For a more cultural emphasis on the panic, see Jessica Lepler, *The Many Panics of 1837: People, Politics, and the Creation of a Transatlantic Financial Crisis* (Cambridge: Cambridge University Press, 2013).

10. Robert E. Wright, "Specially Incorporated Transportation Companies in the United States to 1860: A Comprehensive Tabulation and Its Implications," *Journal of Business and Economics* 5, no. 7 (July 2014): 972–989. Before the Civil War, state and municipal governments assumed about 70 percent of the costs for canal construction, but private investment for the building of railroads accounted for the same percentage. Songho Ha, *The Rise and Fall of the American System, 1790–1837* (London: Pickering & Chatto, 2009), 130.

11. John Lauritz Larson, *Internal Improvement: National Public Works and the Promise of Popular Government in the Early Republic* (Chapel Hill: University of North Carolina Press 2001), 193–233. Laissez-faire, as a theory of political economy, originated with eighteenth-century French philosophers. In the early republic, the word "corporate" almost always meant state-sanctioned, but today it is often equated with a private business. John, *Network Nation*, 90.

12. Crenson, *The Federal Machine*, 115–135.

13. The relative lack of private investment in transportation in the South vis-à-vis the North was at least partially due to the institution of slavery and the unique mix of clay-based soils in the South. Both of these factors discouraged the growth of large towns necessary for the accumulation of investment capital, and thus, state or mixed public-private funding of transportation was more common in the South. John Majewski, *Modernizing a Slave Economy: The Economic Vision of the Confederate Nation* (Chapel Hill: University of North Carolina Press, 2009).

14. Larson, *Internal Improvement*, 229; William Novak, *The People's Welfare: Law and Regulation in Nineteenth Century America* (Chapel Hill: University of North Carolina Press, 1996), ix, 3–36; John, *Network Nation*, 90.

15. Although Kendall himself often critiqued the wealthy in his anti-BUS writings, it was more common for Jacksonians overall to invoke the language of antimonopolism, which differed in some ways from the discourse of class conflict.

16. Richard White, "Information, Markets, and Corruption: Transcontinen-

tal Railroads in the Gilded Age," *Journal of American History* 90, no. 1 (June 2003): 19–43.

17. Ibid., 24–36.

18. For more on the Credit Mobilier scandal, see Paul Kens, "The Credit Mobilier Scandal and the Supreme Court: Corporate Power, Corporate Person, and Government Control in the Mid-nineteenth Century," *Journal of Supreme Court History* 34, no. 2 (June 2009): 170–182.

19. Bray Hammond, *Banks and Politics in America, from the Revolution to the Civil War* (Princeton, NJ: Princeton University Press, 1957), 451–548; Thomas Payne Govan, *Nicholas Biddle, Nationalist and Public Banker, 1786–1844* (Chicago: University of Chicago Press, 1959), 285–393.

Appendix 1: How the Bank Worked

1. For example, see H. R. Rept. No. 121, 22nd Congress, 2nd Session, Serial Volume 236, 154–159; and *De Grand's Boston Weekly Report*, January 27, 1827.

2. Compare H. R. Rept. No. 460, 22nd Congress, 1st Session, Serial Volume 227, 267, with S. Doc. No. 17, 23rd Congress, 2nd Session, Serial Volume 267, 128.

3. See "Other People's Money: How Banking Worked in the Early Republic," SHEAR blog post by Mark Cheathem, May 16, 2017, at http://www .shear.org/2017/05/16/other-peoples-money-how-banking-worked-in-the-early -republic/, accessed June 30, 2017.

4. Susan Previant Lee and Peter Passell, "Banks and Money before the Civil War," in *A New Economic View of American History: From Colonial Times to 1940* (New York: W. W. Norton, 1979), 108–129.

5. Howard Bodenhorn, *A History of Banking in the Antebellum Era: Financial Markets and Economic Development in an Era of Nation-Building* (Cambridge: Cambridge University Press, 2000); Robert Wright, *The Wealth of Nations Rediscovered: Integration and Expansion in American Financial Markets, 1780–1850* (Cambridge: Cambridge University Press, 2002).

6. H. R. Rept. No. 121, 57.

7. Ibid., 14–17.

8. House Document 3, 22nd Congress, 2nd Session, Serial Volume 233, 1–4; Jane Knodell, *The Second Bank of the United States: "Central" Banker in an Era of Nation-building, 1816–1836* (London: Routledge, 2017), 13–16.

9. Samuel Ingham to Nicholas Biddle, June 19 and December 4, 1829, *Letters to Banks*, NARA II; Ingham to Biddle, September 17, 1830, *Political Papers*, #6365, INHP.

10. *RD*, 21st Congress, 1st Session, Appendix, 128; *National Intelligencer*, December 10, 1832; *New York Spectator*, March 24, 1834.

11. "Merchant" was a generic term that could refer to any number of occupations, including a traveling peddler, an owner of a country store, a dry-

goods retailer, an exporter, a wholesale jobber devoted to one particular line of goods, or an importer. The boundaries between merchant, creditor, factor, and exchange broker were fluid and arbitrary. Many individuals were both merchants and creditors at the same time. In the context of the antebellum South, factors, sometimes defined as commission merchants or middle men, were financial intermediaries that extended credit to planters. As such, they provided information on business conditions, discounted credit instruments, purchased supplies, sold merchandise, kept business records, and endorsed notes, bills, and drafts. Factors charged a commission for helping planters market crops in distant commercial areas like New Orleans, which involved transportation and insurance. George D. Green, *Finance and Economic Development in the Old South: Louisiana Banking, 1804-1861* (Palo Alto, CA: Stanford University Press, 1972); Edward J. Balleisen, *Navigating Failure: Bankruptcy and Commercial Society in Antebellum America* (Chapel Hill: University of North Carolina Press, 2001), 2, 28.

12. Richard Timberlake, *The Origins of Central Banking in the United States* (Cambridge, MA: Harvard University Press, 1978), 2–4; Barry Eichengreen, *Golden Fetters: The Gold Standard and the Great Depression 1919–1939* (New York: Oxford University Press, 1992); Kenneth Mouré, *The Gold Standard Illusion: France, the Bank of France, and the International Gold Standard, 1914–1939* (New York: Oxford University Press, 2002).

13. The Spanish and Spanish American silver peso was legal tender in the United States until 1857. Paper money did not become legal tender until the Civil War. Today's Federal Reserve Note is legal tender.

14. This hypothetical scenario presumes that the Lexington and Albany banks did not regularly conduct business with one another. If they did, the Lexington bank would have likely deposited some specie in the Albany bank (and vice versa) for these types of transactions. This was known as *correspondent banking,* and it obviated the need for transporting specie. See Joseph Van Fenstermaker, *The Development of American Commercial Banking: 1782–1837* (Kent, OH: Kent State University Press, 1965), 32–43.

15. S. Doc. No. 17, 25–26; H. R. Rept. No. 121, 3; Condy Raguet, *A Treatise on Currency and Banking* (Philadelphia: Crigg and Elliot, 1840).

16. The author wishes to thank Robert Wright for patiently explaining the intricacies of this labyrinthine credit system. This example is a simplified version demonstrating only one component of a complex network of trade and credit instruments involving several financial institutions. Even 200 years ago the number of different actors and occupations brought together for a seemingly simple transaction such as transferring Mississippi cotton to Manchester textile factories was surprisingly complex. For each transaction recorded in New Orleans, there was likely a corresponding trade involving other credit instruments from New York banks and London mercantile houses.

17. Walter B. Smith, *Economic Aspects of the Second United States Bank*

(Cambridge, MA: Harvard University Press, 1953), 39–44; Naomi Lamoreaux, *Insider Lending: Banks, Personal Connections, and Economic Development in Industrial New England* (Cambridge: Cambridge University Press, 1994).

18. S. Doc. No. 17, 25–26.

19. Ralph C. H. Catterall, *The Second Bank of the United States* (Chicago: University of Chicago Press, 1903), 137–143; Leland Hamilton Jenks, *The Migration of British Capital to 1875* (New York: Alfred A. Knopf, 1927), 66–95.

20. In the accounting parlance of the times, "drawn on" or "drawn against" meant that the credit instrument, once negotiated or cashed, would deduct funds from that particular locale. A bill "drawn on New Orleans" would deduct funds from the New Orleans branch BUS.

21. Knodell, *The Second Bank of the United States*, 79.

22. S. Doc. No. 17, 126–140; *Niles' Weekly Register*, July 19, 1834; Bodenhorn, *State Banking in Early America*, 72–94, 219–249.

23. H. R. Rept. No. 121, 45–46; S. Doc. No. 17, 130.

24. Jessica M. Lepler, *The Many Panics of 1837: People, Politics, and the Creation of a Transatlantic Financial Crisis* (Cambridge: Cambridge University Press, 2013), 17; *RD*, House, Appendix, 22nd Congress, 1st Session, 52; Thomas Payne Govan, *Nicholas Biddle, Nationalist and Public Banker, 1786–1844* (Chicago: University of Chicago Press, 1959), 320–323.

25. *RD*, 21st Congress, 1st Session, House, Appendix, 104–133; Knodell, *The Second Bank of the United States*, 69–70, 160.

26. Smithian assumptions can be found in the works of many of the major financial theorists of the antebellum era, including Nathan Appleton, *An Examination of the Banking System of Massachusetts in Reference to the Renewal of Bank Charters* (Boston: Stimpson and Clapp, 1831); William Gouge, *A Short History of Paper Money and Banking in the United States* (Philadelphia: T. W. Ustick, 1833); George Tucker, *The Theory of Money and Banks Investigated* (Boston: Charles C. Little and James Brown, 1839); and Raguet, *A Treatise on Currency and Banking*. Only in the twentieth century did fiscal and monetary authorities come to stress the importance of stabilizing prices and employment.

27. This self-correcting feature of international trade is elucidated in Raguet, *A Treatise on Currency and Banking*, 16–38.

28. Internal improvements referred to infrastructure projects like roads, turnpikes, canals, railroads, the widening of a river, or the creation of a harbor. Jenks, *The Migration of British Capital to 1875*, 73–95.

29. This system of "open credits" would stop in 1836, prior to the financial panic. Peter Austin, *Baring Brothers and the Birth of Modern Finance* (London: Pickering and Chatto, 2007), 19–31, 47, 141, 149–150; Bray Hammond, *Banks and Politics in America, from the Revolution to the Civil War* (Princeton, NJ: Princeton University Press, 1957), 461.

30. For the manner in which the BUS was connected to the expansion of slavery in the old Southwest and the broader history of capitalism, see Edward

E. Baptist, *The Half Has Never Been Told: Slavery and the Making of American Capitalism* (New York: Basic Books, 2014), 218–292; Sven Beckert, *Empire of Cotton: A Global History* (New York: Alfred A. Knopf, 2014); and Calvin Schermerhorn, *The Business of Slavery and the Rise of Capitalism, 1815–1860* (New Haven, CT: Yale University Press, 2015).

31. Lepler, *The Many Panics of 1837*, 17; Stephen Campbell, "The Transatlantic Financial Crisis of 1837," in William Beezley, ed., *The Oxford Research Encyclopedia of Latin American History* (New York: Oxford University Press, 2017).

32. For the Jacksonian claims that the bank drained specie from the South and West, see H. R. Rept. No. 460, 1–29; and Thomas Hart Benton, *Thirty Years' View Vol. 1* (New York: D. Appleton, 1856), 187–192, 222–223.

33. While Americans imported goods from China, the Chinese had little interest in American goods. As a result, the United States often ran a trade deficit. Prior to 1827 the Chinese would not accept American credit instruments, and thus, American merchants had to send silver. Alejandra Irigoin, "The End of a Silver Era: The Consequences of the Breakdown of the Spanish Peso Standard in China and the United States, 1780s–1850s," *Journal of World History* 20, no. 2 (June 2009), 209–239; Linda K. Salvucci and Richard J. Salvucci, "The Lizardi Brothers: A Mexican Family Business and the Expansion of New Orleans, 1825–1846," *Journal of Southern History* 82, no. 4 (November 2016): 759–788; Knodell, *The Second Bank of the United States*, 107, 138.

34. H. R. Rept. No. 460, 322; Austin, *Baring Brothers*, 60–64, 146.

35. According to the U.S. federal census of 1830, about 55 percent of the nation's population lived in free states, but the BUS placed 70 percent of its shares of capital stock in branches that were located in free states. U.S. federal census of 1830, University of Virginia Library, Historical Census Browser, Geospatial and Statistical Data Center, available at http://mapserver.lib.virginia.edu/, accessed June 25, 2015.

36. Steven Deyle, *Carry Me Back: The Domestic Slave Trade in American Life* (New York: Oxford University Press, 2005), 96–129.

37. Isaac Franklin to Rice Ballard, October 26, 1831; James Franklin to Rice Ballard, November 14, 1831; Isaac Franklin to Rice Ballard, April 19 and June 8, 1832, in *Rice Ballard Papers*, SHC; Schermerhorn, *The Business of Slavery and the Rise of Capitalism*, 126–135.

38. Gavin Wright, *Slavery and American Economic Development* (Louisiana State University Press, 2006), 50. Like Baptist, Joshua Rothman has focused on the southwestern frontier as a key boom area that helped the United States become a global power. See *Flush Times and Fever Dreams: A Story of Capitalism and Slavery in the Age of Jackson* (Athens: University of Georgia Press, 2012), 14–24.

39. Bonnie Martin, "Slavery's Invisible Engine: Mortgaging Human Property," *Journal of Southern History* 76, no. 4 (November 2010), especially 821–825.

40. Isaac Franklin to Ballard, June 8, 1832, *Ballard Papers*, SHC.

41. Baptist, *The Half Has Never Been Told*, 94 and 239; Richard Holcombe Kilbourne Jr., *Slave Agriculture and Financial Markets in Antebellum America: The Bank of the United States in Mississippi, 1831–1852* (London: Pickering and Chatto, 2006), 2.

Bibliography

Archival Collections

Filson Historical Society, Louisville, Kentucky
    Amos Kendall Miscellaneous Papers
    Arthur Lee Campbell Miscellaneous Papers
    Daniel Bradford Collection
    John Crittenden Collection
    Matthew Monroe Miscellaneous Papers
    Philip Kearny Papers
    Richard M. Johnson Miscellaneous Papers
    William Barry Letters
    William J. Graves Papers
Firestone Library, Princeton University, Princeton, New Jersey
    Blair-Lee Papers
Historical Society of Pennsylvania, Philadelphia, Pennsylvania
    Biddle Family Correspondence
    George M. Dallas Papers
    Simon Gratz Collection
    Thomas Biddle Correspondence
    Thomas Cadwalader Collection
    United States Bank Papers
Independence National Historical Park, Philadelphia, Pennsylvania
    Manuscripts and Political Papers

Library of Congress, Manuscript Division, Washington, DC
  Andrew Jackson Papers
  Biddle Family Papers
  Blair Family Papers
  Blair-Rives Papers
  Joseph Desha Papers
  Martin Van Buren Papers
  Nicholas Biddle Letterbooks
  Nicholas Biddle Papers
Massachusetts Historical Society, Boston, Massachusetts
  Appleton Family Papers
Missouri Historical Society, St. Louis, Missouri
  Duels Collection
  Thomas Hart Benton Papers
National Archives and Records Administration II, College Park, Maryland
  Letters from Banks
  Letters to Banks
Rush Rhees Library, University of Rochester, Rochester, New York
  Thurlow Weed Papers
Southern Historical Collection, University of North Carolina, Chapel Hill
  Duff Green Papers
  Rice Ballard Papers
Western Historical Manuscript Collection, Columbia, Missouri
  Abiel Leonard Collection
  Daniel Dunklin Collection
Yale University Sterling Library, New Haven, Connecticut
  James Watson Webb Papers

Newspapers and Periodicals
Aurora and Pennsylvania Gazette
Christian Register
Frankfort Argus
Frankfort Commonwealth
Globe
Indiana Journal
Jeffersonian Republican
Kentucky Gazette
Missouri Argus
Missouri Free Press
Missouri Intelligencer
Missouri Republican
Morning Courier and New York Enquirer
National Gazette
National Intelligencer

National Journal
New England Galaxy and United States Literary Advertiser
New Hampshire Statesman
New York Courier and Enquirer
New York Spectator
Niles' Weekly Register
Pensacola Gazette and Florida Advertiser
Richmond Enquirer
Scioto Gazette
St. Louis Beacon
United States Telegraph
Workingman's Advocate

Books and Articles, Primary

Appleton, Nathan. *An Examination of the Banking System of Massachusetts in Reference to the Renewal of Bank Charters*. Boston: Stimpson and Clapp, 1831.

Barry, William T. "Letters of William T. Barry." *William and Mary Quarterly* 14, no. 1 (July 1905): 19–23.

———. "Letters of William T. Barry." *William and Mary Quarterly* 14, no. 4 (April 1906): 230–241.

Benton, Thomas Hart. *Thirty Years' View*. Vol. 1. New York: D. Appleton, 1856.

Darby, John Fletcher. *Personal Recollections of Many Prominent People whom I Have Known, and of Events—Especially Those Relating to the History of St. Louis—during the First Half of the Present Century*. St. Louis: G. I. Jones, 1880.

Feller, Daniel, et al. *The Papers of Andrew Jackson, Volume 7: 1829*. Knoxville: University of Tennessee Press, 2007.

———. *The Papers of Andrew Jackson, Volume 8: 1830*. Knoxville: University of Tennessee Press, 2010.

———. *The Papers of Andrew Jackson, Volume 9: 1831*. Knoxville: University of Tennessee Press, 2013.

———. *The Papers of Andrew Jackson, Volume 10: 1832*. Knoxville: University of Tennessee Press, 2016.

Gouge, William. *A Short History of Paper Money and Banking in the United States*. Philadelphia: T. W. Ustick, 1833.

Henshaw, David. *Remarks Upon the Bank of the United States: Being an Examination of the Report of the Committee of Ways and Means, Made to Congress, April, 1830. By a Merchant*. Boston: True and Greene, 1831.

McGrane, Reginald Charles., ed. *The Correspondence of Nicholas Biddle: Dealing with National Affairs, 1807–1844*. Boston: Houghton Mifflin, 1919.

Raguet, Condy. *A Treatise on Currency and Banking*. Philadelphia: Crigg and Elliot, 1840.

Seager, Robert, II, and Melba Porter Hay., eds. *The Papers of Henry Clay, Vol-*

ume 8: *Candidate, Compromiser, Whig, March 5, 1829–December 31, 1836.* Lexington: University Press of Kentucky, 1984.

Shephard, Elihu. *The Early History of St. Louis and Missouri: From Its First Exploration by White Men in 1673 to 1843.* St. Louis: Southwestern Book and Publishing Company, 1870.

Stickney, William. *Autobiography of Amos Kendall.* Boston: Lee and Shepard, 1872.

Tucker, George. *The Theory of Money and Banks Investigated.* Boston: Charles C. Little and James Brown, 1839.

Books and Articles, Secondary

Allgor, Catherine. *Parlor Politics: In Which the Ladies of Washington Build a City and a Government.* Charlottesville: University of Virginia Press, 2000.

Ames, William A. *A History of the National Intelligencer.* Chapel Hill: University of North Carolina Press, 1972.

Austin, Peter E. *Baring Brothers and the Birth of Modern Finance.* London: Pickering and Chatto, 2007.

Baldasty, Gerald. *The Commercialization of News in the Nineteenth Century.* Madison: University of Wisconsin Press, 1992.

Balleisen, Edward J. *Navigating Failure: Bankruptcy and Commercial Society in Antebellum America.* Chapel Hill: University of North Carolina Press, 2001.

Balogh, Brian. *A Government Out of Sight: The Mystery of National Authority in Nineteenth-Century America.* Cambridge: Cambridge University Press, 2009.

Baptist, Edward E. *The Half Has Never Been Told: Slavery and the Making of Capitalism.* New York: Basic Books, 2014.

Beckert, Sven. *Empire of Cotton: A Global History.* New York: Alfred A. Knopf, 2014.

Belko, William Stephen. *The Invincible Duff Green: Whig of the West.* Columbia: University of Missouri Press, 2006.

Bodenhorn, Howard. *State Banking in Early America: A New Economic History.* New York: Oxford University Press, 2003.

Brands, H. W. *Andrew Jackson: His Life and Times.* New York: Doubleday, 2005.

Campbell, Stephen. "Funding the Bank War: Nicholas Biddle and the Public Relations Campaign to Re-Charter the Second Bank of the United States, 1828–1834." *American Nineteenth Century History* 17, no. 3 (Fall 2016): 273–299.

———. "Hickory Wind: The Role of Personality and the Press in Andrew Jackson's Bank War in Missouri, 1831–1837." *Missouri Historical Review* 101, no. 3 (April 2007): 146–167.

———. "The Spoils of Victory: Amos Kendall, the Antebellum State, and the Growth of the American Presidency in the Bank War, 1828–1834." *Ohio Valley History* 11, no. 2 (Summer 2011): 3–25.

Catterall, Ralph C. H. *The Second Bank of the United States*. Chicago: University of Chicago Press, 1903.

Clokey, Richard M. *William H. Ashley: Enterprise and Politics in the Trans-Mississippi West*. Norman: University of Oklahoma Press, 1980.

Cohen, Patricia Cline. *The Murder of Helen Jewett*. New York: Vintage, 1999.

Cole, Arthur Harrison. *Wholesale Commodity Prices in the United States 1700–1861*. Cambridge: Harvard University Press, 1938.

Cole, Donald B. *A Jackson Man: Amos Kendall and the Rise of American Democracy*. Baton Rouge: Louisiana State University Press, 2004.

———. *The Presidency of Andrew Jackson*. Lawrence: University Press of Kansas, 1993.

Cooper, William. *Liberty and Slavery: Southern Politics to 1860*. Columbia: University of South Carolina Press, 1983.

Crenson, Matthew A. *The Federal Machine: Beginnings of Bureaucracy in Jacksonian America*. Baltimore: Johns Hopkins University Press, 1975.

Crouthamel, James L. "Did the Second Bank of the United States Bribe the Press?" *Journalism Quarterly* 36 (1959): 35-44.

———. *James Watson Webb: A Biography*. Middletown, CT: Wesleyan University Press, 1969.

———. "Three Philadelphians in the Bank War: A Neglected Chapter in American Lobbying." *Pennsylvania History: A Journal of Mid-Atlantic Studies* 27, no. 4 (October 1960): 361–378.

Davis, Ethan. "An Administrative Trail of Tears: Indian Removal." *American Journal of Legal History* 50, no. 1 (January 2008–2010): 49–100.

De Kock, Michiel Hendrik. *Central Banking*. London: Crosby Lockwood Staples, 1939.

Dewey, Davis R. *The Second United States Bank*. Washington, DC: Government Printing Office, National Monetary Commission, 1910.

Diamond, Douglas W., and Philip H. Dybvig. "Bank Runs, Deposit Insurance, and Liquidity." *Journal of Political Economy* 91 (June 1983): 401–419.

Edling, Max. *A Revolution in Favor of Government: Origins of the U.S. Constitution and the Making of the American State*. New York: Oxford University Press, 2003.

Einhorn, Robin. *American Taxation, American Slavery*. Chicago: University of Chicago Press, 2006.

Ellis, Richard et al. *Aggressive Nationalism: McColluch v. Maryland and the Foundation of Federal Authority in the Young Republic*. New York: Oxford University Press, 2007.

———. "A Symposium on Charles Sellers, the Market Revolution: Jacksonian America, 1815–46." *Journal of the Early Republic* 12 (Winter 1992): 445–476.

Ericson, David F. *Slavery in the American Republic: Developing the Federal Government, 1791–1861*. Lawrence: University Press of Kansas, 2011.

Fehrenbacher, Don E. *The Slaveholding Republic: An Account of the United*

States Government's Relationship to Slavery. New York: Oxford University Press, 2001.

Feller, Daniel. "Politics and Society: Toward a Jacksonian Synthesis." *Journal of the Early Republic* 10 (Summer 1990): 135–161.

Gatell, Frank Otto. "Secretary Taney and the Baltimore Pets: A Study in Banking and Politics." *Business History Review* 39, no. 2 (Summer 1965): 205–227.

———. "Spoils of the Bank War: Political Bias in the Selection of Pet Banks." *American Historical Review* 70, no. 1 (October 1964): 35–58.

Govan, Thomas Payne. *Nicholas Biddle, Nationalist and Public Banker, 1786–1844.* Chicago: University of Chicago Press, 1959.

Green, Fletcher M. "Duff Green, Militant Journalist of the Old School." *American Historical Review* 52, no. 2 (January 1947): 247–264.

Green, George D. *Finance and Economic Development in the Old South: Louisiana Banking 1804–1861.* Palo Alto, CA: Stanford University Press, 1972.

Greenberg, Kenneth. *Honor and Slavery: Lies; Duels; Baseball; Gambling Etc. in the Old South.* Princeton, NJ: Princeton University Press, 1996.

Grimsted, David. "Robbing the Poor to Aid the Rich: Roger B. Taney and the Bank of Maryland Swindle." *Supreme Court Historical Society Yearbook* (1987): 53–123.

Ha, Songho. *The Rise and Fall of the American System: Nationalism and the Development of the American Economy, 1790–1837.* London: Pickering and Chatto, 2009.

Habermas, Jurgen. *The Structural Transformation of the Public Sphere: An Inquiry into a Category of Bourgeois Society,* translated by Thomas Burger with the assistance of Frederick Lawrence. Cambridge, MA: MIT Press, 1989.

Hammond, Bray. *Banks and Politics in America from the Revolution to the Civil War.* Princeton, NJ: Princeton University Press, 1957.

Holt, Michael F. *The Political Crisis of the 1850s.* New York: W. W. Norton, 1978.

———. *The Rise and Fall of the American Whig Party: Jacksonian Politics and the Onset of the Civil War.* New York: Oxford University Press, 1999.

Howe, Daniel Walker. *What Hath God Wrought: The Transformation of America, 1815–1848.* New York: Oxford University Press, 2007.

Huntzicker, William E. "The Popular Press, 1833–1865." In *The History of American Journalism, Number 3,* edited by James D. Startt and William David Sloan, 36–37. Westport, CT: Greenwood Press, 1999.

Irigoin, Alejandra. "The End of a Silver Era: The Consequences of the Breakdown of the Spanish Peso Standard in China and the United States, 1780s–1850s." *Journal of World History* 20, no. 2 (June 2009): 207–243.

Jenks, Leland H. *The Migration of British Capital to 1875.* New York: Alfred A. Knopf, 1927.

John, Richard. "Affairs of Office: The Executive Departments, the Election of 1828, and the Making of the Democratic Party," in Meg Jacobs et al., *The*

Democratic Experiment: New Directions in Political History. Princeton, NJ: Princeton University Press, 2003.

———. "Governmental Institutions as Agents of Change: Rethinking American Political Development in the Early Republic, 1787–1835." *Studies in American Political Development* 11 (Fall 1997): 347–380.

———. *Network Nation: Inventing American Telecommunications*. Cambridge, MA: Harvard University Press, 2010.

———. *Spreading the News: The American Postal System from Franklin to Morse*. Cambridge, MA: Harvard University Press, 1995.

Karp, Matthew. *This Vast Southern Empire: Slaveholders at the Helm of American Foreign Policy*. Cambridge, MA: Harvard University Press, 2016.

Katznelson, Ira. "Flexible Capacity: The Military and Early American State-building." In Ira Katznelson and Martin Shefter, eds., *Shaped by War and Trade*. Princeton, NJ: Princeton University Press, 2002.

Kens, Paul. "The Credit Mobilier Scandal and the Supreme Court: Corporate Power, Corporate Person, and Government Control in the Mid-nineteenth Century." *Journal of Supreme Court History* 34, no. 2 (June 2009): 170–182.

Kielbowicz, Richard. *News in the Mail: The Press, Post Office, and Public Information, 1700–1860s*. New York: Greenwood Press, 1989.

Kilbourne Jr., Richard Holcombe. *Slave Agriculture and Financial Markets in Antebellum America: The Bank of the United States in Mississippi, 1831–1852*. London: Pickering and Chatto, 2006.

Knodell, Jane. "Rethinking the Jacksonian Economy: The Impact of the 1832 Bank Veto on Commercial Banking." *Journal of Economic History* 66, no. 3 (September 2006): 541–574.

———. *The Second Bank of the United States: "Central" Banker in an Era of Nation-building, 1816–1836*. London: Routledge, 2017.

Lamoreaux, Naomi. *Insider Lending: Banks, Personal Connections, and Economic Development in Industrial New England*. Cambridge: Cambridge University Press, 1996.

Larson, John Lauritz. *Internal Improvement: National Public Works and the Promise of Popular Government in the Early Republic*. Chapel Hill: University of North Carolina Press, 2001.

Leonard, Thomas C. *The Power of the Press: The Birth of American Political Reporting*. New York: Oxford University Press, 1986.

Lepler, Jessica M. *The Many Panics of 1837: People, Politics, and the Creation of a Transatlantic Financial Crisis*. New York: Cambridge University Press, 2013.

Lomazoff, Eric. "Turning (into) 'The Great Regulating Wheel': The Conversion of the Bank of the United States, 1791–1811." *Studies in American Political Development* 26 (April 2012): 1–23.

Lyon, William. *The Pioneer Editor in Missouri 1808–1860*. Columbia: University of Missouri Press, 1965.

Malka, Adam. "'The Open Violence of Desperate Men': Rethinking Property and Power in the 1835 Baltimore Bank Riot." *Journal of the Early Republic* 37, no. 2 (Summer 2017): 193–223.

Mallalieu, William C., and Sabri M. Akural. "Kentucky Banks in the Crisis Decade: 1834–1844." *Register of the Kentucky Historical Society* 65, no. 4 (1967): 294–303.

Marshall, Lynn. "The Authorship of Jackson's Bank Veto Message." *Mississippi Valley Historical Review* 50 (1963): 466–477.

McChesney, Robert W., and John Nichols. *The Death and Life of American Journalism: The Media Revolution That Will Begin the World Again.* New York: Nation Books, 2010.

McCormick, Richard P. *The Second American Party System: Party Formations in the Jacksonian Era.* Chapel Hill: University of North Carolina Press, 1966.

McFaul, John M. *The Politics of Jacksonian Finance.* Ithaca, NY: Cornell University Press, 1972.

Meerman, Jacob P. "The Climax of the Bank War: Biddle's Contraction, 1833–34." *Journal of Political Economy* 71, no. 4 (August 1963): 378–388.

Mihm, Stephen. "The Fog of War: Jackson, Biddle, and the Destruction of the Bank of the United States." In Sean Patrick Adams, ed., *The Companion to the Era of Andrew Jackson.* Malden, MA: Wiley-Blackwell, 2013.

Morrison, James A. "This Means (Bank) War! Corruption and Credible Commitments in the Collapse of the Second Bank of the United States." *Journal of the History of Economic Thought* 37, no. 2 (June 2015): 221–245.

Moss, James Earl. "William Henry Ashley: A Jackson Man with Feet of Clay." *Missouri Historical Review* 61, no. 1 (January 1966): 1–20.

Murphy, Brian Phillips. *Building the Empire State: Political Economy in the Early Republic.* Philadelphia: University of Pennsylvania Press, 2015.

Nash, Gary B. *The Unknown American Revolution: The Unruly Birth of Democracy and the Struggle to Create America.* New York: Penguin Books, 2005.

North, Douglass. *The Economic Growth of the United States.* New York: W. W. Norton, 1961.

Novak, William. "The Myth of the 'Weak' American State." *American Historical Review* 113, no. 3 (June 2008): 752–772.

———. *The People's Welfare: Law and Regulation in Nineteenth Century America.* Chapel Hill: University of North Carolina Press, 1996.

Padgett, James A. "Correspondence between Governor Joseph Desha and Amos Kendall, 1831–1835." *Register of the Kentucky Historical Society* 38 (January 1940): 5–24.

Parsons, Lynn Hudson. *The Birth of Modern Politics: Andrew Jackson, John Quincy Adams, and the Election of 1828.* New York: Oxford University Press, 2009.

Pasley, Jeffrey L. "Minnows, Spies, and Aristocrats: The Social Crisis of Congress in the Age of Martin Van Buren." *Journal of the Early Republic* 27, no. 4 (Winter 2007): 599–653.

———. *"The Tyranny of Printers": Newspaper Politics in the Early American Republic.* Charlottesville: University of Virginia Press, 2001.

Peart, Daniel. "Looking beyond Parties and Elections: The Making of United States Tariff Policy during the Early 1820s." *Journal of the Early Republic* 33, no. 1 (Spring 2013): 87–108.

Perkins, Edwin J. *Financing Anglo-American Trade: The House of Brown, 1800–1880.* Cambridge, MA: Harvard University Press, 1975.

———. "Lost Opportunities for Compromise in the Bank War: A Reassessment of Jackson's Veto Message." *Business History Review* 61, no. 4 (Winter 1987): 531–551.

Prince, Carl E. "The Great 'Riot Year': Jacksonian Democracy and Patterns of Violence in 1834." *Journal of the Early Republic* 5, no. 1 (Spring 1985): 1–19.

Rao, Gautham. *National Duties: Custom Houses and the Making of the American State.* Chicago: University of Chicago Press, 2016.

Ratcliffe, Donald J. *The One-Party Presidential Contest: Adams, Jackson, and 1824's Five-Horse Race.* Lawrence: University Press of Kansas, 2015.

———. *The Politics of Long Division: The Birth of the Second Party System in Ohio, 1818–1828.* Columbus: Ohio State University Press, 2000.

———. "Popular Preferences in the Presidential Election of 1824," *Journal of the Early Republic* 34, no. 1 (Spring 2014): 45–77.

Reed, George Edward, and W. W. Griest, eds. *Pennsylvania Archives Fourth Series: Volume VI. Papers of the Governors 1832–1845.* Harrisburg: State of Pennsylvania, 1901.

Remini, Robert V. *Andrew Jackson and the Bank War.* New York: W. W. Norton, 1967.

———. *Andrew Jackson and the Course of American Freedom, 1822–1832.* New York: Harper and Row, 1981.

———. *The Election of Andrew Jackson.* Philadelphia: J. B. Lippincott, 1963.

———. *Henry Clay: Statesman for the Union.* W. W. Norton, 1991.

Rohrs, Richard C. "Partisan Politics and the Attempted Assassination of Andrew Jackson." *Journal of the Early Republic* 1, no. 2 (Summer 1981): 149–163.

Rothenberg, Winifred B. *From Market-Places to a Market Economy: The Transformation of Rural Massachusetts.* Chicago: University of Chicago Press, 1992.

Rothman, Joshua D. *Flush Times and Fever Dreams: A Story of Capitalism and Slavery in the Age of Jackson.* Athens, GA: University of Georgia Press, 2012.

Schermerhorn, Calvin. *The Business of Slavery and the Rise of Capitalism, 1815–1860.* New Haven, CT: Yale University Press, 2015.

Schlesinger Jr., Arthur M. *The Age of Jackson.* Boston: Little, Brown, 1945.

Schweikart, Larry. *Banking in the American South from the Age of Jackson to Reconstruction.* Baton Rouge: Louisiana State University Press, 1987.

Sellers, Charles G. *The Market Revolution: Jacksonian America, 1815–1846*. New York: Oxford University Press, 1991.

Shalhope, Robert E. *The Baltimore Bank Riot: Political Upheaval in Antebellum Maryland*. Champaign: University of Illinois Press, 2009.

Skocpol, Theda. "Bringing the State Back In: Strategies of Analysis in Current Research." In Peter Evans, Dietrich Rueschemeyer, and Theda Skocpol, eds., *Bringing the State Back In*. New York: Cambridge University Press, 1985.

Skowronek, Stephen. *Building a New American State: The Expansion of National Administrative Capacities, 1877–1920*. Cambridge: Cambridge University Press, 1982.

Smith, Culver. *The Press, Politics, and Patronage: The American Government's Use of Newspapers, 1789–1875*. Athens: University of Georgia Press, 1977.

Smith, Elbert. *Francis Preston Blair*. New York: Free Press, 1980.

Smith, Walter Buckingham. *Economic Aspects of the Second Bank of the United States*. Cambridge, MA: Harvard University Press, 1953.

Starr, Paul. *The Creation of the Media: Political Origins of Modern Communications*. New York: Basic Books, 2004.

Steffen, Charles G. "Newspapers for Free: The Economies of Newspaper Circulation in the Early Republic." *Journal of the Early Republic* 23, no. 3 (Autumn 2003): 381–419.

Stevens, Walter Barlow. *St. Louis: The Fourth City 1764–1911, Volume I*. St. Louis: S. J. Clarke, 1909.

Stokes, Melvin, and Stephen Conway. *The Market Revolution in America: Social, Political, and Religious Expressions, 1800–1880*. Charlottesville: University of Virginia Press, 1996.

Stowe, Steven M. *Intimacy and Power in the Old South: Ritual in the Lives of the Planters*. Baltimore: Johns Hopkins University Press, 2007.

Sylla, Richard E., et al. "Alexander Hamilton, Central Banker: Crisis Management during the U.S. Financial Panic of 1792." *Business History Review* 83 (Spring 2009): 61–86.

Temin, Peter. *The Jacksonian Economy*. New York: W. W. Norton, 1969.

Thornton III, J. Mills. *Politics and Power in a Slave Society: Alabama, 1800–1860*. Baton Rouge: Louisiana State University Press, 1978.

Timberlake, Richard. *The Origins of Central Banking in the United States*. Cambridge, MA: Harvard University Press, 1978.

Van Fenstermaker, J. *The Development of American Commercial Banking: 1782–1837*. Kent, OH: Kent State University Press, 1965.

Wainwright, Nicholas B. "The Life and Death of Major Thomas Biddle." *Pennsylvania Magazine of History and Biography* 104, no. 3 (July 1980): 326–344.

Watson, Harry. *Liberty and Power: The Politics of Jacksonian America*. New York: Hill and Wang, 1990.

White, Leonard D. *The Jacksonians: A Study in Administrative History 1829–1861*. New York: MacMillan, 1954.

White, Richard. "Information, Markets, and Corruption: Transcontinental Railroads in the Gilded Age." *Journal of American History* 90, no. 1 (June 2003): 19–43.

———. *Railroaded: The Transcontinentals and the Making of Modern America*. New York: W. W. Norton, 2011.

Wilburn, Jean Alexander. *Biddle's Bank: The Crucial Years*. New York: Columbia University Press, 1967.

Wilentz, Sean. *The Rise of American Democracy: Jefferson to Lincoln*. New York: W. W. Norton, 2005.

Wilson, Major. "The 'Country' Versus the 'Court': A Republican Consensus and Party Debate in the Bank War." *Journal of the Early Republic* 15 (Winter 1995): 619–647.

Wright, Robert E. *The First Wall Street: Chestnut Street, Philadelphia, and the Birth of American Finance*. Chicago: University of Chicago Press, 2005.

Wyatt-Brown, Bertram. *Southern Honor: Ethics and Behavior in the Old South*. New York: Oxford University Press, 1982.

Dissertations and Theses

Forderhase, Rudolph Eugene. "Jacksonianism in Missouri, from Predilection to Party, 1820–1836." PhD diss., University of Missouri, 1968.

Kindig, Everett William. "Western Opposition to Jackson's 'Democracy': The Ohio Valley as a Case Study, 1827–1836." PhD diss., Stanford University, 1974.

McCandless, Perry. "Thomas Hart Benton, His Source of Political Strength in Missouri, 1815–1838." PhD diss., University of Missouri, Columbia, 1953.

Government Documents

1830 United States Federal Census. *University of Virginia Library*. Historical Census Browser. 2004. Available at http://mapserver.lib.virginia.edu/php/start.php?year=V1830. Accessed June 2013.

1840 United States Federal Census. University of Virginia Library. Historical Census Browser. 2004. Available at http://mapserver.lib.virginia.edu/php/start.php?year=V1840. Accessed June 2013.

American State Papers. Advances for Printing, & C. 1830. 251.

———. *Post Office Department*. 1829. 184.

———. "Receipts and Expenditures to April 1, 1829." 21st Congress, 2nd Session, Senate. March 1, 1831. Document 106.

Annals of Congress. 2nd Congress, 1st Session. House. December 28, 1791. 289–290.

———. House, 14th Congress, 1st Session, Appendix, 1812–1825.

Biographical Directory of the United States Congress, 1774–present. http://bioguide.congress.gov/biosearch/biosearch.asp. Accessed July 25, 2015.

Congressional Globe, 25th Congress, 2nd Session, House, 326–333.

House Journal, 21st Congress, 1st Session, 11–28.

———. 21st Congress, 2nd Session, 8–33.

———. 22nd Congress, 1st Session, 1066–1075.

House of Representatives Document No. 3, 22nd Congress, 2nd Session, Serial Volume 233.

———. No. 8, 22nd Congress, 2nd Session, Serial Volume 233.

House of Representatives Report No. 121, 22nd Congress, 2nd Session, Serial Volume 236.

———. No. 460, 22nd Congress, 1st Session, Serial Volume 227.

———. No. 849, 24th Congress, 1st Session, Serial Volume 295.

Journal of the House of Representatives of the State of Missouri at the First Session of the Sixth General Assembly. Bowling-Green, MO: Office of the Salt River Journal, 1831.

Register of Debates. "Postage on Newspapers and Periodicals." 22nd Congress, 1st Session. House. January 13, 1832, 1.

———. 22nd Congress, 1st Session. House Report, 128.

———. 22nd Congress, 1st Session. House. February 9, 1832, 139–142.

———. 22nd Congress, 1st Session. House. 2651–2671.

———. 23rd Congress, 1st Session. Senate. 518, 1138–1205.

———. 23rd Congress, 1st Session. Senate. 1538–1539.

———. 23rd Congress, 1st Session. Senate. Document 422. "Report to the Committee on the Post Office and Post Roads." June 9, 1834, 4 and 55.

———. 23rd Congress, 1st Session. Senate. Document 462. "Memorial of Francis P. Blair." June 20, 1834, 1–8.

———. 24th Congress, 1st Session. Senate. Document 11.

———. 29th Congress, 1st Session. House. Document 37. "Memorial of Amos Kendall." December 15, 1845.

Senate Document No. 17, 23rd Congress, 2nd Session, Serial Volume 267.

———. No. 31, 22nd Congress, 1st Session, Serial Volume 212.

———. No. 37, 22nd Congress, 1st Session, Serial Volume 212.

———. No. 104, 21st Congress, 2nd Session, Serial Volume 193.

Senate Journal, 22nd Congress, 1st Session, 91, 345–346.

Miscellaneous Sources

Imbert, Anthony. "Set to between Old Hickory and Bully Nick." Lithograph. New York: 1834. Library of Congress. American cartoon print filing series. Available at https://www.loc.gov/item/2008661767/.

Johnston, Louis, and Samuel H. Williamson. "What Was the U.S. GDP Then?" *MeasuringWorth.* 2013. Available at http://www.measuringworth.com/usgdp/.

Pasley, Jeffrey L. "Editorial Officeholding." "Tyranny of Printers" website. Available at http://pasleybrothers.com/newspols/officeholding.htm.

Peters, Gerhard, and John T. Woolley. "1832 Presidential Election." *The American Presidency Project*, 1999–2016, available at http://www.presidency.ucsb.edu/showelection.php?year=1832.

Index